Enigmatic Proconsul
Sir Philip Mitchell and the
Twilight of Empire

ENIGMATIC PROCONSUL

Sir Philip Mitchell and the Twilight of Empire

RICHARD FROST

The Radcliffe Press
London · New York

To Kenneth Kirkwood, Professor Emeritus of Race Relations,
University of Oxford

Published in 1992 by
The Radcliffe Press
45 Bloomsbury Square
London WC1A 2HY

175 Fifth Avenue
New York
NY 10010

In the United States of America
and Canada distributed by
St Martin's Press
175 Fifth Avenue
New York
NY 10010

A full CIP record is available from the British Library

Library of Congress cataloging-in-publication card number: available
A full CIP record is available from the Library of Congress

ISBN 1–85043–525–1

Contents

List of Plates

Abbreviations

MD	=	Sir Philip Mitchell's Diaries
EAS	=	*East African Standard*
EA&R	=	*East Africa and Rhodesia*
HCD	=	House of Commons Debates
LCD	=	Legislative Council Debates
CO	=	Colonial Office papers in the Public Record Office (PRO) at Kew.
CU	=	Closer Union
CS	=	Chief Secretary
PC	=	Provincial Commissioner
DC	=	District Commissioner
DO	=	District Officer
TT	=	Tanganyika Territory
NA	=	Native Administration

General Foreword to the Series

A whole generation has passed, nearer two in the case of the Indian sub-continent, since Britain's colonial territories in South-East Asia, Africa and the Caribbean, achieved independence. In the Pacific the transfer of power came about a decade later. There was little interest in recording the official or the personal experience of empire either in the inter-war years – viewed by some, often among those personally involved, as the apogee of the British empire – or in the immediate aftermath of empire. And in this latter period attitudes were critical, largely condemnatory and even purposively hostile. This is not surprising: such a reaction is usual at the end of a remarkable period of history.

With the passing of time and with longer historical perspective it was possible to see events in a better and more objective light and the trend was gradually reversed. In due course there came about a more sympathetic interest in the colonial period, both by those in Britain or in the countries of the former empire who were intrigued to know how colonial government operated – in local, everyday practice, as well at the policy level of the Colonial Office and Government House. Furthermore those who had themselves been an integral part of the process wanted to record the experience before, in the nature of things, it was too late. Here was a potentially rich vein of knowledge and personal experience for specialist academic historians as well as the general reader.

Leaving aside the extensive academic analysis of the end of empire, the revival of interest in the colonial period in this country may be said to have been stimulated by creative literature. In the late 1960s there were novels, films, radio and TV programmes now and again tinged with a touch of nineteenth-century romance and with just a whiff of nostalgia to soften the sharp realism of the colonial encounter. The focus was primarily on India and the post-1947 imagery of the 'Raj': there were outstanding novels by Paul Scott – surely destined to be one of the greatest twentieth-century novelists – JG Farrell and John Masters. Later appeared epic films like *A Passage to India*, and *Gandhi*, the charming and moving vignette of *Staying On*, and, for Africa, *Out of Africa* and *Mister Johnson*.

In the second half of the 1970s there emerged a highly successful genre of collective 'colonial' memoirs in the *Tales of . . .* format: Charles Allen's splendid trilogy *Plain Tales from the Raj* (1975), *Tales from the Dark Continent* (1979) and *Tales from the South China Seas* (1983), followed by others with *Tales of Paradise: Memories of the British in the South Pacific* (1986) and *Tales of Empire: the British in the Middle East* (1989), all good history and good reading.

Throughout the period from India's independence until that of the last crown colony there had, of course, been those splendid works which combined academic history and creative literature: for example, Philip Woodruff's *The Men Who Ruled India: The Founders* (1953) and *The Guardians* (1954); and Jan Morris's *Heaven's Command, Pax Britannica* and *Farewell the Trumpets* (1973–8).

Finally as the 1970s gave way to the 1980s, those voices which had remained largely silent since the end of empire now wanted to be heard. The one-time colonial official, be he district officer, agriculturist, veterinary, medical or forestry officer, policeman or magistrate, and just as often their wives, began to write about their experiences in one of Britain's overseas civil services. They wrote with relish and enthusiasm, with a touch of adventure and few personal regrets. There was a common feeling of a practical and useful task well done, although some thought that more could have been achieved had independence come about more slowly.

These memoirs often began as little more than a private

record for the family, children and grandchildren, some of whom had never seen a colonial governor in full fig, shaken hands with an emir or paramount chief, discussed plans with a peasant or local politician, or known at first hand the difference between an *askari* and *alkali*, an *amah* or an *ayah*.

By 1990 the colonial memoir had begun to establish itself as a literary genre in its own right.

The initiative of the Radcliffe Press in harnessing and promoting this talent, primarily autobiographical but also biographical, promises to be a positive addition to both the historical and literary scenes. Here is a voice from the last Colonial Service generation, relating from personal experience the lives and careers involved in the exercise of latterday empire. They were part of what was arguably the most influential and far-reaching international event of the second half of the twentieth century, namely the end of empire and the consequent emergence of the independent nations of the Third World. It could perhaps also be argued that this is part of an even greater process – decolonisation 'writ large', a sea-change in world affairs affecting greater and lesser powers into the late twentieth century.

It may well be that by 2066, the centenary of the closing down of the Colonial Office, great-great-grandchildren will find the most telling image of Britain's third and final empire in these authentic memoirs and biographical studies, rather than in the weightier imperial archives at the Public Record Office at Kew or in Rhodes House Library, Oxford.

AHM Kirk-Greene, lecturer in the Modern History of Africa, University of Oxford, and formerly of the Colonial Administrative Service, Nigeria.

Acknowledgements

Philip Mitchell's cousin, Randolph Vigne, gave me very great help by introducing me to members of the family who were able to supply letters and photographs in their possession. I am sincerely grateful for the constant interest he has shown in my book.

Because of my acute arthritis I have been largely confined to a wheelchair and my daughter, Katherine Jones, has been of the utmost help in going for me to the library at Rhodes House where I was unable to go myself because of the stairs. I should like to acknowledge my indebtedness to her.

Richard Frost
July 1992

I

The Early Years

Philip Euen Mitchell was born in London on 1 May 1890. His father was Scottish, his mother the daughter of an English father and a Scottish mother, and Philip never let it be forgotten that he was a Scot. His father was Captain Hugh Mitchell, who had been in the Royal Engineers but retired from the Army, studied law at the Inner Temple and was called to the Bar. His wife, Mary Catherine, always called Katie, was a member of the Creswell family. Both the Mitchells and the Creswells had a record of distinguished service in the army and the professions and the union of Hugh and Katie produced a family of seven very able children, of whom Philip was the sixth and, it was thought, the most brilliant. Hugh had been at school at Harrow and had a bookcase full of prizes, mainly for classics. In his generation in the family and later among his children conversation was enlivened by puns in Greek and Latin and a dry wit and humour, which were shown by Philip throughout his life.

Katie died when her youngest child was born, a few days after Philip's second birthday. Her husband was devoted to her and her death was an incurable loss and grief to him. He had always been rather dour and, when his wife died, he became more withdrawn and unable to enter into the childish atmosphere of his family. One of his granddaughters remembers him as 'a patriarchial and terrifying figure', of whom all his family were somewhat afraid.[1]

In 1822 Philip's grandfather, Edmund Creswell, known in the family as Exodus Edmund, left England and was appointed to

1

the post of supervising mails in the Mediterranean and became 'Admiralty Agent for the management of packets' in Gibraltar. His daughter, Maggie Creswell, Philip's aunt, became postmistress there, where the Creswells had a family home, Mount Pleasant, with a large fig tree in the garden. When the figs were ripening, the Barbary apes used to invade the garden, climb all over the house and go into the bedrooms, if windows had been left open, to the delight of visiting nephews and nieces from England. Mount Pleasant and the Creswell aunts were well known to the Mitchell children and when friends in London suggested to Hugh that, as he had been called to the Bar rather late in life, he might find it easier to get work in Gibraltar than in London, he decided to leave England and settle in practice in Gibraltar. Not only would he be better able there to earn the money needed for the education and maintenance of his seven children but a new life there might help him to overcome his sorrow at the loss of his wife. So he left London and built up a practice in Gibraltar and Tangier. First he and his children lived at Mount Pleasant but in 1896 they moved to Campamento, a village three miles away on the Spanish coast, where Aunt Maggie had a house, which became Philip's childhood home. Philip was educated there by a French tutor and his father, and won a scholarship to St Paul's School in London direct from home. His holidays were then spent partly at Campamento and partly with various of his mother's relatives in England, mainly at Hitcham in Suffolk, where his mother's cousin, Canon Alexander Ronald, was Rector. After his death the cousins moved to Hitcham Hall, a house belonging to them, and that became the holiday home of Hugh's family when they were at school at St Paul's. Philip was always something of a rebel. One day, when he was a small boy, he was sent to have his hair cut and on his return was told that it was still too long and he must go back to have it shortened. When he went home after that second visit to the hairdresser's he said rather defiantly, 'Is that better?', as he exhibited a completely shaved head. His was an unsettled childhood, but it had one blessing: he became completely trilingual in English, Spanish and French, and a flair for learning languages stood him in good stead later on.

To win a scholarship at a leading public school in England without any previous time spent at school was a remarkable feat. His school reports give indications of his lack of earlier school discipline. At Christmas 1905 it was said that he 'Would be good if he did not work so fast and if he were more careful', and in 1908 he was said to be 'capable and industrious. Very bright and sound in both Classics and English', but a year later his Latin showed that he had 'suffered from a complete absence of grounding'. In Divinity he had 'any amount of individuality'. He had 'a fair knowledge of French but works very little'. As he spoke French fluently, he probably thought there was no need to spend time studying the niceties of grammar. During his life in the Colonial Service he was meticulous and went to great trouble in phrasing his letters and despatches, and his official and semi-official correspondence, when he was a colonial governor, could have earned the comment made about his Rugby football prowess at St Paul's – 'Is very plucky and attacks well'.[2] Perhaps his disaster at Oxford was a necessary antidote to his earlier upbringing.

The circumstances of his childhood profoundly affected his character and behaviour. There was no air travel when he was a child and Gibraltar was a long way away from St Paul's. 'The child is father to the man,' and the lack of a mother and a home in his childhood days was probably the cause of a feeling of insecurity which remained with him in adult life and which he compensated by tall talk and which made him afraid of women. One of his sisters-in-law in fact always terrified him. As he grew up he hid his instability by an exuberant exterior. This tendency to show off was intensified by the fact that as a young man he was extremely handsome and whenever he entered a room he became the centre of attention. He was described as 'larger than life'. He was socially very polished and endowed with dynamic energy.

From St Paul's he won a classical scholarship at Trinity College, Oxford. The classical course at Oxford is divided into two parts of two years each. He took the first part, Honour Moderations, but his name then passes out from the college records. He did not return from the summer vacation to start his two years work in Literae Humaniores, known as Greats. One escapade had followed another. None was vicious, but the University and the colleges in those days were less tolerant of what he described as 'undergraduate pranks' than they have become in recent years. He frequently had to escape from the 'bulldogs', the bowler hatted constables of the University proctors, often no doubt for not wearing a gown in the town after dark, which was then an offence. Once, when he was escaping from the 'bulldogs', he climbed through a college window and landed in a room whose undergraduate occupant was sitting on the floor smoking a hookah and merely looked up and said, 'Make yourself at home'. But at last Trinity became exasperated by his numerous and varied 'pranks' and, when he went round with a pot of red paint with which he painted the noses of any statues he happened to see, the authorities decided that enough was enough and took his scholarship away from him. At that very time the transfer of Morocco to France deprived Philip's father of his Moroccan practice and he would have been unable to pay for Philip to remain at Trinity, even if the college had agreed to allow him to return as a commoner; so his 'pranks' ended in his having to leave Oxford. This was a great shock to him. Five years at St Paul's were all he had spent at school and the free and easy life which he had known at Campamento, where the cost of living was low and the Creswells and Mitchells had a wide circle of friends, had not prepared him for the harsh realities of life in Britain.

He then lived a rather wild life in London and was a thorn in the flesh of his family. His elder brother Kenneth, who went into the Indian Civil Service, was studying engineering at the Imperial College in Kensington. He gave Philip a key to his lodgings and on several occasions, when he went into his sitting room in the morning, he found Philip in evening clothes and an opera hat sprawled on the sofa recovering from a hangover after an evening in town. The family wondered what was to be done

4

with its most brilliant member, who had had to leave Oxford without a degree. He had thought of the Diplomatic Service, but his University fiasco made that impossible. Fortunately entry to the Colonial Service was conducted on a different basis from the normal entry to the Civil Service. There was no Colonial Service examination and applicants were chosen or refused as the result of interview, preceded by testimonials and enquiries of people best able to assess a young man's qualities. It was a method which required an interviewing staff with great experience and understanding and perspicuity and, when carried out by the small group of interviewers at the Colonial Office, could reveal what a candidate's potential and aptitude were for the various branches of colonial service. 'Interviewing', wrote Sir Ralph Furse, who became head of the Colonial Office recruitment department, 'is an art . . . it takes all that the interviewer can give. Every faculty must be awake and concentrated . . . on the business of apprehension'.[3] A colonial administrative officer, 'while still in his twenties . . . might find himself in charge of a slice of Africa as big as Yorkshire, and quite possibly alone. Qualities of character and personality (not excluding physical presence, and bearing and some rather elusive facets of a man's intelligence and temperament like imaginative sympathy) were therefore factors of prime importance'.[4] Those were qualities which Mitchell displayed in abundance in the various stages from district officer to governor. When he applied for acceptance in the Colonial Service, it was Furse, himself then only 24 years of age, who interviewed him and appreciated the potential of the wild young man who had no university degree. Many years later, when Mitchell was Governor of Uganda and Furse was staying with him at Entebbe, Mitchell said to him: 'Whenever I have thought that you were doing something peculiarly silly or outrageous I have said to myself, "Stop – there must be some method in Furse's madness; otherwise he would never have put me into the Colonial Service when I had just come down from Oxford without a degree".'[5]

Mitchell was posted to Nyasaland and in the first week of January 1913, off the Chinde mouth of the Zambese in Mozambique, he was put overboard in a cage suspended from a derrick and arrived at Port Herald from where he went on to Zomba with the title of assistant resident. The administrative staff was small and he was the only assistant resident in a district covering 1674 square miles with 79,700 inhabitants, of whom about 30 were Europeans and 40 Indian traders.[6] The resident was struggling with a terrible famine, due to failure of the rains, followed by excessive rains and disastrous floods, and the young assistant had little spare time to give to the important work of learning Nyanja, the local language. In spite of his natural gift for learning languages, he found that learning a Bantu language, so different from any European languages, took 'a deuce of a time'. That was a difficulty which he soon overcame, however, and before the end of the year he success-fully took the Higher Standard Nyanja Examination. When he went to Tanganyika six years later, after service in the King's African Rifles, he was as proficient in Swahili as he was in Spanish and French. From the start he began to love Africa and found his 'black brother on the whole a very pleasant person'.[7]

Working so much on his own in a large district demanded qualities which Ralph Furse looked for in candidates for admis-sion to the Service — 'self-reliance, for instance, self-sufficiency in loneliness, foresight, imaginative sympathy'.[8] A year after his arrival Mitchell wrote a very short letter to his family — very short because spare time was almost non-existent:

Times have been quite exciting recently, and I have not spent a consecutive fortnight under my own roof since September. I've had three cheery murderers to catch — one of them ... not at all a pleasant customer, especially as I was sent out at 1 a.m. and you can't arm native police for that kind of job, as when their blood is up they are like Tweedledum, they will 'probably kill everything within reach'.[9]

Another of his early tasks faced him with a problem which was not fully catered for by the legal studies he had followed during his period of training in England. Two chiefs had had a

6

dispute over a land boundary. In former days they would have fought about it, but the government disapproved of that method of settling disputes and a meeting to discuss the matter was arranged instead. It was far from friendly and, when the visiting deputation was returning to its own village, the rival chief turned himself into a leopard and killed one of them at a lonely spot in the dusk. It was a difficult problem for the new young assistant resident. Hold an inquest? That was the right procedure. Several highly respected witnesses testified to having seen the chief, Nyalugwa, turn himself into a leopard and follow the rival envoys. 'What was I to do?' Mitchell asked later. 'Prepare an indictment against Nyalugwa for murder by becoming a leopard? . . . It began to appear to a very perplexed young magistrate that the English laws of evidence and the African belief in magic might often not really go together very well.'[10] Fortunately for Mitchell the rains, heralding the end of the dry season, started in earnest that night and everyone hurried to the fields to engage in the more important work of hoeing and planting. Mitchell enjoyed talking with people of all kinds. His quick mastery of the Nyanja language made it possible for him to mingle easily with Africans of every kind and he was able, as he wrote, to learn 'something of the people among whom I was to spend my life; a few tea and tobacco planters, Scots and French missionaries, Indian storekeepers, an obliging race of men who treated very young cadets with a deference they greatly enjoyed; African clerks, policemen, artisans, chiefs, headmen and common people of the district, and the endless stream of Nguru immigrants'.[11]

When the First World War – the Kaiser's War as it is known in East Africa – broke out in August 1914, Mitchell asked leave to join the army, but his request was refused. Nothing daunted, he enlisted as a private soldier in the King's African Rifles and, because there had been so many casualties among the officers in the first engagement of the campaign, he escaped any penalty for his disobedience and was given a commission. He had a high opinion of the African soldiers. They had been selected and trained by British officers and regimental sergeant majors and were 'self-reliant, smart, efficient and wholly dependable', and Mitchell thought that the way in which they adjusted themselves to working with a large number of European volunteers was remarkable. The warrant officers won his greatest admiration. 'No one, in those days,' he wrote later, 'would say bluntly that those African warrant-officers were our superiors, but that was the fact; and they dealt with us, while they taught us our business, tactfully and sensibly, so that they were respected and obeyed.'[12]

His service in the East African campaign strengthened his idealism and devotion to the service of Africa. Hardships and dangers shared with African soldiers 'had a profound effect', Mitchell believed, 'on all of us young Britons who served with the regular African troops, so that, with the exception of a few misfits, we came, consciously or unconsciously, to a relationship which took no – or anyhow only a very restricted – account of difference of colour, race or background'.[13] It certainly had that effect on Mitchell. Many years later, when he was Governor of Kenya and was commending an appeal for funds for the African Section of the British Legion, he said: '. . . twice in 30 years [we] have owed our immunity from invasion as much to the African soldier as to any other single factor . . .'[14]

His ability to mix and talk with people of all kinds, which he used so well when he was learning 'the rudiments of [his] trade' in Nyasaland greatly enriched his life in the army during the war, and he learned then that there were things which the illiterate Africans could do better than the graduates of Western universities. Long chats with African private soldiers in the field were interspersed by games of *Bau*. This game is a favourite in Africa. It is difficult to learn. It needs no equipment; little holes in the ground and pebbles, nuts, seeds or what you will for pieces are all that is required. The average European looks with amazed bewilderment at the speed with which Africans play it and wonders at the mental agility which they show. Mitchell learned it and discovered that 'once one had learnt it, one could always play 'Bau' with one's men and be beaten'.[15] His experiences in the army were a useful part of the training of a future Secretary for Native Affairs and governor.

He had four years full of interest, excitement, often of danger, and variety, but after the war he felt that the story of his enlistment, which had not been forgotten in Nyasaland, was not likely to make him popular among the administrative officers who had stayed to carry out their civil duties in an understaffed service. He was not mistaken. He returned to Nyasaland and, after a spell as private secretary at Government House, he was posted to a district to work under a district commissioner who had joined the Service during the war and was in fact three years his junior in the Service.

The DC's years in Nyasaland had been dull in comparison with Mitchell's experiences in the bush. It was not a happy partnership and Mitchell successfully applied for a post in the temporary military administration of Tanganyika. His first District was in the southwestern part of the territory among the Fipa tribe. His proficiency in Swahili enabled him immediately to make contact with the thoughts and traditions of the people of his district. Each of the two parts of the tribal area was ruled by a lady. They were kinswomen, of Hima origin, and the sister of one of them was given authority as a sort of liaison officer near Mitchell's station. He learned much from this 'first experience of ladies in authority in a tribe',[16] and much about the problems of African marriage and social customs and the impact of the Christian missionaries on the traditional patterns of African life.

Promotion came quickly and in 1922 he became District Commissioner at Tanga at the northern end of the coast of Tanganyika. It was a particularly interesting district. Tanga was a sea port with a very mixed population composed of Arabs, Swahilis, coastal Africans and Africans from the interior, with some Indian and European traders. The district included sisal estates developed by the Germans, and African peasant communities. Three years later he went on leave and married Margery Tyrwhitt-Drake, daughter of an Admiral of the Royal Navy, who lived in South Africa.

9

Philip was no stranger to South Africa, having frequently stayed with relatives there. His South African connections stemmed from his mother's brother, Colonel FHP Creswell (Uncle Fred), a mining engineer, who had gone to the Transvaal in 1894 and become manager of a gold mine. He later became Minister of Labour and Defence in the South African Cabinet. Philip often spent parts of his leaves with his own and his wife's relatives in South Africa. Uncle Fred believed in a white labour policy and went into an alliance with the Afrikaner nationalists with the aim of achieving it. It was a policy of full apartheid, with white people doing all the manual work in the white areas and the Africans confined to their own allotted areas, where they would slowly progress through many generations. Uncle Fred did in fact successfully manage a gold mine with only white labour, but his example was not followed elsewhere and young Philip, when on leave from East Africa, saw apartheid with Africans doing the manual work everywhere and, as he wrote later on, the whites being intent on maintaining privilege and repression. His personal knowledge of South Africa did much to strengthen his determination to serve the African people of East Africa where almost all of his life was to be spent. He studied South African labour legislation and native agricultural policy and experiments, and learned much that could be of use in East African economic and agricultural development. At the same time he increasingly detested the whole apparatus of apartheid and the race relations existing in the Union. However, his intelligence accepted what was of practical value and, when he became Governor of Kenya and embarked on his campaign for solving the problems of African agriculture, he sent agricultural advisers to study the agricultural systems and experiments in South Africa, while at the same time working for the improvement of human contacts and race relations in Kenya.

His early days in Nyasaland and his service in southern Tanganyika and then at Tanga were not unusual for a young officer in the Colonial Service, but his obvious ability gave him promotion to the important post of District Commissioner at Tanga unusually quickly and caused him to be removed from

10

service in a district three years later. In the middle of 1925 Sir Donald Cameron arrived from Nigeria as Governor of Tanganyika. He was 'a sort of human atom bomb'[17] and immediately looked round his new territory for someone who might have the same dynamic qualities as himself. Mitchell's service in the field was gone forever.

Notes

1. Personal details in this chapter supplied by members of family.
2. Information supplied by St Paul's School.
3. Major Sir Ralph Furse, *Acuparius*, (London, 1962) p. 230.
4. Ibid., p. 228.
5. Ibid., p. 38.
6. Letter by Mitchell to his family, undated but presumably written about four and a half months after his arrival.
7. Ibid.
8. Furse, *Acuparius*, p. 230.
9. Letter by Mitchell to his family, 7 February 1914.
10. Sir Philip Mitchell, *African Afterthoughts* (London, 1954) pp. 28–9.
11. Ibid., p. 27.
12. Ibid., p. 46.
13. Ibid., p. 47.
14. EAS, 25 January 1946.
15. Mitchell, *African Afterthoughts*, p. 41.
16. Ibid., p. 76.
17. Ibid, p. 103.

II

Tanganyika: Secretary for Native Affairs

The governor under whom Mitchell first served in Tanganyika was Sir Horace Byatt, who had had the task of restoring order and reviving the economy of the territory after the First World War. German resistance in Tanganyika had collapsed in 1916 and Byatt arrived as governor late that year. His task was made all the more difficult by the Hague convention on control of occupied territories, which forbade immediate innovation in methods of administration. German administration was at variance with British colonial philosophy but had to be followed at the beginning of the new regime. The Germans had disregarded tribal loyalties and Byatt found himself governor of a country in which tradition had been completely neglected in favour of efficiency, deriving from the governor right down to the village headmen or *jumbes*.[1] It was a system which neither the principles of the League of Nations Mandate nor the traditions of British colonial administration could accept and even before Cameron arrived in 1925, a conference of senior administrative officers opted for a system of indirect rule with a Secretary for Native Affairs to supervise its development. Byatt had been well aware of the need to reform the system bequeathed by the Germans and as his Report for 1922 shows, gave the establishment of a system of government by native authority top priority in his plans for the administration of Tanganyika.[2]

When Cameron arrived as Governor in 1925 he found – not unnaturally at the end of a period of rebuilding a country shattered by the war – that 'there was no settled policy and at

12

the time Administrative Officers in charge of Districts seem to have been severely left alone to work out their own salvation'.[3] The ground work had been ably done by Byatt, and Cameron with Charles Dundas as Secretary for Native Affairs and Mitchell, who was made Assistant Secretary for Native Affairs in 1925, took up the work of introducing a system of native administration founded on the customs and traditions of the people. Mitchell had shown his outstanding qualities while he was District Commissioner at Tanga and, although in 1925 he returned from leave, newly married, to be District Commissioner at Iringa in the beautiful Southern Highlands, Cameron, the new Governor, countermanded this posting and brought him to Dar es Salaam.

Cameron's main aims were to form a legislative council, to complete the reform of the provincial administration and to establish a system of indirect rule. He quickly got approval from the Colonial Office to form a legislative council, a necessary step in the development of Tanganyika towards ultimate self-government. It was a small council with unofficial members nominated by the governor 'without regard to representation of particular races or public bodies as being particularly fitted to be of assistance to the Governor in the exercise of his responsibilities, having regard to the interests of all communities, in the Territory, native and non-native'.[4] Educational standards and ability to speak English confined membership to Europeans at that time, but it was the first step towards a more democratic system of government.

Dundas left Tanganyika in 1929 to be Colonial Secretary in the Bahamas and Mitchell, who took over his post, carried out the work of Secretary for Native Affairs without an assistant secretary. Later on, when he became chief secretary in 1934, the office of Secretary for Native Affairs was allowed to lapse. Native Administration had been firmly established by then and Mitchell could not accept the idea of anyone else being in charge of it and so continued to supervise it from the chief secretary's office.

In Nigeria Cameron had admired the system of indirect rule

13

which Lugard had established, but he disagreed with certain aspects of the Nigerian model. He believed that 'a system of Native Administration of an indirect character ... should be built, if it is to be genuine and not a sham and a snare on the indigenous institutions of the people themselves that still exist',[5] but Mitchell's service in Nyasaland had shown him that blind adherence to traditional forms would be the wrong policy there. Missionaries had been active for 50 years or more and policy had to 'take account of the highly educated Christian native' there. In Tanganyika the Germans had used the missionaries to good effect in education and the percentage of literacy among Africans was higher than it was in Uganda or Kenya.[6] Cameron saw that education of an African élite was necessary for the very existence of indirect rule and he did all he could to foster it. He gave special encouragement to the government school at Tabora and his élitist policy made possible the development of native courts, which could not have been integrated into the system of administration without an adequate supply of clerks.

An adequate supply of Africans with some secondary education was certainly needed for the running of native administration, but exhaustive research into the customs of each tribe and an understanding of African outlooks were basic to the very existence of the idea of indirect rule. It was essential to find out where traditional authority lay, but then Mitchell demanded that that knowledge should be interpreted in terms of African life and thought and not according to British political thinking. 'The whole outlook of life and the whole philosophy of life of the African people is group action,'[7] he said, and research had to establish who were the people who traditionally had the right to advise the chief. He himself spent much of his time travelling round the country. 'I believe I saw every Commissioner of a Province or District on his own ground at least once a year,' he wrote, 'and met and talked to every Chief and other important man in the country.'[8]

The Local Government memorandum, which was written by Mitchell, reminded the officers of the Administration that 'the original strength of the system derived not from the native treasuries as is the case to-day but from the native courts which in most areas were novel institutions, in respect of which a considerable degree of support and tuition was, and still is, necessary'.[9] Things might have been easier if there had not been any previous European administration. As the memorandum pointed out, 'The Germans, with no initial colonial experience, deliberately adopted at first the Arab "akida" system of local rule by paid minor officials selected for efficiency and not by tradition'.[10] This system, originally emanating from the Sultanate in Zanzibar, had to be replaced by a system of direct participation by the African people themselves, who had to realize that their new European rulers were rejecting the system which their former, equally white skinned, rulers had imposed. Indirect rule derived from 'the traditional authority of the Chiefs', the attorney general told the Legislative Council 'and the exercise of judicial functions by the Chief sitting alone, or sitting with his Council, is an essential part of that authority. There is no division of authority into executive and judicial functions, but his people look to their Chief sitting with such advisers as custom may require as the source of all authority within the tribe'.[11]

Mitchell insisted that the research which had to be undertaken to find out where authority traditionally lay in the tribe should regard the chief as the point of a pyramid, not as a single source of authority. But the chief was the recipient of tribute in kind or service and 'the first step had to be an investigation into the tribute and service due – or at any rate paid – to the Chiefs by their people'.[12] Rapacious chiefs might extract more than their due.

As part of the campaign to find the traditional authorities in the tribes Mitchell suggested, and the governor agreed to, the appointment of an anthropologist and an administrator to delve into tribal customs and traditions. They reported that it was frequently difficult to locate the traditional rulers and, when they were discovered, it was often found that their traditional authority had been irretrievably eroded by German administration.[13] The same conclusion was reached by many of the administrative officers who were required to undertake similar research. The system of government which Britain was developing was therefore not a complete restoration of customary forms. In any case, since the traditional systems were themselves dynamic and subject to change, it was neither desirable nor possible to put the clock back to the days before the advent of the Germans. The indirect rule devised by Cameron and his team was based on a somewhat amended form of tradition.

One of Cameron's first acts was to abolish tribal tribute in kind and in free labour, and substitute for it the hut and poll tax, which was raised from six shillings to ten shillings. It might have been expected that such a change would cause trouble both with the peasants and the chiefs, but the commutation of tribute was accomplished without difficulty. This was due in no small measure to the good relations established by the provincial and district officers of the administration, who were able to build up trust and to explain to chiefs and people what the change really meant. 'Those who had formerly been liable to tribute,' wrote the Deputy Provincial Commissioner of Mwanza Province,

> were happy to be relieved at the cost of an addition of four shillings to the annual tax, and the Chiefs and their subordinate authorities who had to relinquish their tribute dues accepted the new order quietly because they realised that insistence on tribute in many cases embittered their relations with their people, that tribute in kind was uncertain and increasingly troublesome to collect, and that the regular incomes assured to them from the Native Treasuries were sufficient for their proper maintenance in their positions.[14]

Even in Kasulu the 'Watutsi overlords' began to accept happily the task of substituting for a tribute which they were habituated to exact an impost which, by the injunction of the British Government, it became their duty to collect.

The good relations existing between the tribal authorities and the Provincial and District Officers made this revolutionary change in general acceptable to the chiefs and, as one district

16

officer wrote, 'among at least some of the Chiefs an observer may detect the awakening of a sense of responsibility and a desire to make themselves more worthy of ruling'.[15] Almost everywhere in the native administrations, the fusion of old traditions with modern Western standards was happily accepted and at times of crisis, such as the locust invasion of 1929 in the Central Province, in 'a year of drought, locusts and famine . . . the native administration rose to the emergency – insisting on the planting of certain crops, conserving food stocks by prohibiting sale of grain for brewing beer'.[16] The same acceptance of instructions, unpalatable instructions when circumstances made them essential, was seen generally throughout the territory. The native administrations rose to the challenge and 'Responsibility and executive power have raised the Authorities in their own and their people's estimation and they are now of much greater value than formerly',[17] wrote the provincial commissioner.

The European administrative officers were the key. As Cameron wrote in his autobiography, 'It is the primary duty and obligation of the Administrative Officers with tact and patience to educate the Native Authorities in their duties to their people according to civilized standards'.[18] This duty required constant and painstaking supervision of the records of the native courts and treasuries. The whole system of native administration depended on supervision by British officers – a supervision which could only be really constructive if it was based on friendship and sympathetic understanding. The records of native courts and treasuries were first exhaustively scrutinized by the district officers and further inspected by the provincial commissioners. As the Provincial Commissioner for Kigoma Province wrote, 'Generally speaking, although the task of inspecting several thousand records of native court cases is a most laborious one, it is most necessary and at the same time not without interest. With very few exceptions mistakes are at least genuine and the Native Courts are doing excellent work. When jurisdiction has been exceeded it is usually with a laudable desire to assist'.[19]

From time to time still further inspections were conducted by the Secretary for Native Affairs as he toured round the provinces. An aggrieved party had the right of appeal to a higher native court, to a district officer, and from him to a provincial commissioner and lastly to the governor. But the standards of justice were well maintained and appeals were few. In one year in the Iringa Province, for instance, 8,166 cases were heard, but only 93 appeals were lodged,[20] and a similar acceptance of judgements was found throughout the territory. A chief in the Central Province, when asked by the governor to contrast British administration with former times, said 'These days no man is beaten – no man is cheated. For if a man is punished or sued, his case has to be entered in the court register and this register is examined every month by an administrative officer'.[21]

There was a basic problem. What should be the code of justice binding on the decisions of the courts and supervision by the district officer? British standards might be regarded as unjust in the administration of justice in a tribal society and so it was necessary for the district officers to inspect the records. When necessary, they heard appeals with understanding and tried to see the points of the case through the eyes of the simple Africans who had appeared in the courts, while never forgetting the principles of British justice and moral standards. Mitchell appreciated the difficulty. He thought that

> as regards Native Courts and Law a British officer cannot himself depart from our standards of justice, morality and conduct. We can acquiesce in lesser standards for Native Courts and Chiefs because of their more backward state and may refrain from interfering for these reasons. But for his own actions his standards must be those of a civilised society, else chaos follows.[22]

He stressed the need for an understanding of the religious and social forces which influenced the people with whom the administrative officers had to deal. He felt strongly that 'it is the modern African, his social background, religious background, law and customs, and the reaction on them of Islam and the contact of western civilization that cadets should study and not the eccentricities of remote and unheard of Papuans – the scars they make on their bottoms and their unsavoury sexual habits which scarcely any anthropologist can keep off'.[23]

When he was on his travels round the country, he was always ready to talk to young cadets and other junior officers, listening to their views and discussing the problems of native administration and the need for sympathetic understanding of African outlooks.[24] At the same time he was gathering information picked up by the officers of the provincial administration, who worked in close collaboration with the chiefs. 'Unless administrative officers learn from the chiefs,' wrote a provincial commissioner, 'and the chiefs learn from the administrative officers we cannot get the best results.'[25] The Secretary for Native Affairs was like a bridge across which ideas could travel in both directions. It has been said that 'of all the various bodies of opinion which played their part in influencing and formulating government policy that of the territorial administration was by far the most important'.[26]

Although Mitchell personally had friends among the European members of Legislative Council, his championship of the interests of the Africans was feared and resented by them. As the head of an administration working for the programme of Africans, whom he did not regard as being primarily a labour force for the European farmers, he was highly suspect politically in European settler circles. During Cameron's governorship the unofficial members of Legislative Council tried to clip his wings. They tried to get him excluded from the Executive Council and to prevent him from being what in fact was the head of the provincial administration. They were quite open about their aim and a certain Major Wells, when he was a guest at a dinner party at the Mitchells' house, told him that they were going to initiate a debate in Legislative Council on native policy, mainly as a personal attack on him.[27] During this debate they said that he had too much power, particularly when the interests of the 'native communities and the superior races were in dispute' and that in mixed areas there was 'a tendency perhaps at present to take more interest in the native affairs than in those of the Europeans'.[28]

Major Wells had told Mitchell that it was said that the knees of the provincial commissioners knocked together with fright when he travelled round the provinces.[29] Major Wells did in fact use that graphic phrase in the debate and added that it was 'generally understood in the Provinces that the Secretary for Native Affairs does report on the officers in the Provinces', while another member informed the Council that it was thought that the Secretary for Native Affairs did the posting of officers, a fact which the unofficial members considered most undesirable, to which Cameron, the governor, said from the chair, 'I do it'. Of course, he said, he used the Secretary for Native Affairs to prepare the papers for him, but, he stressed, 'no posting is made till it has been approved by me'.[30] To this there was no answer, although no one doubted that Mitchell's recommendations were usually accepted. His dominant position in the provincial administration remained undiminished and he continued to travel round the territory and advise the governor as before.

The unofficial members had made an onslaught on Mitchell a few days earlier during a meeting of the Finance Committee, objecting to his presence in the secretariat and on Executive Council. It was clear to Mitchell why they wanted to limit his scope. 'No doubt they do object,' he wrote, 'since in fact the SNA [Secretary for Native Affairs] is the only voice which the 4,750,000 Africans have.'[31] The man who in 1914 had disobeyed orders, joined the King's African Rifles and been awarded a commission could not be other than appreciative of successful enterprise in the officers of the district administration. Once when he was Secretary for Native Affairs and was visiting Songea, he found that the district commissioner had built a hospital and school without receiving any grant for either. He had used the free services of his architect brother and had saved money from here and there to pay for the buildings. When Wing Commander Francombe, who had flown him from Dar es Salaam, asked where the money had come from, Mitchell said,

'These excellent buildings are a monument to the inefficiency of the Colonial Audit'.[32]

Mitchell's diaries show that throughout his service life one of his major concerns was an improvement of relations between the races and he made friends in a personal way with influential people in other walks of life with interests in colonial and racial matters. One of these friends and allies was JH Oldham, the Secretary of the International Missionary Conference in London. He was a remarkable man – missionary, politician and diplomat with a keen interest in African affairs and a particular knowledge of Kenya, although well informed on East Africa affairs in general. Perhaps more than anyone else he was responsible for the Devonshire Declaration on the paramountcy of African interests in Kenya, which was contained in the White Paper, *Indians in Kenya*, in 1923.[33] He was a member of the Hilton Young Commission on East Africa and was respected and consulted by politicians at Westminster from secretaries of state downwards. Mitchell kept in close touch with him by letter and by personal meetings when he was in London. When in 1930, for instance, he read 'a disgraceful article in the paper; the usual foul abuse of natives and "are such savages to be allowed to keep the land" and so on', his immediate thought was that he must send it to Oldham 'for use in the proper quarters'.[34]

In those days travelling in Tanganyika was no easy matter. The roads were so bad that Cameron, who insisted on visiting the southern part of the country soon after his arrival, 'met officials who, entering the country through Nyasaland, were some of them unknown at headquarters'.[35] In 1929 a new cadet posted to Tunduru found that it took two days to reach his station from Lindi 214 miles away, while the next district headquarters was at Songea 360 miles further on along roads equally primitive; and as late as 1938 there was no telegraph or telephone at Tunduru.[36] The state of the roads is a recurrent theme in Mitchell's diaries. He went by air whenever he could, being piloted by his friend, Wing Commander AN Francombe. The Government had its own aeroplanes and also had a contract with Wilson Airways of Nairobi. In January 1930 Mitchell had to call off a safari altogether because 'at Morogoro he was informed there was no chance of getting thro because of 9 washaways and a 15 mile lake – mostly between Gulwa and Dodoma'.[37] When he decided to go to the Northern Province by air, he found that a hot country with small isolated hills could provide hazards for a little, low-flying aeroplane of the 1930s. 'Just over Same,' he wrote, 'we flew into an air pocket and dropped vertically 200 ft. Francombe shot out of his seat and would have shot out of the plane but for the rudder loops. I came out till my belt stopped me; and my suit case came right on to the fuselage and was only held by a piece of string.'[38]

The fact that the books were well kept showed that the policy of trying to educate an African élite was proving successful. Courts and treasuries had to have clerks to keep their records. Tabora School was providing clerks, but later on it was able to turn out university entrants, many of whom became the leaders of the African community. But there were other schools also turning out young men with a good basic education, sufficient for simple work as clerks, with adequate proficiency in English. A difficulty arose from the fact that they were not spread equally over the country and tribal languages were used in the native courts. Frequent reference to this problem was made in provincial reports. 'In Musoma District,' for instance, a Provincial Commissioner wrote, 'it is difficult to obtain clerks who are sufficiently educated for the clerical work and at the same time proficient in the local languages.'[39] The remarkable thing was the way in which young men, many of them straight from school, responded to the trust placed in them and to the friendly supervision of the district officers. Their ability to keep records in English, a language unknown to the chiefs and elders, gave them a power which could easily have been abused. Almost everywhere, however, they carried out their duties honourably and more efficiently than their lack of experience might have led the administration to expect.

From the beginning Cameron had given high priority to education. Mitchell had seen in Nyasaland that the protestant missions, as became the case in Tanganyika, had been the pioneers in advocating 'a forward native policy which would keep open a road to racial equality in the future'. Then when 'once the policy had been established in Tanganyika, the Roman Catholic missions took their full share in making it work', so much so that in 1928 the apostolic vicar told a conference of bishops and leading missionaries that when they could not carry out both evangelism and education their policy must be: 'neglect your churches in order to perfect your schools'.[40] Church schools like Pugu and Minaki in Tanganyika; King's College, Budo, and Mwiri in Uganda; the Alliance High School and Mangu High School in Kenya, and also the Government School at Tabora, which Cameron fostered so ardently, became the top of the educational pyramid and supplied a great majority of the leading Africans in the governments and administrations at the time of independence. Later on, when he was Governor of Uganda, Mitchell followed this policy at a higher level and made the reorganization of Makerere one of his principal tasks, believing that there was need for an African élite who would be able to supply the leadership which, he thought, must be given by Africans if the colonial power was to fulfil its obligation as trustee to train its wards to stand on their own feet in the modern world. 'African questions are going to be settled in Africa,' he wrote, and 'if they are to be settled on a racially just basis, and not by a series of racial struggles for power, it is clearly necessary to promote to the utmost the integration of an orderly African society capable of taking a part for itself at the earliest possible moment in the political life of the country.'[41]

In matters concerned with native administration Mitchell's power was great, but in the field of education he had no specific authority and was not able to influence policy in the same way. He fully approved of the policy of producing an African élite through Tabora and other schools, but in general he thought that the condition of the Africans and the economy of Tanganyika at that time required less attention to academic education and more to simple agricultural training. He thought that agricultural training was an essential part of the educational system, but only government measures could enable the peasant, living according to age-old custom, to meet the needs of the new life created by the incursion of the West. He made the same point when he was Governor of Fiji and issued a paper on reconstruction there. Honesty and application to duty were what was required. Tribal society was so different from Western society that the synthesising of tribal customs and Western standards and demands was a basic task of education, whether in school or in places of work after school. Sympathetic and intelligent understanding was necessary. On one occasion Mitchell was impressed by a point of view expressed by the influential Chief Makwaia of the Nyamwezi federation of tribes when he and other chiefs were meeting the governor. He wrote in his diary,

> Makwaia spoke very intelligently and I was much struck by one of the things he said. H.E. had been urging upon them the importance of continuing to show the Government that they could be trusted, and he (M) said, 'Yes, we know, and we are very sorry when people prove untrustworthy and bring discredit on us and let you down. But you must regard us as people who are trying to be trustworthy, not yet as people who are trustworthy. For we have not yet got control of our own souls (*mioyo*); we need much more education and civilisation for that. When we have control of our own souls, then we shall be trustworthy in reality; now we are only trying.'[42]

Mitchell felt that Government policy had to appreciate the difficulties which Africans had to face in their progress from primitive society to the modern world. What is loosely called 'the tribal system', he wrote, 'is the whole integrated life of the African and that is of course not static but dynamic.' It was a bridge to the future, but some people seemed to want the African to 'spring from peak to peak like a chamois!'[43]

Notes

1. Tanganyika, *Local Government Memorandum*, No. 1, pt 1, p. 3.
2. Byatt, *Tanganyika Report for 1922* (Govt office, 1922) p. 59.

3. Sir Donald Cameron, *My Tanganyika Service and Some Nigeria*, (London, 1939) p. 23.
4. Ibid., p. 29.
5. Ibid., p. 79.
6. Judith Listowel, *The Making of Tanganyika*, (London, 1965) p. 48.
7. Proceedings of the Legislative Council, 2 November 1932, p. 53.
8. Mitchell; *African Afterthoughts*, (London, 1954) p. 132.
9. Tanganyika, *Local Government Memorandum*, No. 1, pt 1, p. 3.
10. Ibid., p. 3.
11. Proceedings of the Legislative Council, 3 April 1929, p. 26.
12. Mitchell, *African Afterthoughts*, p. 125.
13. G Gordon Brown and A McD Hutt, *Anthropology in Action*.
14. Provincial commissioners' reports 1929–39 (Rhodes House Library), p. 2.
15. Ibid., pp. 13–14.
16. Ibid., p. 27.
17. Ibid., p. 61.
18. Cameron, *My Tanganyika Service*, p. 98.
19. Provincial commissioners' reports 1929–39, p. 6.
20. Ibid., p. 26.
21. Ibid., p. 26.
22. MD, 30 June 1927.
23. Ibid., 21 September 1929.
24. Interview with S Walden, former provincial commissioner, 31 October 1978.
25. Provincial commissioners' reports, 1929–39, p. 27.
26. HF Morris and James S Read, *Indirect Rule and the Search for Justice*, (Oxford, 1972) p. 5.
27. MD, 9 January 1931.
28. Proceedings of the Legislative Council, 13 January 1931.
29. MD, 9 January 1931.
30. Proceedings of the Legislative Council, 13 January 1931.
31. MD, 6 January 1931.
32. Information supplied by Wing Commander Francombe in January 1982.
33. Cmd HMSO *Indians in Kenya: A Memorandum*.
34. MD 24 September 1930.
35. Cameron, *My Tanganyika Service*, p. 52.
36. Interview with S Walden, 31 October 1978.

37. MD, 4 January 1930.
38. Ibid., 27 December 1930.
39. Provincial commissioners' reports 1929–39, p. 8.
40. Listowel, *The Making of Tanganyika*, p. 102.
41. MD, 9 August 1931.
42. Ibid., 30 January 1941.
43. Ibid., 20 August 1930.

III

Tanganyika and Closer Union

While Mitchell was In Tanganyika the question of closer union of the East African territories was a constant matter for enquiry and debate. He felt strongly that from the economic point of view some form of association between them would be of value to them all. The main stumbling block was the white settlers of Kenya and the fear of the Africans elsewhere that closer union would mean an extension of the racial attitudes and policies of Kenya to the other East African territories. The fear of the Tanganyikan Africans was doubtless enhanced by the presence of white settlers in Tanganyika itself, particularly in the Northern Province, where, as in Kenya, many of them were apt to look on the Africans primarily as labour; essential for the white dominion they wanted to establish.

When the Hilton Young Commission visited Arusha in 1928, Mitchell recorded that one settler declared that 'the important thing was to keep the natives as labour for the Europeans', and another said that 'the settlers liked the Governor's system of NA. But the DC and PC must be behind the Chief with strength and the natives must be made to work for the settlers. There were 5,000 armed Moran on the mountain and the Whites were not safe.'[1] The slopes of Kilimanjaro and Mount Meru were not a solid block of European farms like the 'White Highlands' of Kenya. The European farms were grouped together in blocks with blocks of African land between them. These areas were mixed areas in a broad sense although the *individual* European farms were not surrounded by African tribal land.

In 1931 there was what Mitchell described as a 'flood of ridiculous oratory from Unofficials in Legislative Council'.[2] As has been mentioned, one member claimed that the Europeans felt that in the mixed areas more attention was paid by the government to the interests of the Africans than of the Europeans. In Kenya at that time the Africans felt bitterly that the government's policies were the other way round; the interests of the Africans being subordinated to those of the European settlers. Mitchell thought that in both countries in European circles one 'would never guess from listening to the debate that there were any natives in the country except farm labourers and servants',[3] and that a prevailing European attitude was that 'any suggestion that natives are human beings and to be treated as such is intolerable'.[4] Mitchell's insistence on respect for the humanity of Africans remained with him and earned the praise of the African members of Legislative Council in Kenya at the end of his governorship there.

Neither Mitchell nor Cameron was averse to settlement by Europeans. Cameron, the governor, although he came to Tanganyika from Nigeria, where there was no European settlement, thought that European settlers should be welcomed where, as he subsequently wrote, 'there are certain agricultural processes which European enterprise and capital can undertake but which are beyond the capacity of African tribesmen and will be beyond their capacity for a long time to come'.[5] He made his view clear to the secretary of state. Provided that native interests were not injured, development by the non-natives would be of benefit to the territory and the Empire.[6] Mitchell was in favour of controlled settlement but only if it in no way involved 'depriving natives of their land' or did anything 'to lay the foundations of a native land problem'.[7] What he did not like was the establishment of large white areas as in Kenya. He was in favour of purely African areas and smaller mixed areas where financial and technical ability to farm well rather than race was the criterion regulating sales of land. He hoped that Tanganyika would avoid turning the Northern Province into a copy of the 'White Highlands' of Kenya and he thought that 'a division of white and black areas is not only not possible but is bad in itself'.[8]

In 1929 Mitchell was delighted to be able to record that 'Mange Alanga and 2 others have bought 285 hectares; from old Kilimanjaro Smith. So that is the beginning. Good.'[9] 'My idea for the Northern Province,' he wrote,

> is *not* to admit that there must always be conflict between white and black and to try to separate them, but to get people to realise that some areas are and always must be mixed (if white people are to remain in Africa): that the races are interdependent and must diligently seek a means of peacefully living together. This they can do under the protection and moderating influence of the British Government, but much can be done also by local cooperation, given the proper forms.[10]

He advocated administration of the mixed areas under the central government with equal representation of Europeans, Africans and Asians. No wonder Major Wells and his friends were suspicious of the influence of a high ranking officer who could suggest equality of racial representation. Many years later, when he was Governor of Kenya, he wanted Africans to be able to farm in the 'White Highlands', but he was unable to override the Highlands Board and the order in council which enabled it to exclude members of non-European races from farming in what had come to be regarded as the European Reserve.

When Mitchell became Governor of Kenya, Africans feared that the fact that he had a South African wife and had members of his mother's family living in South Africa might have given him a racialist outlook. That fear was groundless. In fact his knowledge of South Africa sharpened his determination to remain strictly impartial. It had given him ample opportunity for seeing what to guard against, as when he spoke to a white audience in South Africa about native affairs in Tanganyika and doubted 'if any of them have any real conception of the problem or in their hearts any thoughts other than indefinite repression'.[11]

Cameron was opposed to any idea of closer union because he saw no way of harmonizing the interests of the Africans of Tanganyika with the aims of the leaders of the European community in Kenya, who, as he later expressed it, were declaring that the Africans of Kenya 'must never at any time have any political rights in the parliaments of that country, such as they might be'.[12] In 1926 Sir Edward Grigg (later Lord Altrincham), the Governor of Kenya, called a conference in Nairobi, at which he and Sir William Gowers, the Governor of Uganda, argued for closer union. Cameron stood firm in opposition to it, being 'committed', wrote his biographer, 'to justice for the Africans.'[13]

Mitchell, on the other hand, advocated some form of closer union but was no less 'committed to justice for the Africans' than Cameron was. He disliked the racial outlook of Grigg as much as Cameron did, but he thought that the interests of the Africans of Tanganyika could be preserved while the *economic* advantages of closer union could be enjoyed. He felt that the overheads of government could be cut down and that the expertise of the Europeans of Kenya in agriculture and other fields could be of great value to the Africans of all East Africa (to which he would have liked the addition of the Rhodesias and Nyasaland). He had no doubt that constitutionally policy was determined by the secretary of state and so the security of the Africans of Tanganyika, a mandated territory, would lie in London. He entirely disagreed with Cameron's successor, Sir Stewart Symes, who told him one day that 'it was no business of a colonial governor in matters of policy to be the mouthpiece of the secretary of state'. Mitchell was amazed at this and recorded: 'When I suggested that policy was determined by HMG and Governors were employed to carry it out, he said no, that he would do as he liked'.[14]

In later years, when he was himself a Governor, Mitchell

continued to be guided by his view of the constitutional position. He initiated policy and, when he thought it necessary, he argued against the proposals of the Colonial Office, but he never doubted that the final decision must be that of the secretary of state. So important a matter as closer union in East Africa, however, caused such discussion and debate in London that it was felt that further investigation was necessary and enquiries followed each other in rapid succession.

The Hilton-Young Commission of 1928 was followed by the visit to East Africa of Sir Samuel Wilson, the Permanent Undersecretary at the Colonial Office, and that again by the appointment of a joint select committee of both houses of Parliament. The whole debate seems to have been carried on in a state of muddle and lack of firm purpose. What the British Government meant by closer union was never clearly stated. Much of the suspicion felt by the Africans of Uganda and Tanganyika would have been averted if the Imperial Parliament had agreed its strategy and then announced it in East Africa. What was envisaged was a central authority to deal with services common to the whole of East Africa, with the internal affairs of each territory continuing to be its own responsibility, subject as in the past to the directives of the secretary of state in London and the terms of the various orders in council, Royal instructions and letters patent, which were drawn up in London for the administration of each territory. Even if a dominion of East Africa were formed, the governor-general would not have power over the internal affairs of the individual territories such as native administration. The danger lay in the secretary of state. It was feared, for instance, that Leopold Amery had too many friends among the settlers of Kenya, whose influence within the Conservative Party at Westminster was considerable, and that the idea of a dominion of East Africa dominated by white people was a danger to the preservation of African interests. Many of the settlers in Kenya admitted openly that they did not take the Devonshire Declaration of 1923 seriously, but that for tactical reasons they had not then opposed its assurance of the para-mountcy of African interests. Cameron feared that there might

31

be secretaries of state who would give way to the wishes of the Kenya settlers, but Mitchell put greater faith in the trusteeship of the Imperial Parliament. Nearly 20 years later his hope of inter-territorial cooperation was achieved with an East African assembly and a high commission, which might, if desired, lead later to a federation and he, then Governor of Kenya, was its architect.

Cameron decided that Mitchell should go to London at the end of 1931 with three Africans to give evidence before the Joint Parliamentary Committee. The choice was left to Mitchell. He chose Martin Kyamba, chief clerk of the district office at Tanga, who spoke excellent English; Chief Makwaia of Shinyanga in the central part of the country; and Mwami Francis Lwamgira, Secretary of the Chiefs' Council at Bukoba in the far west beyond Lake Victoria: an Anglican, a Muslim and a Roman Catholic. They, together with Mitchell, sailed from Mombasa on 1 April 1931. During the preceding few months all of them visited Dar es Salaam and had discussions with the governor. They were all personal friends of Mitchell's and in Tanganyika and on the voyage they unreservedly expressed the opinions of their fellow Africans. Mitchell noted at the beginning of January that Lwamgira said that 'the Bukoba natives are dead against CU partly from fear of Uganda but mainly of Kenya. He thinks that if there is CU, Kenya will dominate the position and land will be insecure. He says natives generally are determined to defend, if attacked, their Native Admin, Courts and Treasuries'.[15] Later that month they had been to see Cameron, the Governor, and 'they expressed very strong aversion to incorporation in Uganda and to any sort of association with Kenya, and they said the first thing was to make secure the Native Administrations'.[16] When Mitchell visited Mwanza he found that the chiefs there were equally opposed to closer union – especially with Kenya – and they, like all the others, insisted on the security of the native administrations with their scope extended still further. They also said that they regarded themselves as subjects of the King and understood no other form of authority, but Mitchell continued to advocate closer *economic* union and union for common services.[17]

At Mombasa the Tanganyika delegation joined the Kenya Africans whom Mitchell found pathetically different from the witnesses from Tanganyika. 'But what can one expect?' he said. In a strange contrast to the relationship of friendship existing between him and his African companions he found the senior officers accompanying the delegates from Kenya to be 'curiously detached with little if any contact with Africans in any shape or form'.[18]

The three witnesses from Tanganyika gave their evidence in London without any shyness and Mitchell was well pleased. He recorded also that alone among the witnesses, the chairman made him a speech of thanks and congratulation.[19] Lord Stanley of Alderley, the chairman, thanked him for the 'very careful thought' which he had given to the preparation of his memorandum and the very full answers which he had given to the questions put to him: 'A great deal of what you have said will obviously be of great value to those who are the permanent custodians of the interests of East Africa as a whole.'[20]

The visit was a great success. The Africans were impressed by the courtesy shown to them by the members of the committee and the various important people whom they met, and by the friendly way in which they were treated everywhere by the ordinary people around them.

Mitchell returned to Tanganyika in December 1932. While he was away Sir Stewart Symes had arrived as governor. For Mitchell it was the beginning of a new era. He found the new Governor 'very anti-SNA'. Mitchell was certainly very anti- the new governor. In the middle of January he wrote that he was 'coming to the conclusion that Symes is the complete feckless nonentity – one really cannot explain all of him any other way'.[21]

Behind the appearance of assurance and sometimes of arrogance which he exhibited throughout his career Mitchell was a man of deep feeling and volatile emotions with a strong unswerving sense of vocation. Although he admitted that promotion to a chief secretaryship would be welcome, he told the authorities at the Colonial Office that he 'was not looking for jobs but for the opportunity to get on with what matters'.[22] There was his own position to be safeguarded. He had no doubt that Symes wanted to reduce the status of the Secretary for Native Affairs to a mere political secretaryship but, as Mitchell quite rightly felt, in those still early years of native administration the influence and enthusiasm of a Secretary for Native Affairs permeating down through the provincial commissioners was a much needed life-giving force to the whole system. He was also quite sure that he was the best man to hold that office – a belief with which the whole administration agreed. Only two days after his first meeting with the new governor he wrote, 'Briefly Symes must make up his mind if he is going to throw me to the wolves or not: the position must be cleared up or I shall remove myself'.[23]

He poured out his feelings into his diary: 1 May 1932. 'My 42nd birthday. The years slip by and one does not seem to do anything with them. Certainly if in the next half dozen I do not find myself so situated as to be of some use in the world, I never shall. We rub along our poor little official round writing our little papers – it is really terrible to think of, and that I suppose is why so few people think.'[24] But the next day he was cheered by Sir Armitage Smith, the Secretary-General of the Reparations Commission, who said that in Tanganyika they had 'a very fine service and a higher standard than the home civil'.[25] And ten days later he was in the heights again because he could reckon that land was in a 'satisfactory and safe condition' and 'as I have been struggling for seven years to get this done I naturally feel elated'.[26]

He was always watchful for any harmful measures arising from Symes's enthusiasm for European settlement. He was particularly glad that African land had been made safe from encroachment, especially when he thought that 'Symes was obviously hoping to tear up the Land Development Convention and do the "Land for Nordics" act.'[27] He wanted the Europeans to be reminded by the government that there were '4,000 of them and four and three quarter million Africans'.[28] He told Symes, who had said that he was greatly attracted to settlers as a class, that he also was attracted 'to individuals, but that one should not let oneself be blinded to the fact that in the sense of colonisation they were predestined to failure'. There is 'a place for planters, a useful and valuable one, but none I fear for colonists'.[29] In later years, when he was Governor of Kenya, his views were different. European settlement was such an important part of the colony's economy that he approved of white farmers of mixed farms as well as of planters, though he never saw any sense or justice in a white area barred to African farming. Proper and full use of the land was his aim. He wanted closer and more intensive settlement on European farms and he wanted Africans to be able to farm in the 'White Highlands' under the supervision which could have been exercised if they had been allowed to become tenants on crown land in the scheduled areas.

During his years in Tanganyika Mitchell rejoiced in two areas in which there was an African breakthrough into a previously European preserve. His pleasure when some Africans bought land from a European, 'Kilimanjaro Smith', in 1929 has already been mentioned. In 1932 he was again delighted when he managed to persuade the governor to appoint Martin Kyamba, who had been a member of the party which went to London to give evidence before the Joint Parliamentary Committee, an assistant secretary in the secretariat in the Native Affairs branch. This was a foretaste of his scheme to appoint African assistant administrative officers in Kenya in the early years of his governorship there. He was not surprised when 'The EA Standard [came] out with an offensive *leader* about Kyamba's appointment, as one might expect, the real grievance being an African, because African, getting a job'.[30] The Second World War caused considerable alterations in thought and the *East African Standard* became in many respects more liberal than the majority of European residents in Kenya. When Africans were appointed to junior posts in the Provincial Administration in

35

Kenya in the late 1940s, this development was accepted as wise and Mitchell's policy was approved of in the press.

In October 1933 Symes was appointed Governor-General of the Sudan. Mitchell, as had already been shown, had taken a violent dislike to him from the start. He had revised his opinion for a short time but had soon reverted to it. Adverse opinions, strongly held, were not unusual with him, but he was ready to revise them and admit that he had been wrong if greater knowledge showed that he had been mistaken. It was so in the case of Sir Stewart Symes. Mitchell's diary contains many bitter attacks on him, but in October 1933 he recorded that Symes had been appointed Governor-General of the Sudan and wrote, 'I never thought I should be sorry to see Symes go, but I shall be very sorry, for he has, or has developed, quality for which I fear I did not give him credit. He has done a great deal here and I have learnt much from him.'[31]

A few months later Jardine, the chief secretary, also left Tanganyika. Of him Mitchell wrote, 'He has been a splendid chief and partner, admittedly not a man of tremendous intelligence, but shrewd, able, honourable and straight: a man in whom everyone has confidence and everyone likes.'[32] The territory was then without a governor and a chief secretary. Mitchell was the senior officer in the administration and took the oath as acting governor on 16 February, and was appointed chief secretary a month later. 'That is wonderful,' he wrote, when he received a cable from London telling him of the appointment, 'and I have hoped and hoped for it. It is the nicest thing bar one that ever happened to me.' Soon telegrams began to pour in – they came from as far afield as Mwanza, Shinyanga, Lindi and Lushoto, and schools from Tanga. 'Macmichael wrote a charming note and everyone seems pleased anyhow.'[33] He was not replaced as Secretary for Native Affairs but continued to watch the progress of native administration from his chief secretary's desk.

The new Governor was Sir Harold Macmichael, who had been in the Sudan political service, becoming civil secretary and at times acting governor-general. Mitchell liked him and the new governor had a high opinion of his chief secretary, which he expressed publicly in Legislative Council after Mitchell had made his first budget speech.[34]

In November Mitchell sailed to England on leave. 'So ends a remarkable tour,' he wrote.

> I came back to find a low intrigue to get me out of the job of SNA and undo all my work and start the miserable Kenya methods here: and I go home CS with, I believe, the general confidence. It has been a hard fight and I must have been very near the edge of the precipice several times. But it has turned out well and I ought to be able to see the country out of its troubles and full sail for prosperity.[35]

But his days in Tanganyika were numbered. He arrived back from leave on 14 May 1935. On the following day the governor went on leave and Mitchell was sworn in as acting governor. On 15 June, when on a visit to Mbeya in the Southern Highlands, he received a cable telling him that he was to be appointed Governor of Uganda. It was an appointment which he had 'often dreamed of as possible 4–5 years hence'.[36] He was 'almost frightened' at his 'good fortune' but cabled acceptance on the following day.

In August he visited the Lake Province and 'the many friends, white and black', he had there.[37] He had a special feeling for the Lake Province where he felt he had done his best work in building a society firmly rooted in the traditional past but learning the skills and standards needed for the future. 'I am of course pleased to have been promoted,' he told the Legislative Council. 'I should be insincere if I suggested otherwise. But it will be hard to leave Tanganyika, where I have so many friends and where a great part of my working life has been spent. Indeed, I think some of me will always remain here.'[38]

When he left Tanganyika the Dar es Salaam chamber of commerce entertained him at a farewell dinner at which the chairman said that much of the territory's sound position in 1935 was due to Mitchell, whom he described as 'the most outstanding businessman the country has possessed'.[39] His scrutiny of finance was aimed at affecting economies without impairing efficiency. In his reply he stressed what he was to maintain throughout his career, that 'What matters is people – especially in the business of Government. The longer I live,' he said, 'the less importance I attach to systems and theories and the more I realise that Government is in the first place, and indeed all the time, a vast complexity of human relationships and that it is persons and personalities that matter.'[40] He left Dar es Salaam on 28 September and, after staying for a fortnight in Kenya, arrived in Kampala on 17 October.

Notes

1. MD, 22 February 1928.
2. Ibid., 14 January 1931.
3. Ibid., 14 January 1931.
4. Ibid., 9 January 1931.
5. Cameron, *My Tanganyika Service*, p. 39.
6. CO691/83/X2971. Governor to Secretary of State, 25 February 1926.
7. MD, 18 June 1925.
8. Ibid., 9 April 1929.
9. Ibid., 11 April 1929.
10. Ibid., 10 April 1929.
11. Ibid., 15 June 1928.
12. Cameron, *My Tanganyika Service*, p. 226.
13. Harry A Gailey, *Sir Donald Cameron, Colonial Governor*, (Stanford, 1974) p. 44.
14. MD, 15 October 1932.
15. Ibid., 5 January 1931.
16. Ibid., 24 January 1931.
17. Ibid., 27 January 1931.
18. Ibid., 31 March and 1 April 1931.
19. Ibid., 5 May 1931.
20. Joint Select Committee on Closer Union in East Africa: HC Paper No. 156, vol. II, p. 475.
21. MD, 17 January 1932.
22. Ibid., 5 June 1931.

23. Ibid., 10 December 1931.
24. Ibid., 1 May 1932.
25. Ibid., 2 May 1932.
26. Ibid., 12 May 1932.
27. Ibid., 22 September 1932.
28. Ibid., 14 January 1931.
29. Ibid., 19 September 1932.
30. Ibid., 17 January 1933.
31. Ibid., 26 October 1933.
32. Ibid., 15 February 1934.
33. Ibid., 29 February 1934.
34. Proceedings of the Legislative Council, 1 November 1934, p. 199.
35. MD, 13 November 1934.
36. Ibid., 12 June 1935.
37. Ibid., 23 August 1935.
38. Proceedings of the Legislative Council, 27 June 1935, p. 288.
39. EAS in account of Mitchell's career, 3 June 1952.
40. Ibid.

IV
Uganda

From before the year 1900 Entebbe had been the administrative headquarters of the British Protectorate and, when
Sir Hesketh Bell, who had arrived as British commissioner
in 1905, became the first governor in 1907, Entebbe was
recognized to be the administrative capital of Uganda. The site
was on the shore of Lake Victoria some 20 miles from Kampala
where the Kabaka of Buganda had his capital on Mengo Hill.
As the agreement of 1900 recognized Buganda as a kingdom in
relationship by treaty with the British crown, the seat of British
administration was advisedly situated at a tactful distance from
the native capital. As time passed, this isolation produced certain
inconveniences and some government departments were moved
to Kampala, which became the commercial capital of the
protectorate.

When Mitchell and his wife arrived in Kampala by train from
Nairobi on 17 October 1935 he immediately went to the law
courts there and took the governor's oath, which was administered by the chief justice. Then they motored to Entebbe and
Government House, which was built like a comfortable English
country house on a hill with wide lawns round it and a view
over the lake. It was no wonder that Mitchell wrote in his diary
that evening, 'We are going greatly to love this place I can see'.
The Mitchells made some improvements to the house and added
a rose garden to make the grounds even more beautiful. The
new roses, which came from near Nairobi, did well at Entebbe
and in the middle of the following year Mitchell was happy to
admit that he had 'an idle day during which I gave more

40

attention to my rose garden than anything else'.[1] He was no stranger to Uganda, which he had visited several times during his years in Tanganyika. He had met Ugandan officials on many occasions and his East African outlook had led him to maintain a general knowledge of the affairs of the protectorate.

In Tanganyika he had realized that indirect rule, with which he was so deeply concerned, was not possible unless the chiefs had some measure of traditional authority. He soon found that in Uganda many of the chiefs were arbitrarily chosen by the administration: often they were Baganda, not members of the tribes over which they were given authority.

It did not take him long to come to the conclusion that all rule in Uganda was in fact direct with the exception of Buganda where, if he did not intervene fairly quickly, there too what he regarded as 'protected' rather than 'indirect' rule would soon become rule by the colonial power. In a note on native administration, which he wrote in 1939 he said, 'I am not now dealing with the case in which an African subordinate administrative officer is placed in charge of an area, but with the case in which he is appointed to masquerade as a tribal chief . . . You might as well try to appoint Mr John Smith as chieftain of the Macdonalds.'[2] When he visited Arua, for instance, he found that the chiefs whom he met at the Baraza were the same sort of sub-AO's or Akidas as in so many other places in Uganda.[3] Even where there was no tribal difference between chief and people, if the chief was imposed and was not 'entitled by custom to the power which he wields', the rule was really direct, although to his great surprise Mitchell found that many administrative officers sincerely thought that it was indirect.

A salaried chief, arbitrarily appointed by the government, was really no more than a subordinate government officer directed by the British District Officer, and local administration was direct rule by the protectorate administration. 'This substitution of employees for chiefs was carried further in Uganda than in the other EA Territories and on this framework an elaborate system of NA was built up with the DC at the head of it.'[4] It was the same with such councils as were needed. 'It is synthetic or artificial councils deriving from no real native or natural authority, which are a snare and a delusion,' he said.[5] Since the district commissioner was foreign, serving a foreign government, the system was regarded as a foreign imposition. It had to be centrally controlled and there was 'thus an inevitable neglect of communal feelings and loyalties'.[6] It was only in the Kingdom of Buganda that by virtue of the 1900 Agreement Mitchell saw a measure of sovereignty in the Kabaka and of independence in his government.

It is not fanciful to say that Mitchell was a revolutionary in every post to which he was appointed. Some members of the administration in Fiji, when he was governor there, said that they were afraid that, if he went to lunch in one of their houses, he would have reorganized the whole household by dinner time! In Uganda from the beginning of his government he delved into the problems of native administration and reached some unexpected conclusions. In the very primitive and undeveloped areas in the north rule could not be other than direct. Elsewhere he saw that the control of native funds exercised by the Provincial Administration enabled the 'foreign' officers to play an increasingly detailed role in local government, although at the same time education was producing an increasing number of Africans capable of being given responsibility in local affairs. He was keenly aware of Britain's responsibilities as trustee for the *people* of the colonies and so native administration had to be made to serve the interests of the peasants as well as the traditional privileges of the chiefs. Within a year of his arrival he told the Uganda Society that 'Indirect Rule, to use the commonly accepted label, is no more than a means to an end, like any other administrative system or practice'; and he warned against 'the error of mistaking the means for the end, and thus to sacrifice the true interests of the people to a doctrinaire devotion to administrative theory'.[7] He had made the same point some years earlier in Tanganyika when he wrote that 'the policy cannot be static, but must always be capable of development or modification; it is a means and not an end, a means of achieving at least certain minimum requirements.'[8] And in his lecture to the Uganda Society he stressed a principle which was always fundamental to his thinking: 'in the matter of administration you are dealing with human beings and not with chessmen, and it is humanity, human contacts, personalities and the realities of everyday life among ordinary people, which must condition every means which you may adopt, to discharge the functions of administration.'[9]

He had been an enthusiast for Cameron's plans for indirect rule in Tanganyika because he thought that local government could only be properly developed by building on tribal tradition and custom and that national representative government would at some future time evolve from the training experienced in local government; but when he became Governor of Uganda he found himself in new circumstances.

Up to that time, wrote Cranford Pratt, Uganda had not had 'a governor who took a major interest in native administration'.[10] The goal was the same as in Tanganyika, but the means of achieving it could not always be the same. When Mitchell wrote to the Colonial Office about his ideas, officials there failed to appreciate what fundamental changes they implied. His aims were towards the development of native responsibility, whereas under previous governors protectorate policy had always been 'towards greater control and increased bureaucratization'.[11]

In Tanganyika Mitchell had been the main intellectual architect of the system which he called native administration rather than indirect rule. He looked on it as a system 'designed to provide the framework within which the administration, social and economic progress of the people might be promoted from foundations resting on their past compatible with their present, and suited to their future'.[12] As tribal society was not static but dynamic, so a system of native administration in the colonial context had to be capable of development. When he became Governor of Uganda he saw that the system devised for Tanganyika was not appropriate to some parts of Uganda in the second half of the nineteen thirties. But as HF Morris, surveying the earlier years in Tanganyika concluded, 'Given the state of the territories at the time, the prevailing attitudes of the metropolitan countries towards colonial rule, and the limited revenues at the government's disposal, it is hard to see that there was any alternative system of administration which could in fact have proved more equitable or effective.'[13]

During recent years the system of native administration or indirect rule has been attacked by African historians as being a brake on African advance towards responsibility in administration and participation in national government. One Nigerian historian has criticized it for giving British 'political officers' great influence over the chiefs and so showing everyone that there was an authority greater than the chief's. He also claims that 'In Tanganyika, as elsewhere, native administration tended to prevent rapid progress. The concept of the African, chief or peasant, as a child who required guidance and constant supervision left initiative in the hands of the colonial administrators.'[14] This criticism seems to ignore the fact that when the Native Authority Ordinance was issued in 1926 Tanganyika was little more than a quarter of a century away from complete illiteracy and was only a geographical area inhabited by separate, often warring, tribes. Any idea of a national state would imply an authority above the local authority of the chiefs and it would be clear that there was an authority greater than theirs. Ultimately that authority would be a nationally elected government. In the meantime the administering power was the only cohesive element in the territory. No area in tropical Africa became a nation without the influence of a colonizing power. Even Liberia owed its national cohesion to American economic aid and, through that, American administrative influence.

Without the educative rôle of the administration the leaders of the present day African nations would not have learned the art of government in the twentieth-century world. To say that the administrators held 'the concept of the African, chief or peasant, as a child' is somewhat of a caricature. To hold with Mitchell the conception of 'wards in trust' is more accurate. A ward is being trained for responsibility, for standing unsupported on his own feet, and the trustee envisages a day when his task will have been accomplished. In the 1920s and 1930s there were but a handful of Africans in Tanganyika who could have taken part in modern government. The native courts and treasuries provided the opportunities for Africans to accept greater responsibilities when the changed circumstances of subsequent decades provided greater scope. Mitchell in Tanganyika, travelling all over the country with his abundant energy and enthusiasm, had seen in native administration the best means of fulfilling Britain's trusteeship.

When he became Governor of Uganda he saw at once that the native government of Buganda had progressed beyond the stage in which the system of native administration, with which he had been involved, could be applied. He told the Executive Council that the traditional system in Buganda, must be preserved although purified by the reform of abuses of power.[15] Sir Charles Dundas, who succeeded him as Governor of Uganda, thought that Buganda showed 'how conflicting were the two policies of Indirect Rule and Representative Government'.[16] Mitchell, however, had believed that Buganda was an example not of indirect rule but of protected rule – at that time a traditional hierarchical rule – and for that to become representative government was a process within the normal Western governmental development. He did not suggest that 'protected' rule meant the complete withdrawal of the paramount authority. For instance he believed that the protectorate government had to ensure the financial solvency of the 'protected' state and on one occasion he told the resident that he must make the native government of Buganda understand that, if they did not submit their estimates to the governor and went on spending money without approval, he would cut off supplies. True independence was impossible without financial self-sufficiency.

In Karamoja and other northern and eastern parts of Uganda the tribes could only be ruled directly. The people were very primitive and the Baganda agents used by the protectorate government had introduced a semblance of Kiganda administration in the earlier years of the century, which only tended to conceal the fact that protectorate administration was effectively direct. In the western kingdoms there was a fairly effective system of indirect rule, which Mitchell encouraged. The danger in such a situation was that the existing pattern was apt to make it possible for the native rulers to find ways of still further increasing their powers.

Buganda was different from all other parts of Uganda. The 1900 Agreement had created an entirely new constitution and a special relationship between Buganda and the Imperial Government. Alone among the African rulers in Uganda the Kabaka had the status of His Royal Highness. Mitchell called Buganda a protected state, but that did not mean that he felt himself unable to intervene in the affairs of Buganda when he thought it necessary to do so; but he intervened as the representative of the paramount power in accordance with the terms of the treaty. This was different from indirect rule based on the supervision by British officers of tribal agencies of administration.

In the west of Uganda, Bunyoro, Toro and Ankole were, like Buganda, communities which had agreements with Great Britain. Although they were smaller and far less important than Buganda, they had always been, at any rate in theory, different from ordinary districts, being in treaty relationship with the imperial power. They all, like Buganda, had traditions of kingship and hierarchical organization, but the royal house and the Ganda hierarchy in Buganda, largely through cooperation with the British in the 1880s, had become a much more powerful institution with a much larger territorial dominion than any of the Agreement states in the west. But the basic consideration applied to all of them, that they had agreements with Britain and so had some elements of 'protection' in their relations with the administration. However, as had happened in Buganda, the protectorate administration had steadily extended its interference with the internal affairs of the western states and agreements had tended to lose their strength as treaties and became arrangements capable of such changes as were required by general policy. As in Buganda, Mitchell soon saw that the British administrative staff in the Agreement states was excessive and was bound to cause confusion. '... either British or Native

Government,' he wrote, 'must administer but not both simultaneously'.[17] However, as he explained, pressure of work on the comparatively small secretariat and treasury staffs made it impossible for him to deal with all the problems facing him at the same time and so the west would have to wait for definite administrative arrangements until he had settled the affairs of Buganda.[18]

He told the Secretary of State in a despatch in August 1936 that Buganda was 'far the most important and advanced of the units with which Agreements' had been made and that the Uganda Agreement of 1900 went 'in important respects much further than the Agreements with Bunyoro, Toro and Ankole'.[19] He did not think there was any need for haste in the west. 'There was a difference, significant in constitutional law,' he wrote later, 'that the Kabaka retained a limited sovereignty and the others did not.'[20]

He proposed adding Bunyoro to the Western Province, which already included Toro and Ankole. There was no question in his mind of appointing residents to these states. They were small communities and, although there was no harm in their rulers maintaining their traditional customs and style of living, he thought that in their relations with the protectorate government they had too high ideas of their own importance. An Agreement had been made with Bunyoro in 1933. He did not like it and thought it would have been wiser to stick to the broadest and most general terms possible, and he had no doubt that the other kings were fairly certain to compare what was offered to them with arrangements offered to the Mukama of Bunyoro. He was not gravely worried, because, as he wrote to Bottomley at the Colonial Office, 'these people are very small beer – any ordinary Sukuma Chief amounts to a good deal more than His Nibs of Toro or Ankole' and they were on very good terms with the provincial commissioner.

The idea of 'Agreements' could become absurd, he said: 'I am now being asked to make an "Agreement" with the Basoga whose Chiefs are simply Government nominees appointed in exactly the same way as AOs and whose divisions are of our making, like District or Provinces. I might as well make an Agreement with the PC!'[21] He expected trouble with the Mukama of Toro and he did not have to wait long for it.

Land and status were the main points at issue. The Imperial Government was trustee for the people in the empire and the responsibilities of trusteeship were bound to bring conflict with the rulers and chiefs of the hierarchical states of Uganda. The administration of the protectorate had to be vigilant in opposing the attempts of the chiefs to increase the size of their estates at the expense of the peasants and also had to prevent the chiefs from increasing the dues which they demanded from them. The tribal organizations in Tanganyika had an element of democracy which was lacking in the kingdoms of Uganda and, when he became Governor of Uganda, Mitchell found problems which he had not experienced when he was Secretary for Native Affairs in Tanganyika.

In Tanganyika the substitution of a fixed tax paid to the government for the personal dues formerly paid to the chiefs received general approval. In western Uganda, on the other hand, it was bitterly resented by the rulers when imposed by the protectorate government. The loss of personal tribute weakened their position and, although the money levied on the peasants through tax, and paid into the native administrative funds provided equivalent incomes, they saw that this arrangement made it impossible for them to increase the dues demanded from the peasants and also altered their status. 'The personal tribute had been a witness of an acknowledged authority. It had confirmed the position of the chiefs as local rulers rather than paid employees. Its replacement by a local tax weakened this authority.'[22]

It was the Mukama of Toro who felt most aggrieved. A despatch written by Mitchell in April 1936 about tribute in Toro and Ankole curtailed his power to increase his income by levying higher tribute. This might be financially frustrating, but what really offended him was the fact that the measure attacked his traditional position as a ruler with an unlimited authority to levy tribute, a power which, even if not exercised, was a witness to his hereditary status. He was also affronted by being referred to as 'the Ruling Chief'. Chiefs, he felt, were two a penny, but Mukamas were quite different and he wanted to be called 'His Highness' as the Kabaka of Buganda was. The Protectorate of Uganda was a country made by the British. One 'protected state' was difficult enough to fit into the whole and later events in Buganda led to the tragic deportation of the Kabaka. Over the years the Colonial Office had gradually accepted the view that agreements made with 'protected' states could be interpreted in ways which fitted in with colonial policy, but in the case of Toro, Mitchell seemed to lose patience altogether with the ruler and his claim to status. He was certainly not going to have a collection of western 'Bugandas'.

Residents instead of the provincial commissioner were out of the question in little communities like Toro and Ankole, but 'Local Government' and 'Ruling Chiefs' were very distasteful words to a man who wanted to be called 'His Highness' in unfettered charge of his own native administration. Reports reached Government House that the Mukama had shown signs of oppressing the peasants. Mitchell seized on these rumours as an excuse for lecturing the Mukama on his status. 'I told him,' he wrote, 'that, if he had any idea that his position was similar to that of the Kabaka of Buganda, he had better drop it quickly.' Fortunately Sandford, the provincial commissioner in the west, was well liked by the chiefs and managed to calm the discomforted Mukama.

Pressure of other work in any case prevented Mitchell from initiating further administrative changes in the west at that time. But he continued to ponder over the position of Toro and Bunyoro in the protectorate and on 8 April 1940 he had a talk on administration in Uganda with Sir Malcolm (later Lord) Hailey, who was visiting him at Entebbe. He told Hailey that education and other matters in Buganda must be devolved into the Kabaka's Government, although being 'subject to control and inspection by the Central authorities', and the British Government must sooner or later remove from Buganda or ruin the native government. In the west only local government matters arose, but local government could no longer be based on weak remnants of tribal authority, but native courts would have to be composed of people whose decisions would carry respect, and councils must be developed, consultative at first, as an antidote to the chiefs.[23] In June Mussolini declared war on the Allies and in July Mitchell ceased to be Governor of Uganda and went to Nairobi to supervise the East African war effort. He was therefore unable to implement any of his plans for administrative development in Uganda.

Notes

1. MD, 26 June 1936.
2. CO536/202/40080, Sir Philip Mitchell, *Uganda Protectorate: Native Administration*. Note by the Governor, 15 April 1939.
3. MD, 17 April 1936.
4. Note by the Governor, *Uganda Protectorate*.
5. Sir Philip Mitchell, 'Indirect Rule', a lecture given to the Uganda Society on 17 July 1936, *The Uganda Journal*, Vol. IV (1937).
6. Note by the Governor, *Uganda Protectorate*.
7. Mitchell, 'Indirect Rule'.
8. Introduction by Mitchell in Brown and Hutt, *Anthropology in Action*, p. xi.
9. Mitchell, 'Indirect Rule'.
10. RC Pratt: 'Administration and Politics in Uganda, 1919–1945' in Vincent Harlow and EM Chilver (eds), *History of East Africa*, Vol. II, (Oxford, 1965), p. 491.
11. Ibid., p. 493.
12. Brown and Hutt, *Anthropology in Action*.
13. Morris and Read, *Indirect Rule*, p. 10.
14. O Adewoye, 'Native Administration in a Mandated Territory', *Tarikle* (Historical Society of Nigeria) No. 3 (1970), p. 47.
15. MD, 2 July 1938.
16. Sir Charles Dundas, *African Crossroads*, (London, 1955), p. 213.
17. MD, 10 January 1936.
18. CO536/190/40174. Governor to Secretary of State 23 November 1936.
19. CO536/188/40080/1. Governor to Secretary of State, 28 August 1936.

20. Mitchell, *African Afterthoughts*, p. 172.
21. CO536/40140 Mitchell to Bottomley.
22. RC Pratt, 'Administration and Politics in Uganda', p. 495.
23. MD, 8 April 1940.

V
Buganda

Buganda presented Mitchell with the most difficult problems in a country full of matters which seemed to him to need reform. He was not interested in making merely minor changes in administration. Uganda was not a homogeneous colony but a protectorate made up of widely divergent parts and it seemed to him that its various fundamental differences were not fully understood either at Entebbe or in the Colonial Office. At the end of his first year as governor he told the Colonial Office about his views and plans in semi-official correspondence and in a despatch to the secretary of state, but the extent of the radical changes which he had in mind does not seem to have been fully appreciated in London. An Office minute stated that:

> Mr Mitchell, who is tentatively embarking on a very long-range policy, visualises a new era in the relationship between the Protectorate and the Native Governments.
>
> Mr Mitchell also seems to envisage a future black Bar practising in the native Courts. This may be a logical development of the present situation, but there are obvious risks in admitting the right of a pleader trained in English law to argue on matters which may not be governed by it.
>
> Generally speaking I do not imagine that Mr Mitchell's proposals are at all revolutionary, but that he is simply aiming at filling up the gaps in the picture of administrative control which is already existent in rough outline.[1]

Mr Mitchell's proposals were in fact distinctly revolutionary. It is true that he wrote in his despatch, 'I do not propose any drastic or immediate general reorganisation,' but he had much more in mind than 'filling up the gaps in the picture of administrative control,' which, he thought, was on entirely wrong lines with regard to Buganda and needed drastic changes elsewhere. With regard to native barristers he took a realistic look at the future and saw that, however grave the risks might be, there were facts which had to be faced wisely and realistically and not be put in files which, he sometimes feared, were used to give a deep underlay to Colonial Office carpets.

He soon came to the conclusion that Buganda was at that time a state directly administered under a camouflage of traditional institutions and ought in any case not to be administered by indirect rule but be treated as a protected state. For him the problem was complicated by the provincial commissioner, AH Cox. Mitchell saw within a fortnight of his arrival that there was 'evidently some personal trouble between Cox and the Kabaka', but Cox said that he got on 'very well with the Ministers'.[2] Here another difficulty was revealed. There was lack of harmony within the Buganda hierarchy itself and the intrigues employed against each other by the Kabaka and the ministers complicated the Buganda situation.

Mitchell believed that the Colonial Office was not thinking along the right lines and that Cox had little understanding of his proper relationship with the native government. He wrote to Sir Cecil Bottomley, the assistant undersecretary of state at the Colonial Office, that he thought that a despatch, sent by the secretary of state in the previous July, was 'a disastrous document, implying, as it did, that the Uganda Agreement must be textually interpreted as if it were a statute whereas it is a treaty and is to be interpreted broadly to mean full control by "advice" in matters of policy'. He hoped 'they would see reason'.[3] It was clear under the Agreement, he thought, that the Kabaka, to whom resolutions of the Lukiko were sent for ratification and who had to forward them to the governor for his perusal, could not implement anything if the governor advised against it, which

53

in fact meant forbad it. However, if one of the Lukiko's resolutions was something which the governor wished to see put into effect, could the Kabaka refuse to implement it? In a particular case which led to the despatch in which Mitchell deplored his predecessor, Sir Bernard Bourdillon had thought that the governor's wishes must be paramount, but his legal advisers had said that the governor's power in such cases was only negative. He could exercise a veto but could not order the implementation of a Lukiko resolution which the Kabaka did not want to implement. Bourdillon referred the matter to the Colonial Office which upheld the legal advisers in Uganda.

During Mitchell's first months as governor the Kabaka was proposing to introduce an element of parliamentary democracy into the Lukiko. This, Mitchell saw, though highly desirable, might at times produce friction between the Kabaka and the Lukiko and he pointed out that something like the dispute between King Charles I and the English House of Commons might occur in Kampala unless he, as governor, had power to compel the Kabaka to implement the wishes of the Lukiko if he considered that they ought to have effect.[4] Mitchell caused the Legal Advisers in the Colonial Office to think again and the earlier ruling was reversed.

But there was more than that. Mitchell felt that in general and not only in the case of Lukiko resolutions 'in matters of policy it is obligatory upon the Kabaka and his Government to act upon the advice of the Governor',[5] because Article 6 of the Agreement said that 'The Kabaka, chiefs and people . . . shall co-operate loyally with His Majesty's Government in the organisation and administration of the . . . kingdom'. The Colonial Office found this claim by Mitchell difficult to answer and after much thought by the secretary of state's legal advisers Mitchell was told that in general the Kabaka was not obliged to ask for or follow advice, although, if some important point of principle were involved, the acknowledgement of the king as overlord could be invoked by the governor.

It was not necessary to point out to Mitchell that such a power could only be used on rare and particularly important

occasions. His aim always was to avoid collision and create a
basis of harmony, but it was reassuring that, if such occasions
arose, he would have the support of the Colonial Office. Great
changes had taken place in Buganda and in 1936 issues might
arise which would have been unthinkable in 1900:

> The 1900 Agreement had introduced many changes which
> fundamentally modified the traditional system of political and
> social organisation. In particular the introduction of private
> ownership of land had changed the basis upon which political
> and economic power rested, while the neo-parliamentary
> Lukiko of the twentieth century was a very different insti-
> tution from the levee of chiefs of Mutesa's time.[6]

He decided that a despatch on the whole question was
necessary but first he had to make Cox and his district officers
understand the fundamental issues. He found that very difficult
and it was not till the middle of June that he was able to start to
draft a despatch about Buganda affairs, and it was not till the
end of August that he signed it after it had 'taken months to
write'.[7] The despatch *was* revolutionary because it advocated a
completely new outlook. 'It puts the case,' he wrote in his diary,
'for developing the Native Government and adjusting the organisation of the British Administration so as to exercise a functional rather than a geographical control, gradually abolishing
the DCs.'[8] He had found it very difficult to write because of the
prevailing views – to him mistaken views – of the Uganda
administration and of the Colonial Office and he had asked
advice from London. 'My purpose in submitting these views
now for your consideration,' he wrote, 'is to bring these
questions to your notice and obtain your guidance and advice in
dealing with a situation which is in important respects outside
my previous experience.'[9] But nearly a year and a half after he
sent his despatch, which AJ Dawe at the Colonial Office called
a *damnosa hereditas*, it still lay unattended and Dawe minuted
the head of the department that they 'should clearly try to give
the Governor an answer without further delay'.[10]

The resurrection of the forgotten document merely elicited the comment that 'The delay in dealing with this paper has so far not mattered at all. Sir P Mitchell does not want to make any change while Mr Cox is provincial commissioner in Buganda and we have not been able to provide for him elsewhere.'[11] Mitchell had some justification for regarding the Colonial Office as a 'Department which never even answers despatches'.[12]

On the first page of his 1939 diary Mitchell wrote a quotation from Tobit: 'Ask counsel of all that are wise and despise not any counsel that is profitable.' In this instance, although his request for advice became a neglected *damnosa hereditas* in Whitehall, he was able to discuss his ideas with Sir Malcolm Hailey when he was visiting Uganda and he pursued his aims without waiting for the opinion of the Colonial Office.

When at last the file was attended to in the Colonial Office, a minute by Dawe which it evoked showed a sad lack of under-standing. 'Sir Philip Mitchell,' it said, 'no doubt looks at Buganda with the eye of one imbued with the Tanganyika doctrines of indirect rule.'[13] That would seem to imply that he thought that Buganda ought to be treated along Tanganyika lines. In fact, it was because he had been to so great an extent the intellectual architect of indirect rule in Tanganyika that he thought that indirect rule was *not* applicable to Buganda. His diary and his correspondence with the Colonial Office as well as the unpublished material in the secretariat archives at Entebbe, used by Low and Pratt, leave no doubt that 'Mitchell regarded Buganda as being under protected rule rather than indirect rule'.[14]

It had not taken him long to realize that the existing system, which was intended to achieve indirect rule, was becoming more and more a system of direct administration by British officers, headed by the provincial commissioner, who interfered in local Buganda affairs at all levels. In January 1936, when he passed the Buganda estimates, which provided for an expenditure of £136,000, Mitchell was impressed by the way in which they were presented but wondered what 'twelve British AOs were

doing on top of so elaborate an institution'.[15] The native
government at Mengo, the native capital in Kampala, contained
the Kabaka, the ministers and the Lukiko (the parliamentary
council) but, Mitchell complained, 'One keeps on coming across
cases where the AOs function instead of the native government.
One such I had to-day where Cox and the DC Masaka have
given orders about settlement on one of the Sesse Islands;
eventually ordered a man off and burnt his huts – and all direct
with the Saza chief as if there were no ministers.'[16] All over
Buganda he found that the situation was 'complicated by the
fact that the AOs and Secretariat quite seriously believe that
they leave the Kabaka and his Ministers and chiefs to run the
Kingdom when in fact there is scarcely a detail with which they
do not interfere'.[17]

The difficulty was made worse by lack of harmony within the
native government. The Kabaka and the ministers constantly
intrigued against each other and the Kabaka disliked the provincial commissioner, who himself failed to appreciate the constitutional position of the Kabaka. Mitchell believed that under
the previous Governor the Kabaka had been allowed to get
more and more difficult in his dealings with the provincial
commissioner and the governor himself and that the nettle had
to be firmly grasped. 'But at every turn,' he wrote, 'we find the
infernal PC/DC system throwing sand in the works.'[18] Only
fundamental changes would have any effect.

His plans to develop the native government and adjust the
British administration accordingly were accompanied by a
review of the relations between the native courts and the High
Court, and the rival views about how justice based on English
concepts and models could best be achieved in an African
society. When that society was a 'protected state', an autono-
mous state internally as far as could be, in treaty relationship
with the Imperial power, a special solution had to be found. In
Mitchell's view, as the Uganda Agreement was a treaty and
existing administrative procedure was therefore entirely wrong,
the need was to reform and strengthen the native government of
Kabaka, ministers and Lukiko at Mengo. This done, they needed

to ensure that the Saza chiefs worked within the framework of that government and did not bypass the ministers to work with the British administrative officers in their respective localities, establishing a chain of authority, not to Mengo but to the provincial commissioner.

A district officer, however, would not remain idle and Mitchell thought that the solution lay in getting rid of the district officers and making a clear chain of authority from the peasants through the chiefs to the ministers and the Kabaka. Of course he accepted the necessity of having a London-appointed administrative service in Buganda, but he thought that its officers should be appointed on a functional instead of on a geographical basis. As it was, the members of the senior staff spent much time on junior work and Mitchell believed that this waste could only be obviated by the creation of a subordinate service. The creation of a local civil service, however, which was one of Mitchell's aims, was not viewed favourably in the Colonial Office.

The first thing to do seemed to be to improve personal relations with the Kabaka. A week after his arrival Mitchell had the Kabaka, Daudi Chwa, Lady Chwa and the Kabaka's brother, Prince Suna, to lunch and he thought they 'made a beginning of contact'.[19] As always, he believed that good personal relations were of basic importance; but he saw that the Kabaka could not be expected to have any very friendly feelings towards the administration until there was a change in the administration's attitude towards the native government. The interpretation of the Uganda Agreement of 1900 was therefore fundamental. In Mitchell's view the Colonial Office interpreted it wrongly and he was convinced that his plans for the future depended on a different interpretation of this basic document. He wrote in his despatch of 28 August 1936:

> The Uganda Agreement is regarded by His Highness the Kabaka, his Ministers and Chiefs, and all educated Baganda as having an almost scriptural authority and inviolability. In their eyes it is, like a statute, a document to which precise

verbal interpretation is appropriate in any matter under discussion or in dispute with the Protectorate Government.

That view of the agreement, which the Colonial Office seemed to accept, would make administration impossible in certain cases. There was no need to be in a very great hurry, but he continued:

> It is, I suggest, highly undesirable that there should be acquiescence, or the appearance of acquiescence, in the view that the Agreement is to be interpreted in a narrow textual manner as if it were a statute enforceable in a court of law, with the corollary that in matters in which it is silent there is no power of intervention at all.[20]

The agreement, considered textually, was 'by no means a satisfactory document on which to base the relations between the parties'. The situation would become worse as the Baganda became more experienced and politically conscious. There was a fundamental incompatibility between the constitutional status of the Kabaka and his government and the organization of the kingdom into British administrative districts.

Mitchell had pointed out to Bottomley what serious situations could arise if the agreement were regarded as if it were a statute:

> If the Agreement is to be interpreted like a statute to authorise only those things which are specifically and verbally provided by it, the position seems to me to be very disturbing. For example, we have it on the authority of a previous Chief Justice (in a judgement) that a Writ of Habeas Corpus does not run in Buganda: suppose the Kabaka were to order his Prime Minister to be put in prison and were to refuse to try him, am I to say I am sorry I cannot intervene because the Agreement says nothing about it?[21]

In May, while Mitchell was wrestling with writing the despatch, a hint had been vouchsafed that the Colonial Office might be willing to reconsider their attitude when Bottomley wrote to him saying that 'The Uganda Agreement is not a very satisfactory work in itself'.[22] In November 1935, Mitchell had written in a memorandum: 'It does not seem to me that anything could be plainer or that any other form of words could state more definitely that in matters of policy it is obligatory upon the Kabaka and his government to act upon the advice of the Governor.'[23] His opinions were stated three years later in a secret memorandum communicated 'to the Resident and such senior officers serving under him as, in his discretion he may decide: and to the members of the Executive Council'. One paragraph had a tragic effect 12 years later:

It is on this constitutional theory of 'Advice' that depend the ultimate supervision and control exercised by the British over the Native Government. In an extreme case failure to accept the 'Advice' tendered by the Governor on behalf of the Crown might lead to the deposition of the Native Ruler and to the suspension or cancellation of the Agreement and the substitution for it of alternative arrangements.

No such extreme should be permitted to occur, if it can be avoided, and political officers must always have this in mind.[24]

An interpretation of the agreement, fully accepted and acted on, was essential. The district commissioners and district officers were in a very difficult and delicate position without well defined rules to work to and, although Mitchell told the secretary of state that he was 'able to pay an unhesitating tribute to the sincerity of the officers of the Administration',[25] he found it amazing that they failed to see how far their actions contradicted the policy which they thought they were following. The provincial commissioner seemed to be unable to understand that the Kabaka was 'in fact King of Buganda and must not be treated like a petty village headsman'; but Mitchell stressed to the Colonial Office that Cox was 'a man of exceptional ability', who would do well as a chief secretary but in Buganda was in 'a

60

political post for which he is temperamentally and by experience unsuited'.[26]

Mitchell was afraid that the British staff was so excessive that, unless a change could be made soon, the 'probable result might be the extinction of the Kabaka'.[27] His feeling for the national consciousness of Buganda and for the value of the African heritage was so strong that he told his Executive Council that 'The Buganda NG [Native Government] is something precious – far more precious than a mere organ for the administration of Buganda'.[28] He wanted to 'have in lieu of PC a "Resident"' and to 'canalise revenue supervision so that one or two AOs specialise in that and have a Judicial Adviser with one or more Assistants for the Court work to act as a link between the High Court and the Native Courts and bridge the gap to some extent by helping to bring them together'. He also 'contemplated technical department functions becoming gradually part of the Native Government with the Protectorate Government retaining research and advisory duties'.[29]

His proposals were embodied in the despatch of 28 August. The formerly geographically placed DOs would become advisers on the resident's staff. Each would carry out duties related to a particular ministry and the ministers would each deal with the appropriate adviser. The post of judicial adviser was of the greatest importance. He saw the administrative difficulties which the judicial adviser would face and the clear thinking and tact which would be required. Such matters as staffing and legislation would concern him as a member of the staff of the provincial commissioner (or resident), but in the exercise of his judicial functions he would have to be as independent of his official superiors as the chief justice was of the governor.

Throughout this period of radical discussion of Buganda affairs Mitchell explained his ideas to Cox, who gradually came to agree that 'he would be more properly described as Resident and his DCs as Assistant Residents and that the day was coming when it would be necessary to divide their work functionally rather than geographically'.[30] These radical proposals became the *damnosa hereditas* in the Colonial Office, which has already

61

been mentioned. Mitchell would not let it lie hidden indefinitely and he set about educating the Kabaka as well as the provincial commissioner in his ideas. On several occasions he invited the Kabaka to lunch or tea at Government House and in such an informal atmosphere discussed the difficult problems of constitutional reforms and human relations. The Kabaka agreed to have tea with the provincial commissioner once a week, alternately in each other's house, and Mitchell hoped that this would save the Kabaka from being sent for to the provincial commissioner's office, to which he naturally objected.[31] To Mitchell it seemed 'obvious that friendly personal relations are by far the most effective means of getting what has to be done by agreement and by mutual confidence'.[32]

His efforts to create a more friendly relationship between the Kabaka and the provincial commissioner had some temporary success, but progress along personal lines was made impossible by the Kabaka's private life and the rift which it caused within the Baganda hierarchy. His way of life became so deplorable that a group of leading Baganda eventually asked the governor to take action to keep the Kabaka away from public affairs.

In 1938 the title of provincial commissioner was abolished and Cox became resident. This was a visible recognition of Mitchell's conception of Buganda as a 'protected' state. In 1939, when action against the Kabaka had to be taken, it was possible for the governor to act in the spirit of the treaty without becoming himself embroiled in the internal affairs of the native state or allowing a personal encounter to take place between the Kabaka and Cox.

The Kabaka continued to be destructive and discourteous and he showed that his feelings were no more friendly than they had been before Mitchell tried to win him over. 'I had hoped,' Mitchell wrote to Dawe at the Colonial Office, 'that the situation could have been prevented from deteriorating – as it is deteriorating – and I believe that had I been able to make a change in the Resident by the appointment of Cox to another place, things would not have reached their present stage,' but he appreciated the fact that the Colonial Office had not a suitable post elsewhere to which to move Cox.[33]

At the same time discord grew between the Kabaka and the ministers, and the Lukiko at Mengo. At the beginning of November he unwisely went so far that he played into the governor's hands. He told the resident that 'for health reasons' he could not attend the ceremony of laying the foundation stone of the new Makerere buildings by the Duke of Gloucester, the King's brother, and Mitchell commented in his diary that 'In the end I shall have to say that as his health is so bad there will have to be a regency'.[34]

The situation got steadily worse. A month after the ceremony at Makerere, Prince Suna went to see the governor and spoke to him about the Kabaka. 'He does not like Mr Cox,' he said, 'nor me; nor you, Sir, either. He does not like me because I get on well with Europeans. He is drinking very heavily and his legs are swollen badly. He will die soon; his days are finished.'[35] The Kabaka 'has practically broken off relations with Cox,' Mitchell told Dawe, 'and, indeed, with Government. At present I am the only person, as far as I know, who ever sees him and I have difficulty in getting him to come to see me.'[36] The Kabaka's days, however, were not quite finished, but he withdrew more and more from public life and in July 1939 Mitchell wrote to the Colonial Office that the Kabaka 'has completely withdrawn into his lake-shore home, where drunken orgies are, I fear, becoming more frequent . . .'. Things reached such a pass that two of the ministers went to the resident and told him that they would like him to ask the Kabaka to get rid of his 'people given to drinking' and appoint others. 'It was explained to them,' Mitchell wrote, 'that the matter lay between them and their Ruler, and they fully understand that.' Mitchell had stressed to Cox the need to have necessary reforms at Mengo carried out by the ministers and not as a response to pressure by the protectorate government, and that discussion and action should be on a constitutional basis. He said that all the ministers should realize that they should push on with the liberal reform of the

Lukiko so that future criticism and discontent should be heard there and not in outside factions.

The two ministers, who were Protestants, wrote accordingly to the Kabaka, but the Omulamuzi, who was a Catholic, refused to sign the letter. 'I mention this,' Mitchell told the Colonial Office, 'because religious rows are never far below the surface in Uganda, and this may be relevant later.' Then Cox advised the two ministers privately that they must be careful to act constitutionally and that, if they intended to go to extremes, they would have to summon the Lukiko. Public opinion was very strongly against the Kabaka and Mitchell told the Colonial Office that, if the Lukiko 'presents a petition to me saying that His Highness's health is such that they have been driven to decide that he is no longer able to discharge his functions and praying me to establish a Regency, I shall do so'.[37]

Mitchell felt sure that a crisis was inevitable, sparked off by the customary celebrations for the Kabaka's birthday on 8 August. Normally a salute was fired and ceremonies were performed attended by the chief secretary and other senior officials and, of course, by the Kabaka himself. Mitchell decided that, if nothing had happened to show that the Kabaka was mending his way, the usual salute would be fired, but because of his 'ill health' the customary ceremonies would not be held. 'I cannot take the risk,' he explained, 'of his simply failing to turn up and thus making a public fool of the Protectorate Government, as I feel sure he would do ... I do not think a crisis can be avoided: I am hopeful that I may be able to keep it within the Native Government, between Ruler and Lukiko: but if the Lukiko puts its foot down I shall give it my support.'[38] To be able to leave such a crisis to the native government and to act decisively as the supreme power when final action had to be taken was in Mitchell's view an instance not of indirect rule but of protected rule. The native government was left free to discuss and, if possible, to settle its affairs subject to the terms of the agreement without interference from the Imperial power, which would act only if the terms and spirit of the treaty were being ignored or if the native government asked for Imperial support.

The Colonial Office, while assuring Mitchell that the secretary of state agreed with the action to be taken in the crisis, which he expected should be left primarily for Mitchell to decide, was unable to appreciate his distinction between protected and indirect rule. '. . . The time has gone,' they wrote, 'when we can allow "indirect rule" to mean the bolstering up by British authority of native rulers who are incapable of playing a useful role.'[39] To Mitchell the important point was that the proper authorities as constituted by the 1900 agreement in Buganda would have reached a decision themselves. It would not be the decision of a provincial commissioner made in the name of a native ruler. It would be a decision which would have to be implemented by the governor, but up to that point deliberations would have been conducted constitutionally at Mengo without British interference or pressure. That, he maintained, was protected rule, not indirect rule; and, far from 'bolstering up' a native ruler, it would show the governor upholding what, under the 1900 Agreement, was the constitutional native government against a native ruler who had shown himself unfit to discharge his duties. The matter went up to the king, whose private secretary wrote to the Colonial Office to say that the king, having seen Mitchell's letter, agreed that 'the action proposed by the Governor is the only possible course should a crisis arise'.[40] The governor was convinced that the Kabaka would not attend the curtailed birthday ceremonies and so it turned out. The *Uganda Herald* printed a tactful report: 'A Service was held at Namerembe Cathedral, His Highness the Kabaka was unable to be present, but Lady Chwa and Omulangira Mutesa and other members of His Highness's family attended.' The report went on to say that prayers that the Kabaka 'should regain his health soon' were offered. 'The Hon. the Resident of Buganda and two other British Government officials were present' and after the service 'a semi-private Baraza was held at Mengo.'[41]

The Kabaka Daudi Chwa died on 22 November 1939. The three senior officers of the Buganda Government chose from among the princes Frederick Mutesa to succeed him and their choice was unanimously accepted by the Lukiko. By the terms of the 1900 Agreement their choice had to be approved by the governor. Mutesa was a schoolboy at King's College, Budo. Mitchell had seen him several times there and would himself have chosen him as successor to Daudi Chwa. A regency was appointed. Mutesa remained at school, but had to appear as Kabaka at important ceremonies. Mitchell invited him from time to time to Government House and found him a well poised and charming visitor, but what seemed to remain in Mutesa's memory was, as he wrote later, that 'Sir Philip Mitchell . . . used to come to see me occasionally and gave me chocolates'.[42]

Although the immediate problem of Buganda had been settled, Mitchell realized that the development of the kingdom would have to be carefully watched. Detailed intervention would become increasingly difficult and he had no doubt that it was the wrong policy. Accordingly, he explained why the provincial commissioner had become the resident, why a functional basis of administration had replaced a geographical basis, and why a judicial adviser had been appointed to the residency staff to be a link 'bringing the Native system into closer accord with the basic principles of judicial practice and procedure upon which the supreme judicial authority must in the last report insist'.[43]

The Second World War led to Mitchell's transfer to other work before his policies were finally agreed with the Colonial Office; but during the next governorship it was fully accepted that his declaration that the main objectives of the British and native governments were the same, and his policy that 'for all important matters touching his government the Head of the Protected State must seek, and be guided by, the advice of the King's Representative, that is to say, the Governor'[44] became the officially pronounced policy of the Colonial Office.

Notes

1. CO188/40080/1, Minute by SM Campbell, 29 October 1936.
2. MD, 14 November 1936.
3. Ibid., 31 March 1936.

4. CO188/40080/1, Memorandum by the governor enclosed in Mitchell's d/o letter to Bottomley, 3 April 1936.
5. Ibid.
6. Kenneth Ingham, *The Making of Modern Uganda*, (London 1958) p. 191.
7. MD, 17 June 1936.
8. Ibid., 28 August 1936.
9. CO536/188/40081/1, Despatch from governor to secretary of state, 28 August 1936.
10. CO536/188/40081/1, Minute by Dawe, 18 January 1938.
11. Ibid., Minute to Sir C Parkinson, 25 January 1938.
12. MD, 19 June 1937.
13. CO536/188/40080/1, Minute by Dawe, 18 January 1938.
14. DA Low and RC Pratt, *Buganda and British Overrule*, 1900–1935, (London 1960) p. 310.
15. MD, 17 January 1936.
16. Ibid., 18 June 1936.
17. Ibid., 22 July 1936.
18. Ibid., 3 November 1935.
19. Ibid., 24 October 1935.
20. CO536/188/40081/1, Despatch from governor to secretary of state, 28 August 1936.
21. Ibid., Mitchell to Bottomley, 3 April 1936.
22. Ibid., Bottomley to Mitchell, 14 May 1936.
23. CO536/188/40080/1, Memorandum by governor enclosed in letter to Bottomley, 3 April 1936.
24. CO536/202/40081/1, 15 April 1939.
25. CO536/188/40080/1, Despatch from governor to secretary of state, 28 August 1936.
26. CO536/188/40080/1, Mitchell to Bottomley, 9 June 1937.
27. Ibid., 9 January 1936.
28. Ibid., 2 July 1938.
29. Ibid., 24 February 1936.
30. CO536/188/40080/1, Despatch from governor to secretary of state, 28 August 1936.
31. Ibid., 7 June 1937, and the same hope was expressed in a letter to Bottomley, 9 June 1937 (CO516/188/40080/1).
32. Mitchell, *African Afterthoughts*, p. 171.
33. CO536/197/40080/1, Mitchell to Dawe, 24 August 1938.
34. MD, 1 November 1938.

35. Ibid., 2 December 1938.
36. CO536/197/40080/1, Mitchell to Dawe, 24 August 1938.
37. CO536/202/40080/1, Mitchell to Dawe, 15 April 1939.
38. Ibid.
39. Ibid., Dawe to Mitchell, 1 August 1939.
40. Ibid., A Lascelles to IJ Parkin (CO), 8 August 1939.
41. *The Uganda Herald*, 25 August 1939.
42. The Kabaka of Buganda, *The Desecration of My Kingdom*, p. 82.
43. CO536/202/40080/1, Note by the governor, 15 April 1939.
44. Ibid.

VI
Uganda's Economy

On their way from Tanganyika to Uganda Mitchell and his wife spent a fortnight on leave in Kenya. They stayed for a few days at Government House in Nairobi, where Mitchell learned from Sir Joseph Byrne, the governor, that he was deeply worried about the extreme policies of those Europeans who were aiming at the establishment of a European-dominated independent Kenya, and about the financial problems of the colony. Mitchell had long thought that some form of closer union was needed to lessen the cost of the overheads of government, but his conversations with Byrne reinforced his determination to see that no interterritorial cooperation could be contemplated if it gave the Europeans of Kenya power over the other territories. He also concluded that 'there are no patent medicines for public finance'.[1]

In his book, *The Making of Modern Uganda*, Kenneth Ingham says that the treasurer's report on revenue and taxation, which appeared in October 1936, contained ideas which 'commended themselves to the Governor, Mr Mitchell, because they involved a simplification in the taxation of Africans'.[2] Certainly, as Ingham says, there had been 'numerous promptings from unofficial opinion' for a review of the revenue and taxation of the protectorate.

While he was in Tanganyika Mitchell had kept himself informed about affairs in the other territories and the very day after he took the governor's oath in Kampala he asked the treasurer to undertake that enquiry. He told the treasurer that he was 'concerned for the peasant who had to pay for the whole

69

business'. He wanted to be assured that 'the revenue was fair and reasonable' and that 'expenditure was not being increased on a rising market'.[3] The peasant, above all the Baganda, not only provided the largest share of government revenue but through the traditional system of tribal dues maintained the wealth of African landlords and the hierarchical structure of the native kingdoms. Although the provincial commissioner in Buganda did not think that taxes were too high, Mitchell continued to work for a reduction and simplification of taxes and dues. Throughout his career he thought that the collection of tax was the basis of good administration.

When he opened Legislative Council on 20 November he confined his address mainly to finance. The protectorate budget had £1,200,000 in hand, but he warned against spending for its own sake and then stressed that the whole finance of Uganda depended on the peasant, by whose capacity to pay, everything had to be measured. Two days after his arrival he had found that there was a proposal to increase expenditure by £88,000, 'a great deal of it on what seem to me to be frills' and he wrote that he was 'clearly going to have to use the pruning knife with a heavy hand'.[4] To have £1,200,000 in hand 'made a very pretty picture, being so good as to be almost embarrassing',[5] but he felt that this surplus had been unwisely amassed by leaving undone essential maintenance which would have to be attended to sometime at a higher cost than would have been necessary if it had been met earlier. As he put it to the secretary of state, 'The strong financial position of the Protectorate is in part due to the policy of strict economy which has been followed for some years and it was to be expected that substantial arrears of maintenance and replacement would be found to exist'.[6] However, he thought a few months later that capital expenditure could no longer be delayed. The cotton crop in 1936 was expected to be unusually good. A peasant agriculture had been better able than capitalist systems to withstand the world depression and he appointed a development committee to examine the financial priorities of the protectorate and the means of paying for them.

When the development committee published its report, he thought it 'an excellent and painstaking document', but it was 'a little disappointing that so much of it should be rehabilitation and so little productive development, but the parsimony of the last five years has got to be made good.'[7] Uganda had got through the early years of the world depression with financial surpluses. This certainly 'made a very pretty picture', but the cost of the picture had to be borne by the new governorship, and in consequence of this policy of economy, public services like electric light and power, water supplies, sanitation and roads had been neglected, and so conditions in Kampala were 'far more primitive in these respects than in any of the neighbouring territories'.[8]

The Colonial Office was not very sympathetic and one of the officials to whom Mitchell's despatch was passed for comment minuted: 'There is no need for any of these things and they can all be provided gradually.'[9] It was fortunate that this was an internal minute and not a comment in a letter to Mitchell, who often felt that the Colonial Office was lacking in real understanding of local problems and who, being himself enthusiastic and efficient, found the frequent delays in the Colonial Office in answering letters very irksome. Although he had no doubt that in the last resort a colonial governor was the servant of the secretary of state, he resented niggardly interference and thought that the CO might at least 'take the trouble to conceal the contempt it feels for Colonial Governors'.[10]

The danger of being beguiled by the large financial surplus into unwise spending was real and within a week of Mitchell's arrival an example appeared. New police department lines were needed. Plans had been drawn up and were sent to the governor for approval. £50,000 seemed to him to be an unnecessarily high cost and he asked for a discussion and further details[11]. He then found that 'the whole thing could be done for £15,000 – a very different story but very typical of this country'.[12]

He was also concerned about delay in administration in Uganda and he showed his feelings when, for instance, in January 1936 he saw the managing director of an Indian sugar company and commented, 'They have not yet got leave to buy their new sugar mill which was agreed upon in November 1934. O Uganda!'[13] In general it seemed to him that many things in Uganda had been allowed to drift and that decision and action ought to be more definite. The position of Buganda and the worsening relations between the Kabaka and the provincial commissioner had to be tackled. In Bugishu the finances were in a very bad state and 'They are all sails set for bankruptcy'.[14] The police struck the new governor as being slack and inefficient. In the west the Mukama of Toro, as has already been seen, was arguing that his position was similar to that of the Kabaka of Buganda, which expressed a highly exaggerated view of his status. The important question of the relation between the High Court and the native courts needed careful scrutiny.

In other matters also, Mitchell saw a need for decision and action and change. Perhaps the matter which had the most personal appeal to him was the education of Africans and his vision of establishing a college of higher education leading to the University of East Africa at Makerere. His hopes for the future could not be realized without an educated African leadership who would be far better able than the colonial government to explain to the people what constructive policies required. One task facing Britain as trustee for the African peasantry was to educate their leaders according to the ideals of British culture and it was necessary to devise an economic system within which their standard of life could be gradually improved.

The economic system which he had in mind required low taxes. The actual level would have to be decided with social as well as economic considerations in mind, as he told the secretary of state in a despatch at the end of his first year as governor. Opinion was bound to play a large part in deciding whether taxes were oppressive or not. Some people thought that anything was oppressive which interfered with the primitive level and customary mode of 40 years ago but, he wrote:

To others, of whom I am one, it appears that our first and most important function is to interfere as fundamentally and

72

effectively as possible with this customary mode of living and actively to promote the social and economic developments of the people towards the only standards of civilisation open to them – our own.[15]

He did not think that conditions for the peasant could be quickly improved. A simple economic base had to be secured with a simple and not costly level of taxation at light rates, combined with a good custom house revenue slowly developing a civilization in the economic security that can only come from avoiding haste and overtaxation. He thought that none of his officials, except Merrick, the Treasurer, understood the position and were in too great a hurry.[16] He felt that sometimes administrators and policy makers forgot that they were dealing with human beings whose traditions and capacity could not be disregarded.

The protectorate government and the native governments both had to raise revenue, but it could only come 'from the same body of taxpayers – that is to say from the same cotton, tobacco and earnings'. The peasant's capacity to pay depended, in Mitchell's view, not just on the money available in the pockets of the peasants before the payment of taxes but on the amount of money available after they had grown or bought the food which was required for an adequate diet: a poorly nourished peasantry would not have the strength needed to dig the land and tend the crops on which an adequate diet depended, and an ill-conceived system of taxation would generate a spiral leading to general poverty.

He pointed out to the Colonial Office that hut and poll taxes were originally taxes at a low rate imposed upon primitive people who grew their own food, made their own clothes from skins or bark cloth, built their own homes and in fact were economically self-sufficient. But in Uganda, in addition to low taxes covering tribal obligations, there were now numerous fees and licences to be paid as well as customs and excise duties; a fiscal system had arisen entirely different from that for which the poll tax was originally devised. 'It may seem out of place,'

73

he wrote, 'to refer to the question of nutrition in discussing taxation, but the two things are by no means as far apart as may at first appear.'[17]

Taxation at light rates and a good custom house revenue appealed to Mitchell, and poll tax had great advantages over other forms of taxation in the peasant society of Uganda. It could be adjusted as required by changing economic conditions, adjusted even in specific districts, if necessary. Moreover in a peasant society, in many places a rather primitive society, new ideas were difficult to explain, but poll tax, though a tax imposed by the foreign government, was akin to the dues and tribute which Africans were accustomed to pay to their chiefs and so did not appear unnatural. One advantage was that it was simple to collect and so to be approved 'on grounds of cost alone, an important consideration for communities of peasants dependent on small scale farming'. An all-embracing poll tax could dispense with the collection of tribal tribute, fees, licences and various existing dues, which required a larger and more expensive administration. As an example of the reforms which he wanted to introduce he cited the fees for the registration of bicycles, which were to be abolished on 1 January. On the inclusive poll tax basis of taxation the fees for the registration of bicycles would be paid in the poll tax; and the same was true of other fees such as those for the inoculation of cattle. He told the Legislative Council that taxation ought not to deprive the peasants of the highest attainable standard of living. He thought that taxation ought regularly to be subjected to the closest examination. He was glad to report that at that time 'the whole of the proceeds of their taxes [were] spent, directly or indirectly, for the benefit of the natives', but the amount which they had to pay ought always to be carefully watched, and he thought the level ought to be brought down.[18] Of course, he said, the non-native part of the population played a valuable part in the economic life of Uganda, but the largest part of the revenue reached the government by way of the native population and 'judged by standards elsewhere in Africa direct taxation of natives in Uganda is very high'.[19] He called his principal officers together and explained his financial ideas to them, and 18 months later he argued for the poll tax to be 'liquidated in labour as well as money on the ground that only thus could there be the necessary flexibility'.[20]

When he opened the budget session of Legislative Council in 1939, Mitchell spoke in strong terms about the dependence of the living standards of what later came to be known as the developing countries on the world markets for primary products. He made the same point three years later when he was governor of Fiji. He was concerned about the way in which prices of raw materials from tropical countries were depressed in world markets by competition among industrial nations where minimum wage legislation was 'so generally thought indispensable while the urgent need of minimum prices received so little support.' 'I have taken these questions up with the Secretary of State,' he said, 'and hope that many others similarly situated will do the same, and press for concerted Empire-wide action.'[21]

Racial discrimination was anathema to him unless disparity in racial conditions made discrimination the only way of achieving acceptable results. In the case of wages, for instance, he realized that, if African technicians had to be paid as much as was paid to the Indian technicians, who were in general much more skilled, they would become unemployed. But his attitude towards trading licences showed that, where equality would not injure the Africans, discrimination would not be tolerated. 'Racial discrimination appears to me,' he told the Colonial Office, 'to be quite out of place in connection with trading licences, and when the law is under reconsideration I propose, if possible, to abolish special rates for natives *qua* natives. I agree that there ought to be a special rate for small village shops (if indeed they should be required to pay a licence at all) but the criterion ought not to be the race of the propriertor.'[22]

The more he studied the fiscal system of Uganda the more he came to the conclusion that the whole system of taxation needed overhauling. Even if taxes were not oppressive, he wrote to the secretary of state, they might be 'financially imprudent'. His ideas about taxes in Uganda were set in the wider framework of colonial economic and financial practices. His diary often records his thoughts and in the middle of 1938 the financial question must have worried him a good deal. On 25 July he wrote:

> I also worked on a note about our economic and financial methods and the progressive impoverishment of the people as the wealth of the country apparently increases. The causes are of course the continuous deflation we practise by withdrawal of large sums for investment abroad and to meet charges in London and elsewhere. Unless large drafts of capital are introduced it means in effect that annually nearly the whole country's savings are taken away from it, and no country can stand that.[23]

In 1937 he was much occupied with the question of *luwalo*, a traditional form of communal labour in Uganda. In his view it was closely bound up with the consideration of taxes and he wrote a despatch putting suggestions of ways of making what he said was 'a very unpopular imposition' more acceptable to the peasants. One noticeable fact about Uganda was that the roads were much better than those in Tanganyika and Kenya. This was due to *luwalo* labour, or financial commutation, by which they were constructed and maintained. The system was good for the roads but bad for public relations and Mitchell suggested that the protectorate government should assume financial responsibility for the maintenance of roads, bridges and ferries. This done, *luwalo* should be converted into a money rate to be legalized as soon as possible in Buganda and on 1 January in the Eastern and Northern Provinces. Certain complications made it impossible to fix a date for the change in the Western Province, but he hoped it would be effected there before long. There would be some people unable to pay the rate and for them the rate should be 'convertible by an equivalent period of labour'. That should be the first step, but he suggested that later on, when it became possible, the rate and poll tax should be 'consolidated into a single impost to be shared by Government and NAs in agreed proportions'.[24]

At the same time he wrote to Bottomley that '*luwalo* now a labour tax with money in lieu, should become a money tax with labour in lieu'.[25] The Colonial Office agreed that that would not be against the Forced Labour Convention, but that poll tax with labour in lieu would be, and they suggested that perhaps, instead of imprisonment, labour camps might be instituted with discharge being granted on completion of the appropriate amount of work. It was agreed that the matter should be discussed with Mitchell who was on leave at the time. Then, as happened with many other issues, the whole matter was deferred in London.

Mitchell's wish to reduce taxes, with its need to curtail government expenditure, and his desire to enable Africans to participate to the extent of their present capacity in the affairs of their developing country led him to examine the problem of Africanization of government services. He was convinced that every opportunity should be taken to Africanize posts which by that time Africans were qualified to fill. Two months after his arrival in Uganda he told the head of the Public Works Department that he would not have any 'more imported and expensive European storekeepers and accountants and that he must make do with Africans and Asians'.[26]

A task which he therefore saw as being of great social importance was the provision of housing for government African staff. He wanted to establish a junior civil service. That would require approval from the Colonial Office, but housing for the existing Africans in the lower grades was inadequate and he thought that it was important that the government should provide housing which was adequate and financially possible to build, and which would be an example to private employers who were not always adequately concerned about the housing of their African staff. Housing would have to take note of African conditions and social traditions and somehow satisfy both African custom and available finance. 'The African,' he wrote, 'is a family man, often indeed (being polygamous) a man of more families than one and for this alone his first need is for space.' It would not be possible to build permanent buildings which would provide that. Anything more than one small room in some form of barrack would be prohibitively expensive. The problem was not easy to solve but was of great interest and importance and Mitchell intended to initiate further investigations and experiments and he sought authority for expenditure on housing for African staff.[27]

It was not only lower grade staff he had in mind. 'With the staff that Uganda has got,' he told Bottomley, there would soon be boys from Budo and other schools able to fill posts so far filled by Europeans and it would be 'most unfortunate' if they were 'obstructed by a large establishment of young European officers'. He asked to be allowed to include in the estimates a sum to meet the cost of employing experts to investigate the whole question of the employment of Africans and the establishment of a local civil service'.[28] The Colonial Office, however, did not react at all favourably to his request for the etablishment of a local civil service and a reply was sent in the name of the secretary of state which Mitchell must have found far from satisfactory:

> I view with some misgiving the proposal to explore the possibility of creating a local civil service and establishing a Provident Fund . . . Further, in considering the question of a local civil service, I am by no means sure that the circumstances in Uganda warrant too close an imitation of the arrangements obtaining elsewhere.

The last few words were significantly altered in the draft in the Colonial Office file when 'arrangements elsewhere' was substituted for 'arrangements which obtain in Kenya'.[29]

Mitchell failed to see why a local civil service could be good for one territory but not for another even if racial considerations might cause complications. A few months later he arranged a meeting with the heads of all government departments 'to consider the extent to which we could replace imported staff by locals, especially Africans'. 'I stressed,' he wrote, 'that on political grounds alone we must entrench our culture and ideals in the local service and for financial reasons can work through no other agency and that we must therefore accept it as policy that the services have got to be Africanised.'[30] The level of taxation could never be overlooked. He wanted, when possible, to be able to reduce taxation, but he was too much of a realist to think that by curtailing expenditure and making possible a reduction of taxes he could automatically improve the life of the peasants. He had no doubt that in most of the country, as soon as the poll tax was reduced, the 'Native Governments or the native landlords would in one way or another pack it on to the back of the peasant again.'[31]

As with other matters the Colonial Office did not proceed with speed and in March 1940 the idea of a local civil service was still being discussed in Whitehall. A minute written then warned that, as Mitchell proposed a non-racial local civil service with Africans and Indians competing on equal terms, resentment could be expected from the Indians. Uganda was by that time producing 'a sufficiency of educated Africans competent to perform the kind of work hitherto allotted to Asiatics' and so there seemed to be 'no alternative but to accept the theory of no discrimination as between African and Indian'.[32] Mitchell would not have been pleased if he had heard that an officer in the East African department of the Colonial Office came to the conclusion that his non-racial policy had to be accepted because there was no alternative to it. After further discussion, however, the Colonial Office agreed that, although the Asian Civil Service Association would try to preserve their special privileges, Mitchell's scheme was the right one and policy must be aimed at assimilating Asiatics into the rest of the local community in the protectorate.[33]

While the Colonial Office was discussing Mitchell's proposal, he sent a despatch to the secretary of state asking that 'the long overdue improvements in the salaries of serving African staff, which are reflected in my proposals for the formation of a Second Division of the local civil service, should take effect with as little delay as possible'.[34] He saw no reason why the long overdue improvements in the salaries of serving African staff should be held up by discussions in the Colonial Office about the formation of a second division in local civil service.

As expected, the Indians objected to the proposal for a non-racial local civil service. The Indian Unofficial Members of the Standing Finance Committee and the Uganda Civil Service Association declared that the terms offered by the scheme were 'degrading to Asians'. Mitchell wrote to the Colonial Office to say that this contention was based on the assumption that there were two fixed and unalterable standards of living, one for the Asians and a lower one for the Africans – an absurd contention with regard to Buganda, where there were many Africans with a very high standard of living. In any case the standard of living of the Africans for whom the terms of the proposed civil service were designed 'differs no whit from that of the Asians who may be expected to become candidates for appointment'.[35]

The wealth of those Africans with a high standard of living came from the land in one form or another. One of the main tasks of the British administration was to develop crops to take the place of the trade in slaves and ivory, which had previously been the basis of the export economy of the area. The local diet rested on bananas, particularly the plantain which could be turned into banana flour called *matoke*. This with grain crops and live stock supplied a subsistence agriculture in the fertile and well watered southern half of Uganda; but the twentieth-century protectorate needed more from its agriculture than subsistence farming. Fortunately, Mitchell commented, 'With rare foresight the authorities in Uganda had used this *luwalo* labour for a quarter of a century to make roads.'[36] So good were they that 'by 1920 the Provincial Commissioner of the Northern Province was boasting that the 1,400 miles of roads in his province were "swept throughout every Monday"'.[37] The extensive lakes made cheap water transport available elsewhere for the movement of agricultural produce; and the railway through Kenya linked Uganda with the sea. The Lancashire textile mills needed cotton, and cotton was a product which Uganda was ideally fitted to supply and it soon became the leading export crop.

Cotton was not indigenous in Uganda. Some 'wild cotton' had been introduced by the Arabs and between 1903 and 1910 a number of varieties were taken to Uganda by the government and private people. In those early years of the twentieth century plans were made, beginning in Buganda, to develop cotton as a commercial peasant crop and the most suitable substitute for the trade in slaves. Coffee, although less extensively cultivated than cotton, was a useful asset in the economy and the government had encouraged the cultivation of Arabica coffee, which had reached Uganda from Nyasaland to where it had been taken from the Botanic Gardens in Edinburgh, as well as the indigenous robusta coffee. Sugar had been grown in Uganda for centuries, but it was not till 1924 that an Indian immigrant, NK Mehta, founded the sugar industry at Lugazi which made a real contribution to the export and local trade of the protectorate. In the west of Uganda, European planters developed the growing of tea, which had been taken to the Botanic Gardens at Entebbe at the beginning of the century, and this added another item to Uganda's export trade. When Mitchell became Governor however, cotton was so overwhelmingly the main agricultural export that he regarded Uganda as a one-crop country and he felt this to be a great danger, because, if the world price of cotton fell, the economy of the protectorate would be in very great difficulty. With this in mind, he determined to keep recurrent expenditure under strict control.[38]

The export of agricultural products was adversely affected by restrictions imposed by the international marketing bodies. In 1937 an export quota was placed on sugar, giving East Africa a limit of 27,000 tons. Uganda's share was fixed by the interterritorial organization at 12,000 tons which was less than half of the crop produced in that year.[39] An increase of revenue from the export of sugar was thus effectively blocked. Mitchell promised the tea planters that he would support an application for an increased acreage of tea in Uganda, but he feared that he 'had no hope of getting it'.[40]

In 1939 Mitchell wrote to Dawe at the Colonial Office attacking the international restrictions scheme on the growing of tea, which he thought disastrous for Uganda and Kenya, and to a lesser extent for Tanganyika. It prevented development in East Africa while 'in fact holding an umbrella over Belgian, Brazilian and Portuguese' growers, allowing them to 'plant tea to their hearts' content – and eventually ruin the market'.[41] He wanted the Colonial Office to fight for a larger quota for East Africa. Two months later the Second World War broke out, international conferences on agricultural quotas had to wait and he himself soon ceased to be Governor of Uganda. He had asked the Agricultural Department for suggestions for developing other crops. He himself noticed that the climate, altitude and soil of Kigezi in the southwest of Uganda were similar to those of the pyrethrum-growing parts of Kenya and instigated experiments to find out whether pyrethrum could become a peasant crop there.[42]

Some form of closer union of the East African territories seemed to him to be even more necessary when he was Governor of Uganda than it had been before. Soon after his arrival he attended the annual planters' day at Fort Portal and he visited the Indian sugar estates near Jinja. The immigrant planters produced 8 per cent of Uganda's exports and he urged them to organize on an East African basis. This, he pointed out, would not help exports because of the restrictions imposed by the world quota system, but it would enable them to exploit the potentialities of the East African internal markets.[43]

Soon afterwards there was a clear example of the administrative value which could be expected from closer union, which could curtail the power of the Kenya settlers to serve their own needs at the expense of the other territories. Cotton, the main source of income of the Uganda peasants, which they sold to the ginneries, had then to be exported. The main reason for building the Uganda railway had been to link Uganda to the sea at Mombasa and substitute a better mode of transport than the traditional caravan and head-porterage. The line went through Kenya and early in 1936 the export of cotton from Uganda

82

became extremely difficult because all the trucks were used for carrying Kenya's European-grown subsidized maize. Mitchell therefore wrote to the Governor of Kenya to complain and at the same time ordered his officials to make plans for transporting the cotton by lake steamer to Mwanza and then by rail through Tanganyika to Dar es Salaam. The Tanganyika railways, constructed by the Germans, had not been integrated into the Kenya and Uganda railway system. The Governor of Kenya replied that he would do what he could, short of compelling the general manager of the railway, Sir Godfrey Rhodes, to make arrangements with the Tanganyika Railway for the transport of Uganda cotton.[44]

The power of the Kenya Europeans was shown by their monopolizing the trucks for the transport of their maize and the lack of a combined railway organization was clearly a disadvantage to the economy of Uganda which depended on the railway for an outlet to the sea. A system of railways controlled by an East African agency would have prevented the Europeans of Kenya from monopolizing the trucks needed by Uganda. In 1932 the Joint Select Committee on Closer Union had asked for an enquiry into the working of the railways and Mr Roger Gibb was sent from London to enquire and write a report. Among other things he pointed out that the task of fixing railway rates on cotton-seed and maize was bound to cause friction, because cotton-seed was a native crop in Uganda and maize for export was at that time the main crop of the Kenya settlers. The problem reached a crisis in 1936. If the whole railway system of East Africa had been under one authority, Uganda's export problems could have been lessened.

Notes

1. MD, 1 October 1936.
2. Ingham, *The Making of Modern Uganda*, p. 208.
3. MD, 18 October 1935.
4. Ibid., 19 October 1935.
5. Ibid., 25 October 1935.

6. CO536/187/40012/23, Governor to secretary of state, 28 August 1936.
7. MD, 21 July 1936.
8. CO536/187/40012/23, Governor to secretary of state, 28 August 1936.
9. Ibid., 5 October 1936.
10. MD, 3 October 1938.
11. Ibid., 25 January 1937.
12. Ibid., 24 October 1935.
13. Ibid., 25 January 1936.
14. Ibid., 14 November 1935.
15. CO536/189/40141, Governor to secretary of state, 9 October 1936.
16. MD, 20 October 1936.
17. CO536/189/40141, Governor to secretary of state, 9 October 1936.
18. Address by the governor to the Legislative Council, 16 November 1936, *The Uganda Official Gazette* (1936), p. 402.
19. CO536/189/40141, Mitchell to Bottomley, 3 September 1936.
20. MD, 9 March 1938.
21. Address by the governor, *The Uganda Official Gazette* (1939), pp. 514 and 515.
22. CO536/189/40141, Mitchell to Bottomley, 3 September 1936.
23. MD, 25 July 1938.
24. CO536/194/40141, Governor to secretary of state, 14 July 1937.
25. Ibid., Mitchell to Bottomley, 16 September 1937.
26. MD, 24 December 1935.
27. CO536/187/40012/23, Governor to secretary of state, 28 August 1936.
28. CO536/190/40174, Governor to secretary of state, 23 November 1936.
29. CO536/188/40100/18, Secretary of state to governor, 24 December 1936.
30. MD, 10 April 1937.
31. CO536/188/40100, Mitchell to Bottomley, 13 November 1936.
32. CO536/205/40035, Minute by CA Grossmith, 26 March 1940.
33. Ibid., Minute by TA Lloyd, 28 March 1940.
34. Ibid., Governor to secretary of state, 10 February 1940.
35. Ibid., Governor to secretary of state, 13 April 1940.
36. Mitchell, *African Afterthoughts*, p. 164.

37. Cyril Erlich, 'The Uganda Economy, 1903–1945', in Harlow and Chilver (eds), *History of East Africa*, p. 458.
38. CO536/188/40100/18, Mitchell to Bottomley, 13 November 1936.
39. Erlich, 'The Uganda Economy'.
40. MD, 23 February 1937.
41. Ibid., 3 July 1939.
42. Ibid., 11 January 1940.
43. Ibid., 12 December 1935.
44. Ibid., 16 and 22 February 1936.

VII

Makerere

In the colonies and protectorates, as had been the case in England centuries earlier, education was started by the Christian churches. In Uganda from 1877 to 1924 education was left entirely in the hands of the missions, who did great work but who, with their limited resources in finance and staff, were unable to take their pupils beyond an elementary stage. It was they alone, however, who brought literacy to an illiterate country and laid the foundations on which more advanced education could be built. Then in 1924, 'largely as a result of the Phelps-Stokes Commission, it was realised that it was incumbent upon the Government to take a more direct part in education'.[1]

Government neglect of education for Africans had made it necessary for Indians to be recruited as clerks and book-keepers in government offices with the result that, when government did at last accept the responsibility for the education of Africans, the only employment available was at the lowest level and an Indian barrier impeded their advancement in white collar employment. After the First World War a small amount of training of Africans as artisans was started by the government and in 1921 carpenters and mechanics of various sorts began to be trained on Makerere Hill in Kampala.

For some years the education of Africans continued to be geared to an unambitious aim. They were needed to fill technical and low grade clerical staff in government service and in the mid-1920s when the governor, Sir Geoffrey Archer, founded a department and appointed a director of education, there were doubts in Britain as well as in Africa that Africans would be able to absorb a literary education. Makerere remained a technical school with low level training for clerical employment, although the governor himself wanted Africans to be trained for higher level clerical work and so lessen the administration's dependence on Indians. Nevertheless, throughout the 1920s and beyond, ideas for developing literary education were discouraged.

The position which Indians had inevitably acquired made employment of Africans in the higher grades difficult, and in Uganda schools offering Africans secondary education continued to be lacking. In Buganda however there were African landowners able to pay for overseas education for their sons, but the dangers of political subversion abroad and the difficulty of providing suitable employment on their return were of great concern to the administration. The government was active in discouraging and even preventing them from leaving Uganda and issued passports only to those who could be placed in the guardianship of suitable organizations in Britain. Sir Geoffrey Archer's lead, however, was not entirely ignored and literary as well as technical education advanced slowly during the next ten years. Even so, what one critic has called a negative approach to education continued until a sudden change came in 1935. 'It was during Philip Mitchell's remarkable governorship (1935–40),' he wrote, 'that Uganda's educational system ceased to be retarded.'[2] Kenneth Ingham has gone so far as to say that Sir Bernard Bourdillon opposed 'advanced literary education for Africans', but that Mitchell, his successor as Governor, turned policy firmly in the opposite direction. Mitchell believed in the 'overriding importance of education at all levels' and Ingham rated his efforts to get the secretary of state to appoint a commission to study the question of higher education as possibly his greatest contribution to East Africa.[3]

Mitchell's admiration of the educational work of the missions, of which he had experience from his earliest days in the Colonial Service in Nyasaland, and his approval of Sir Donald Cameron's wish to create an African élite in Tanganyika made him keenly interested in the possibilities of the higher education of Africans. He saw no justification for the contention that Africans could never reach high educational levels because their brains did not have adequate capacity; and he never doubted that 'The natives of these parts have it in them to become as civilised as any other race of men'.[4] He believed that Africans ought to be led by Africans and that a well educated élite was essential. To achieve that would take time: an institution of higher education would have to be developed and schools at lower levels would have to be improved and be able to produce students for the higher college. He was insistent that more Africans should be appointed to local clerical posts in the civil service, so making it possible for ex-patriate recruitment to be curtailed, and it was clear that African education at all levels would have to be improved if this was to be possible. While he was still in Tanganyika the possibilities open to Makerere had impressed him and he began to work on plans for developing Makerere as a higher college as soon as he arrived in Uganda as governor.

Just before Christmas 1935, Mitchell made a detailed inspection of Makerere and came to the conclusion that the college, with 11 tutors and 156 pupils was 'altogether wrong in spirit and method'. He thought, however, that the normal and technical schools were 'very good'. They were 'training a type of PWD [Public Works Department] inspectors of works who were said to be admirable men with Makerere leaving qualifications and five years at the Mechanical School'.[5]

Three days later Mitchell made a speech at Makerere on the annual speech day and told his audience that 'A sound education development rooted in the soil of the country is essential to enable them to become a part of the civilisation of the modern world'. He gave the students and staff a glimpse of his vision when he told them that Makerere would become 'a "college" as meaning what it means in our country', and would be the University College and future University of East Africa. But he went on to tell them 'That task must include the widest spread of the best possible elementary vernacular education and', he said, 'it is perhaps in the little schools that to-day the work of the greatest importance is being done . . . in any country it is only a few in proportion to the whole population who seek higher education, and in providing for it we must not forget the many who will not go any further than the elementary schools.' He went on to tell his audience that 'the first call on the limited funds of the Government is the call of the man who pays the bulk of the taxes – the peasant'.[6] The Higher College would provide the élite, for whom Mitchell saw so great a need, but it would also provide a dynamic force in the educational system, every stage depending on the supply of pupils from the stage below.

Mitchell later expressed this idea in a startling way. In August 1939 he spoke at Makerere on 'the theme that the College was the foundation and not the apex of the education system, an idea', he wrote, 'which had most of them spellbound and shocked'.[7] He had already taken a step to put this idea into practical shape by asking the Director of Education to 'get a plan from Makerere downwards which would ensure standards and quality and be within their means.'[8]

The revolution in education which Mitchell envisaged could clearly never be brought about without help from outside to strengthen his hand. He thought that what was needed was a high-powered commission sent by the secretary of state and within a few months of his arrival in Uganda he asked the Colonial Office to appoint a commission in the name of the secretary of state to study the education of Africans and recommend a policy for the future. A minute was sent to the Colonial Office by the Government of Uganda on 'Makerere College in relation to Education for Africans in East Africa'. Closer union or interterritorial cooperation would affect education as well as economic and other common services. 'The impression has gained ground,' said the government's minute, 'that standards have already been achieved which are in fact barely in sight, and the most certain and powerful correction which could be applied would be the report of a Commission such as is desired. Africans in particular could hardly be induced to accept a statement of the facts by any other means.'[9]

On 10 February 1936, four months after he arrived in Uganda, Mitchell signed the Makerere (higher education) despatch.[10] He also wrote to Sir Cecil Bottomley, the head of the East African department of the Colonial Office, pleading for speed. The Governor of Kenya wanted the question of higher education to go to the Governors' Conference. 'I will not oppose it if it must be so,' he wrote, 'but it has been going from Directors of Education to Gov. Conf., to you, to Directors of Education, to Gov. Conf., to you and so on since 1932 and I cannot see any good in more Gov. Conf. on generalities; and so I hope you will let our Uganda Commission go ahead.'[11] Mitchell told the Colonial Office that he would like Sir George Schuster to be chairman. The secretary of state invited him, but other commitments made it impossible for him to accept. An excellent alternative was found in Earl De La Warr, who had just become Undersecretary of State for the Colonies. On 11 January 1937 Lord De La Warr and the other members of the Commission arrived in Uganda.

Having the undersecretary of state as his guest in Government House was very convenient and Mitchell soon discussed with him his financial aims as well as his ideas for the future of education. They were not unrelated, because his overall financial plans provided the possibility of creating an endowment fund for higher education. Later conversations with the chairman gave Mitchell a good idea of what the commission was likely to recommend, and he was anxious to be ready for most of their recommendations so that there might be as little delay as possible.[12] The report reached him when he was on leave in the Outer Hebrides in September 1937 and he wrote to Bottomley saying, 'I have just finished reading the Makerere Commission Report which I find very much to my liking.'[13] In the meantime he had discussed with his treasurer ways of raising money for an endowment fund, because he thought it was essential that the Higher College, which he hoped to get established, should be free from government control. As he expected, the commission recommended that the independence of the college should be secured by an endowment fund and, as Makerere was to be

an East African college, he had no doubt that the other
territories ought to contribute to it.[14]

At this same time, when the commission was considering its
report, he wrote an impassioned letter to Lord De La Warr on
the need for establishing a college of higher education as soon
as possible:

> The more I think of the whole problem the more appalling
> appears the future in East Africa, in which from Egypt to the
> Cape there is no solid foundation for our culture and our
> ideas. Modern factories for the mass production of people
> imbued primarily with bitter hatred of Great Britain and of
> democracy may be expected at any moment to be started in
> Abyssinia. In the Cape, with all its remarkable achievements,
> and excellent as Fort Hare is, there is the inevitable racial
> clash which runs right through the whole structure of edu-
> cation, and whatever else it does it must necessarily be the
> worst possible foundation for the development of culture and
> education in East Africa.
>
> Those of our Baganda who go abroad (and it is quite
> certain the number is going to increase very rapidly in the
> near future unless we meet the need) go generally either to the
> minor universities in the United Kingdom, or to a certain type
> of institution in the United States, the least desirable charac-
> teristic of which is a bitter hatred of the British and of what a
> recently returned product described as 'bloody British
> Imperialism'.[15]

As the report embodied all his ideas, it was small wonder that
Mitchell found it very much to his liking. The main recommendations made by the commission were that primary education
should be improved and extended and that secondary education
should be improved by upgrading existing secondary schools to
the standard of the school leaving certificate, and by the
establishment of new government secondary schools. They
advised that Makerere College and its associated institutions
should be grouped together to form the Higher College of East

Africa. 'We recognise,' wrote the members of the commission, 'in the institution at present associated with Makerere College the beginnings of a university and the full potentialities of a university ... For the immediate future this developing institution might be called "the Higher College of East Africa", but we anticipate that in a few years it will reach the status of a University College.' Even before the commission was appointed, Mitchell was determined that it should be 'open to all of whatever race who wish to make use of it'.[16] 'On the question of the organisation of any new college I intend to press strongly that from the very first we should flatly refuse to take any notice of differences in race or religion.'[17] When financial plans were being worked out Mitchell arranged to have money available for a 'girls' house' at Makerere 'so that there may be room for women at the college from the start'.[18]

His aims were summarized in his own précis of a speech which he made at the Makerere conference in May 1938. 'I opened the Makerere Conference', he wrote,

> in a speech over which I had taken a good deal of trouble and said the things I felt strongly – that you must see that there is an aristocracy of culture to guide and control the masses. A country full of St. VI schoolboys and nothing else would be a horror. That anyhow we needed African professional men and women. That we are a Christian people and propose to found a Christian college and know no other civilisation or culture than that of our own country and to that alone are we fitted to lead Africans. And finally that a bold lead is needed and not a timid hanging back for fear of mistakes.[19]

As soon as the commission's recommendations had been accepted by the Colonial Office Mitchell started work on detailed planning of the site for the Higher College and other buildings. He frequently visited Makerere and discussed the siting of various buildings there. He hoped that it would be possible to have only one chapel, to be used at different times by Roman Catholics and Protestants. He thought that a shared chapel might do something to lessen 'the religious rows', which, he told the Colonial Office in another connection, were 'never far below the surface in Uganda'.[20] He wanted it to be built on the top of the hill – a sign of Christian ecumenism in a multi-racial university serving all the territories of East Africa. He failed to get agreement to this proposal for having only one chapel, but he did succeed in having the two chapels built in the centre of the future university, exactly similar externally.

His interest in the question of the chapels was not an idle whim. He had been pressed 'to let the Catholics understand that they would have a member on the staff of the College' but, he wrote, 'I said I was strongly opposed to any recognition of sectarianism. I probably would have an RC but I disliked any sort of undertaking to that effect.'[21] The Roman Catholic Archbishop of Westminster had gone so far as to ask for joint principals, one of them a Catholic with Catholic teachers as a means of 'safeguarding faith'. This request did not appeal to the Colonial Office where it was felt that 'This kind of thing only means duplication of staff and unnecessary expense on the grounds of denominational religion. It leads inevitably to bigotry and intolerance and sharp division between the Protestant and Roman Catholic sections.'[22] The old rivalry dating from the earliest days was still active and the governor always had to bear it in mind.

His vision of a higher college, which could later become the University of East Africa producing African graduates, who would be the leaders of the African people became a reality when the Duke of Gloucester laid the foundation stone of the Makerere buildings on 3 November 1938. Lord De La Warr and others wrote to congratulate him 'on the actual start of the new college' and, he admitted, 'it does seem almost too good to be true and I can hardly credit it, but I shall wait to rejoice until the endowment fund is invested and the building's really under way'.[23]

Mitchell's satisfaction reached it zenith two months later when George Turner accepted the secretary of state's invitation to become principal of Makerere and he found it 'certainly astonishing that the headmaster of Marlborough, regarded to-day as the leading headmaster of GB, should throw up a post worth £3,000 out of a sense of duty to do what he rightly regards as Imperial work of the first importance'.[24]

The desired endowment fund was created by grants of £250,000 from Uganda, £100,000 from Tanganyika, £50,000 from Kenya and £100,000 from the new Colonial Development vote. The project which was so dear to Mitchell was safely launched before he was moved from Uganda in July 1940. A year later, when he was going from Nairobi to Cairo, he stayed with Turner and 'went all over Makerere'.[25] His affection for Makerere remained after his departure from Uganda. When he was chief political officer on Wavell's staff, one day in the market at Addis Ababa he bought a white metal cross, which he thought would do well for an altar. 'I have in mind to give it to Makerere,' he wrote in his diary.[26]

It was right that the first hall of residence in the University College should be called Mitchell Hall in recognition of the leading part which he played in the development of higher education in East Africa.

Notes

1. *Higher Education in East Africa*, Report of the Commission appointed by the Secretary of State for the Colonies (Colonial 142, September 1937), p. 31.
2. Nizar A Motoni, 'Makerere College 1922–1940', *African Affairs*, vol. 78, No. 312 (July 1979).
3. Ingham, *A History of East Africa*, p. 366.
4. Mitchell, *African Afterthoughts*, p. 129.
5. MD, 18 December 1935.
6. There is a copy of the speech in CO/536/189/40120, 21 December 1925.
7. MD 14 August 1939.
8. Ibid., 18 March 1939.
9. CO536/139/40120, 10 February 1936.
10. MD, 10 February 1936.
11. CO536/189/40120, Mitchell to Bottomley, 10 January 1936.

12. MD, 20 February 1937.
13. CO/536/193/40120, Mitchell to Bottomley, 7 September 1937.
14. MD, 20 March 1937.
15. CO536/193/40120, Mitchell to Lord De La Warr, 27 May 1937.
16. Speech at Makerere College, 21 December 1935.
17. CO536/193/40120, Mitchell to JEW Flood, 9 April 1937.
18. MD, 10 May 1939.
19. Ibid., 21 May 1938.
20. CO536/202/40080/1, Mitchell to Dawe, 15 July 1939.
21. Ibid., 19 February 1938.
22. CO536/114/40120/9, Minute by JEW Flood.
23. MD, 31 October 1938.
24. Ibid., 30 December 1938.
25. Ibid., 16 October 1941.
26. Ibid., 14 July 1941.

VIII
Administration of Justice

In the African tribal society in which Cameron was developing the system of indirect rule or native administration in Tanganyika, the chief in his proper setting with traditional advisers was both judge and administrator. The British principle that the judiciary and the executive must be separate would not have been understood in customary tribal life. The power of the chief as tribal leader depended on the right to judge and to punish as well as to administer and, when Britain accepted the responsibility of government and Cameron set about developing a system of rule through the traditional authorities, it seemed logical that the native courts should be supervised by members of the British administration rather than by some superior judicial authority. It was the district officers, the provincial commissioners and at times the Secretary for Native Affairs who scrutinized the records of the courts, but, as Cameron wrote in a despatch to the secretary of state, in the Tanganyika of which he became governor, the native courts were subordinate to the High Court. This was a situation far from pleasing to him and his enthusiasts for indirect rule. At the same time the district officers were ex officio magistrates in the district courts, where they tried criminal cases which were beyond the competence of the native courts, the limits of whose jurisdiction in criminal matters was well defined. The High Court was the superior court trying cases beyond the competence of the district courts.

At that time the administrators believed that only members of the administration could see that real justice was given to the African peasantry, because British ideas and procedures might seem far from just to a peasantry accustomed to different conceptions of justice. So strongly was this view held by Cameron and his enthusiastic staff that even the attorney-general maintained that judges of the High Court were too far removed from the people to be able to administer a code of justice acceptable to them.[1]

It has been said that Mitchell wrote 'What is perhaps the most eloquent and persuasive apologia for this system of administration as this band of enthusiasts [Cameron and his senior officers] understood it.'[2] He must have been closely involved in the preparation of the governor's despatch, which put the administrative view in strong terms. He wrote that it was impossible to rule through the chief if he was 'deprived of his traditional and customary functions as judicial, as well as executive, head of the community'. The judges of the High Court knew nothing of the language, traditions and mode of life of the Africans and if the faith of the chiefs and people in their local courts became impaired, the system of indirect administration would receive a fatal blow.[3] Mitchell welcomed the secretary of state's approval of Cameron's view which, in spite of the opposition of the chief justice, was accepted with the passing of the Native Courts Ordinance in 1929.

Later developments caused doubts to arise and in 1939 Mitchell admitted that the Cameronian enthusiasts, of whom he was one, failed to realize the full implications of their policy, and his views on the claims of the judiciary had radically changed.[4] Twelve years had passed since Cameron wrote his despatch in 1927. At that time enthusiasm for indirect rule, giving the tribal authorities a great measure of responsibility for the government of the tribe, caused the enthusiasts to fail to see that trusteeship, which was inherent in British colonial policy, would come into conflict with the native administrations which they were creating. At the core of indirect rule was the belief that the colonial power had an obligation to guide the natives towards a future form of government and society resting on their own traditions and customs. But the Imperial Government as trustee had a moral obligation to protect the weaker members of the tribal society from those traditional forms of chiefly power which modern British ethics regarded as uncivilized, and so interference with the tribal authorities was inevitable. HF Morris and James S Read in their detailed and authoritative book on indirect rule express their belief that 'it would certainly appear . . . that a search for justice was a recurrent theme during the colonial period in East Africa'.[5] This search was pursued by colonial administrations and colonial judiciaries and antagonism between them was sometimes heated.

To achieve justice was no easy matter. What might seem to be obvious justice to a British lawyer might be regarded as gross injustice by the illiterate member of an African tribe, and the administration maintained that all the legal knowledge of the Inns of Court in London could not produce justice in East Africa unless the judges and barristers working there had a deep knowledge of the outlooks and customs of the Africans. The administrations in the East African territories often went so far as to say that it was a good thing that district officers usually had little legal training – were certainly not barristers or British solicitors – because they felt that by being unaware of the *technicalities* of British law they were better able to apply the *principles* of British justice to African cases, using their knowledge of local native custom and tradition. The days of pure tribalism were passing, however, and in 1926 the Chief Justice of Tanganyika had claimed that it was no longer possible to say that justice could best be administered by a British officer unencumbered by the rules of legal procedure as 'in the days of Livingstone under his tree'. Mitchell, who read this minute commented, 'Livingstone under his mango tree probably got a good deal nearer to the truth and to justice than a judge on the bench at Dar es Salaam'.[6]

By 1939, however, he had come to realize that what was probably true of Livingstone in the early days could not be accepted as a tenable form of legal administration in the very different circumstances of the 1930s. In 1933 he was a member of the Commission of Enquiry into the Administration of Justice in Kenya, Uganda and Tanganyika Territory in Criminal Matters under the chairmanship; of HG (later Sir Henry Grattan) Bushe, legal adviser in the Colonial Office. What he learned then confirmed his doubts and he signed a report which went against everything that he had so fervently advocated in the 1920s. Historians have wondered how he could have apparently so completely changed sides and we must try to understand why he signed the report without reservation.

The commission was appointed midway between Cameron's despatch of 1927 and an admission by Mitchell that he then wondered how the Cameronian form of indirect rule had ever worked successfully. It depended on the cooperation of the chiefs, and the enthusiasts overlooked the fact that trusteeship exercised on behalf of the peasants was bound to erode the power and prestige of the chiefs. 'Few of us realised . . .' he wrote in 1939,

> that the instrument which we were using could not retain its effectiveness if we deprived it – as we generally did – of most of its powers and responsibilities, to say nothing of its revenues. I have often wondered since those early days that the Chiefs thought it worth while even to try to carry out our wishes, when we had taken from them the power to punish and often looked upon the tribute and service from their people, without which they could not exist, as being corrupt extortion.[7]

That 'I have often wondered' suggests that his doubts about indirect rule were not new and, if he was uncertain in 1933, his two months with the commission could have strongly affected his attitude towards the native courts. In Tanganyika the native courts had become courts of justice with written records and accepted procedures. Although this development was due to the supervision exercised by the district officers, the administration had to admit that the requirements of trusteeship and the ultimate responsibility held by the British Government required a British High Court operating throughout the territory in the most serious criminal cases.

As Mitchell was the youngest member of the commission, if in any place where they stayed to hear evidence accommodation was scarce, he shared a room with the Secretary of the Commission, JB Griffin, later Chief Justice of Uganda. In the evenings the two often discussed the events of the day and, as Griffin was an English barrister, Mitchell was constantly under fire from the legal side.[8] As the commission proceeded with its investigations examples of practices needing reform came before them and it became clear that without the dictates of a high court laying down the requirements of British ideas of justice reform would be impossible. An eye for an eye and a tooth for a tooth was a simple conception common to primitive societies, and even Africans with some measure of secondary education found it difficult in those days to understand how two or more people could be guilty of one murder, for instance, and all deserving of the same punishment. As a former president of the Court of Appeal of Eastern Africa, Sir Robert Hamilton pointed out in 1935, 'The idea of a crime being an offence against the State has no place in the Native conception which looks upon every wrong doing from the point of view of damage done to the individual'.[9]

The commission began its work in Kenya. It had been a miscarriage of justice and subsequent enquiry in Kenya which led to the appointment of the Bushe Commission, and it was in Kenya at the start of the commission's work that Mitchell first fully appreciated the strength of the point of view of the judiciary. He was appalled by evidence of the long sentences given in Kenya by African district councils, whose members had no training in a magistrate's duties, and he had no doubt that there ought to be more professional magistrates and many more judges moving round the country.[10] The need for professional legal supervision of the lower courts and for a strong judiciary became obvious to him as evidence was heard in different parts of the country. In Kenya and Uganda he was horrified by some of the evidence given to the commission by witnesses who 'had some dreadful things to say about the Buganda NCs, their corruption and savage punishments',[11] and before the commission left Uganda he was convinced of the need for a high court authority which was real.[12]

From Uganda the commission went to Tanganyika where at Dodoma the chiefs produced what was to Mitchell a new point: 'Let the AO [Administrative Officer] stick to his European law which he knows and the Native Courts to their native laws'.[13] Clearly that was not possible. Appeals from the native courts could not be heard by a court working on a different system of law and neither a district officer acting as magistrate nor a judge of the High Court could dispense traditional native law.

The enquiries of the commission in the three East African territories must have increased whatever doubt Mitchell had about the administrative case in these developing countries. It could not be denied that hardship was often suffered by witnesses summoned to appear before the High Court when they had to travel long distances to obey the summons and stay in an alien land. If that happened in the planting season, their *shambas* suffered and they and their families found a scarcity of food later on; but that was a matter which could be remedied by sending the High Court round the country like British assizes and so taking it nearer to the people.

The report, which Mitchell signed, was a report in favour of the judiciary but depending on large changes in the working of the High Court.[14] The East African Governors all objected to it. The matter was referred to the East African Governors' Conference and the secretary of state came down on the side of the governors. But their objections were not all alike because the problems of the administration of justice in the three territories were not all alike. When Mitchell became Governor of Uganda in 1935 he had problems which did not face the other two governors and the Governor of Kenya had a white settler situation more difficult than the question of settlers in Uganda or Tanganyika. In general the tide subsequently turned in favour of the judiciary and after the war a new outlook arose. During the nineteen fifties the prospect of independence far earlier than anyone had contemplated began to be discernible and the need for a strong judiciary became evident to all.

101

When he became Governor of Uganda in 1935, Mitchell found the chief justice 'bothered by native courts, in the Northern Province for example, which are unable to keep any records at all but can give up to two years in Prison'.[15] Buganda presented special problems. The chief justice told him that the Lukiko was 'very backward and disappointing', and the whole question of native courts was complicated by the overall question of the position of Buganda as a 'protected state', where Mitchell had no doubt at all about the need for a supreme legal authority in the High Court. The status of the native government and the Kabaka, however, posed special problems in administration and justice. The scheme which he devised replaced the provincial commissioner by a resident and included a judicial adviser who 'would deal with all revision, etc. but under the form of doing it in the Kabaka's name. He would also with an Assistant do the inspection of all Buganda Native Courts and act as it were as a Registrar for High Court appeals.'[16] The chief justice appreciated his proposals for constitutional change and gladly accepted his plan to give the Kabaka's government the maximum freedom to rule and to dispense justice while giving the High Court supreme authority to uphold British standards. As happened in other cases, Mitchell, having conceived the new ideas and done the basic work, was moved elsewhere before the new system was firmly established. The war caused him to be transferred from Uganda, but it was on the foundations which he laid that the future administration was built.

He was also much concerned with African marriage laws, which showed how difficult the harmonizing of tradition and custom and the demands of the modern world could be. During the years of his service in East Africa the laws concerning native marriage caused special difficulties in the legal field. Tribal customs and traditional codes of justice could regulate community life in tribal societies, but, when the tribe was incorporated into a developing territory, traditional practices and the requirements of British ethical standards had to be blended together with a system capable of modern administration. Mitchell gave much thought to marriage laws. Reflecting on this matter after his retirement, when he was asked to write a review of a survey of African marriage and family life, he wrote, 'Orders-in-Council may prescribe that in all cases civil and criminal to which natives are parties every court shall be guided by native law so far as it is applicable and not inconsistent with any Order-in-Council or Ordinance . . .', but, he asked, 'who is to tell "every court" what is native law?'[17] The problem was still further complicated by the fact that the better educated Africans were normally Christian or Muslim and religious considerations came into the reckoning. After his retirement he remembered that during his years of service in Tanganyika he

> was constantly required to adjudicate in disputes between parties supported on the one hand by a crusty old chief and his elders and on the other by a zealous Father Superior with the local authority of a medieval abbot, the matter at stake being for the one party the receipt or payment of cows or goats and for the other eternal damnation. The cows or goats always had it, of course, whatever the DC might order or the abbot threaten; they were at least there 'at that time in those parts' and thus were more convincing than the remote incomprehensible.[18]

The problem affecting Christian marriage among Africans in the 1920s and 1930s when he was working in Tanganyika and Uganda seemed to Mitchell 'to turn on the fact that tribalism is collective and Christianity individual . . . and the institution which Western Christians in the twentieth century call marriage is not even either stable or agreed among them and can hardly be held out to Africans as the only form in which it is possible to be at the same time both Christian and married'.[19] Apart from ethnical considerations there was the practical one that 'when polygamy was a common custom, it was no crime; it ranks as a crime now because it is no longer customary'.[20] Not a crime certainly among the general mass but among the élite who had subscribed to the civil and religious forms of Western marriage. But in all forms of Western marriage laws were

important, because questions of inheritance and social organization could not be settled without them. Could the district
officers, who knew the people, always be expected to understand
the niceties of the law? But could lawyers who did not live close
to the people understand their traditional forms of reasoning?

Mitchell spent a morning in 1939 reading papers 'about
Christian Native Marriage which gets us little further', he wrote.
'The DOs seem to have the most light-hearted views on the
subject based mainly, I think, on an incapacity to think of
natives as people.'[21] He was sometimes a man of apparent
contradictions. He had a very high regard for the officers of the
Colonial Service, but to suggest that they were unable 'to think
of natives as people' might seem to belie this. His strong religious
feeling required an appreciation of every man and woman as an
individual person. He would not have denied the benevolence
and steadfast application of most of the officers of the Provincial
Administration, but he sometimes seemed to feel that they did
not always have the intellectual as well as human approach
which he regarded as so necessary.

Mitchell thought that it was hardly a matter for surprise that
the law in respect of African marriage was, as the survey
showed, a supreme example of muddle. English draftsmen had
been almost completely ignorant of the societies for which they
were required to prepare legislation. One difficulty was that
among Christians the churches disagreed, 'often hotly, about
what in fact constitutes Christian marriage'.[22] He was certainly
an idealist, but he was always a realist assessing how much of
what was desirable was possible. And knowledge of native
tradition was basic to all decisions. Marriage and the family
were joined together in British thinking, but he pointed out that
'if by family is meant anything at all resembling what we mean
by the word when we use it in England, it is confined to a small
minority of Africans.'[23] He recognized that change was taking
place and he agreed with Dr Lucy Mair that in the towns, when
standards of living rose, marriages became more stable and
family life in the Western sense more usual. 'The answer here,'
Dr Mair wrote, 'lies surely as much in the attack on African

poverty as in moral exhortation.' 'Or, I would add, in niceties of dogma,' Mitchell commented, agreeing that every effort should be made to raise living standards.[24] He had much discussion with the Uganda bishops about the problems of Christian marriage and decided in July 1939 that the legal aspects ought to be discussed by a committee of lawyers under the chairmanship of a High Court judge, but almost immediately after this course had been decided on the Second World War broke out and he himself left Uganda in the following year before it was possible to get a committee together.

Sir Philip and Lady Mitchell left by car for Nairobi on 10 July 1940. On the Usasin Gishu plateau in Kenya their car stuck in the mud and was pulled out with difficulty. They stayed that night at the Highlands Hotel at Molo and arrived in Nairobi next day. They stayed for a few days at Government House while they searched for a house and an office to rent. Four and a half years later Mitchell was to return to Nairobi as Governor of Kenya.

Notes

1. Morris and Read, *Indirect Rule*, p. 85.
2. HF Morris, 'Sir Philip Mitchell and Protected Rule in Buganda', *Journal of African History*, xiii, 2 (1972).
3. CO691/88/18087, Governor to secretary of state, 17 February 1927.
4. Mitchell, *Uganda Protectorate*, p. 4.
5. Morris and Read, *Indirect Rule*, p. viii.
6. Ibid., p. 87.
7. Mitchell, *Uganda Protectorate*, p. 14.
8. Information given to the author by Sir John Griffin.
9. Sir Robert Hamilton, MP, 'Criminal Justice in East Africa', *Journal of the Africa Society*, vol. xxxiv, No. cxxxiv (January 1935).
10. MD, 17 April 1933.
11. Ibid., 25 April 1933.
12. Ibid., 23 April 1933.
13. Ibid., 6 May 1933.
14. Report of the Commission of Enquiry into the Administration of

Justice in Kenya, Uganda and Tanganyika Territory in Criminal Matters, May 1933. (Chairman HG Bushe, legal adviser in the Colonial Office).

15. MD, 28 October 1935.
16. Ibid., 10 March 1936.
17. Sir Philip Mitchell: 'The Survey of African Marriage and Family Life', *Africa*, xxiv (1954).
18. Ibid.
19. Ibid.
20. Ibid.
21. MD, 22 July 1939.
22. Mitchell, 'Survey of African Marriage'.
23. Ibid.
24. Ibid.

IX

A Personal Note

Mitchell's diaries, which are kept in the library of Rhodes House at Oxford, began in 1927. In them he recorded the events of each day, including the conversations he had on official matters and personal details such as his morning rides, his games of golf and the sizes of the trout which he caught when he could slip away for a day or two's fishing. If he kept diaries before 1927, it would seem that they have not been preserved. In his diaries he wrote completely candidly about affairs of state and people and his own feelings and emotions. If he thought that someone was like 'a slab of wet fish', he said so in his diary.

Mitchell's intellectual powers and administrative skill were of a high order and, rightly or wrongly, he felt obliged to do work which ought to have been done for him. He frequently thought that the drafts submitted by the secretariat and the departments did not meet the higher standards he insisted on. On the occasion of King George VI's coronation he lamented that he himself had to draft the loyal address for Uganda, 'the Secretariat being quite incapable of doing it'.[1] He felt the same throughout his time in Uganda.

He has sometimes been accused of intellectual pride. He certainly had high standards of intellectual work and if he could not find anyone whom he thought capable of reaching them, he would do the work himself. When he finally signed a despatch he frequently wrote in his diary that he thought it 'a good despatch'. It generally was, but he was never humble about the authorship. He was always anxious, however, to discuss problems and policies before taking action. After he left Uganda the acting governor said of him in Legislative Council on 6 August 1940: 'He was insistent at all times upon the value of consultation with his advisers, both official and unofficial, and there was no important project in regard to which he did not take preliminary counsel with those who were in a position to advise him'.[2] But he was at almost every stage more able than anyone around him and, as the years passed, although he continued to seek advice, he became less and less willing to compromise his views.

In March 1936, while he was struggling with the problem of Buganda and working out his plans for a judicial adviser in Kampala, a personal tragedy brought him a sincere sorrow. Nasero, his Muslim servant from Tanganyika, who had been with him for many years, was killed in a road accident near Entebbe. That evening he described in his diary their many years of friendship. He visited the mortuary of the Entebbe hospital and there, he wrote, 'I found the body of my faithful old servant and friend . . . I was alone with him for a little time.' And 'M. [his wife Margery] and I spent a miserable evening alone together – for she was as devoted to him as he to her. May he rest in peace, for if ever man deserved it he did'. The next day his loss was uppermost in his thoughts. 'I can still hardly believe I shall never again see my dear old friend,' he wrote.[3] Earlier that year the emotional side of his nature produced a remarkable expression of grief when news came of the death of King George V. His diary records vividly his great devotion to the king and the extraordinary effect which the news of his death had on him.

He was a living personality to me and my generation, an inspiration and an example, and as the troubled later years have passed, as my own little responsibilities have grown less insignificant, he has become more and more to me the one sure foundation of honour and justice, of security and of devotion. If I broke down several times to-day and at last on my knees, cried like a child before M. my staff and the

Merricks, as we listened on the wireless to the service in St Paul's it was an excusable weakness.[4]

Soon after he arrived in Uganda Mitchell started the building of a yacht for use on the lake. The work was done by the Technical School at Kampala and *Bluebell* was launched on 18 September 1938. In October he gave a tea party in Kampala 'to the Tech. School boys as some small acknowledgement of their part in *Bluebell*',[5] and he and Lady Mitchell spent the following weekend sailing. She did the cooking and they found two days away from the formality of Government House a refreshing and revivifying experience. On another occasion he stayed on *Bluebell* alone and clearly got great enjoyment and satisfaction from having to look after himself. 'I grilled a chop to perfection,' he recorded, 'and sautéed some new potatoes; and that with a little Gorgonzola and an apple made a meal no one can better.'[6] On another occasion, 'I am still a little clumsy with eggs', wrote the gubernatorial cook on *Bluebell*, 'but yield to none as a sausage fryer.'[7] He derived satisfaction from any work well done and to one side of his nature catching a large trout was as satisfactory as writing a good despatch. He sometimes thought nostalgically of his early days with foot safaris and the wood smoke of the evening fire and greatly enjoyed the experience of a visit of inspection to a district on the slopes of Mount Elgon:

It was delightful to be walking again in the chill of early morning with the cold smells of dew on earth and grass and the cheerful shouting of the porters. The track was very steep in places and before I got the 7 or 8 miles to camp I was aware of 'office legs'. But it was very good and the camp a gem placed on short green grass close to a gorge and looking upon a shere waterfall.[8]

There was something of a poetic trait in his character which showed itself when he was living on his farm after he retired and his well loved horse, Star, died. He wrote in his diary:

109

Poor old Star died last night at 1.30 a.m. He just faded away; he did not suffer and when I said good-night he knew me and his eyes were clear and showing nothing but kindliness and weariness. He had been a great friend and companion and I am happy for him that he is now sleeping on the lower slope of Christopher's Koppe here at Ndiloi in the one place in the world he loved, where he and I have had great rides and great sport. May we meet again when the phantom ducks fly over the Elysian Fields, all guns and killing put away. It will be long before I get used to the absence of his grey muzzle, his quiet companionship and loving wag of his tail.[9]

On the last day of 1935 he contemplated the unexpected promotion which had come to him that year – a promotion which had almost frightened him when he heard of it: 'Thus ends a year for me full of strange happenings which have resulted in great opportunities being given to me: God grant I may be equal to them, or at least never think of rank as being anything more than opportunity, or for any other purpose'.[10]

He wanted to make it possible for Africans to reach any heights, but he never advocated a lowering of standards because they were Africans. And, although he wanted equality of opportunity, he did not want a dull similarity: the traditions of each race, which provided the background of racial characteristics, should be respected insofar as they could be accepted by the moral and ethical standards of the 'civilisation open to them – our own'.[11] If Britain was trustee for the Africans in her colonies, she could only teach them what she herself knew and Mitchell had no doubt that the basis must be the Christian ethic.

He was always a practising member of the Anglican Church and from about the time of his appointment to the Governorship of Uganda he regularly attended church on Sundays. On one Sunday when he was Governor of Kenya great pressure of work prevented him going to any service and he noted in his diary that evening that he very much disliked not being able to attend a Sunday service.[12] His faith was not blind adherence to beliefs inculcated at home and school. It was something which he thought about seriously and pondered over. Bewilderment over the wording of the Anglican communion service caused him to ask the provost of the Anglican cathedral in Nairobi to go to Government House and discuss his difficulty. He found this discussion very helpful and when attending a Communion service on the following Sunday he found his 'old difficulty much less'.[13]

Dr Hugh Trowell, who was secretary of the Uganda Chaplaincy Trustees Committee, was in a position to be

very conscious of the silent influence and example of any Governor to the whole question not only of public worship in the Anglican Tradition but of all that Christianity stood for in the life of Uganda. One soon sensed whether the Governor attended church merely as a formality on the required occasions or whether there was any sincere concern for true religion in public and private life.

About Mitchell he wrote, 'Though he spoke about these matters seldom in public, one came to know how much they meant to him'. And many others who knew him well would agree that 'he was certainly a committed Christian with a quiet unostentatious faith'.[14] When he was Secretary for Native Affairs in Tanganyika one of his junior officers died. He went at once to see the young widow. He told her that he had expected her husband to have 'a distinguished career' and then, he recorded, 'we drifted on to the meaning of religion to persons and I think she derived some comfort from the reflection that Hering was a man who quietly and without fuss or ostentation lived a clean, honourable and charitable life; he lived indeed a Christian.'[15] Mitchell's deep sympathetic understanding and strong emotions did not lead him into sentimentality. When he heard of the death of his father he wrote: 'His great spirit really left him six months and more ago, since when he has been living but not alive. I feel no grief. Sorrow it was that such a man must live on after his frail body and weakened mind were no longer equal to his needs, and not that he should now be at rest.'[16]

He believed that 'every man and woman had a value for his (or her) own sake'[17] and so policy and legislation should aim to make it possible for all people to develop to the extent of their capacity, free from injustice and oppression and fear. But he did not foresee quick change. Progress, he thought, would inevitably be slow, based on the building up of a sound economy and relevant education with an African élite able to deal on equal terms with the expatriates in a multiracial, or non-racial, society. When he was Governor of Uganda he said that the Africans were 'in fact being patiently trained for the enjoyment of that fuller citizenship which they will certainly attain.' He was devoted to the work of leading the natives of East Africa to a brighter future and in 1931 when Sir Donald Cameron left Tanganyika and Mitchell wondered whether he would be able to work successfully under the new governor, he said that he wanted to stay in East Africa even if he had to retire in order to do so. 'I felt,' he wrote, 'I owed the next 20 years of my life to the people who have paid my salary for the last twenty.'[18] Twenty years later he retired in Kenya, but in the end hopes unfulfilled caused him to leave Africa and spend a sad final year in Gibraltar and Southern Spain, which had been his childhood home.

Notes

1. MD, 22 April 1937.
2. *The Uganda Official Gazette* (1940), p. 272.
3. MD, 12 and 13 March 1936.
4. Ibid., 21 January 1936.
5. Ibid., 4 October 1938.
6. Ibid., 10 June 1939.
7. Ibid., 11 June 1939.
8. Ibid., 7 December 1938.
9. Ibid., 8 February 1953.
10. Ibid., 31 December 1935.
11. Mitchell, *African Afterthoughts*, p. 47.
12. MD, 12 December 1948.
13. Ibid., 20 February 1947.

14. Letter to the author from Dr Trowell, 20 February 1980.
15. MD, 18 February 1933.
16. Ibid., 17 August 1937.
17. Mitchell, 'Indirect Rule'.
18. MD, 30 April 1931.

X

Major General Sir Philip Mitchell and Ethiopia

Mitchell went to Nairobi as Deputy Chairman of the Governors' Conference. His task was to coordinate the East African war effort. There were many difficulties. It was not always easy to get the different territories to agree on common policies, and relations between the army and the civil authorities had to be tactfully handled. His most difficult problems arose from Tanganyika's refusal to cooperate with the other territories in the arrangements for exchange control. 'They are passed all enduring,'[1] he commented. He found Tanganyika uncooperative in the sale of produce also and 'too stand-offish'.[2] At the same time he found that some of the Kenya farmers were 'clearly preparing to obstruct in their usual way'.[3] His position was difficult. His office was in Nairobi, where naturally he was in closer contact with the Governor of Kenya than with the Governors of Uganda or Tanganyika, but he had to maintain an East African status and not seem to be tied to Kenya. He and the Governor of Kenya agreed that the secretary of state must accord him the title of His Excellency, putting him on the same level as the three governors, and that it was he, not any of the territorial governors or chief secretaries, who was the civil link with the military general-officer-commanding in East Africa. He thought the question of address was 'itself a silly trifle, but if I am to be useful on this job, I must maintain its standard and authority'.[4]

In September 1940 he sailed for India to attend a conference called by the viceroy to discuss questions of economics and supply. The conference was attended by representatives from

India, Ceylon, Malaya, Australia, New Zealand, South Africa and East Africa. The ship on which he sailed called first at Madras, where his first action was, with the aid of an official serving there, to buy a bracelet of zikorns as a present for Lady Mitchell and 'five carefully matched unmounted stones to be made into a brooch to match the bracelet. They are very beautiful,' he wrote, 'and will, I believe, give her great pleasure.'[5]

After his return it became clear that the Army Supply Commission was not working well, a fact which complicated an already difficult situation in the control of timber, in which Colonel Ewart Grogan, a Kenya settler with important timber interests, was trying to interfere. Mitchell made it clear that he would not have 'outside interference from Grogan or anyone else.' The army seemed to want to take over the control of timber. If they proposed this and the War Office, the Secretary of State for the Colonies and the governments concerned agreed, well and good, but, he said, 'If we were to run it, they must keep out of it', and Grogan and his friends would have to be told 'to lay off'.[6] Three days later the War Supplies Board settled the machinery for timber control, and, as he wrote, he was firmly 'engaged in the wholesale grocery and timber trade on behalf of the forces, my little exercise in colonial governorship apparently at an end'.[7]

In his autobiography Mitchell describes how on his way back from the conference in Delhi he landed in Cairo on 7 December and found a message from General (afterwards Field Marshal Lord) Wavell inviting him to dinner that night at the Turf Club. The occasion was a party given to the commander-in-chief by the generals of the Dominions. Mitchell was amazed to find himself seated next to Wavell and even more astonished when Wavell himself drove him back to his hotel and spent some time walking about on the pavement, talking.[8] The dinner was in fact arranged to deceive the commander of the Italian forces in North Africa, Marshal Graziani. Who would have expected that, with all the British and Dominion commanders enjoying a social occasion in Cairo, in the early morning hours of that very night the great attack which shattered the Italian army was to be launched at Sidi Barrani?

Mitchell had no idea that the commander-in-chief was using the occasion to decide whether or not to ask him to become his chief political officer. Nothing was said that evening and Mitchell flew on to Nairobi three days later to resume his work of organizing the East African war effort. That work was not to last for long. On 4 January he received what he described as 'a bombshell' in the form of a cable from Lord Lloyd, the Secretary of State for the Colonies, asking him to go to Cairo as an administrator on Wavell's staff 'to examine problems and formulate plans for administration of enemy territory in Italian EA when occupied'.[9] He saw that he would have to accept and that it would be wise for Lady Mitchell to go to South Africa and settle there. 'I am very tired,' he wrote, 'but that cannot be helped.'[10] Another cable from the secretary of state informed him that Wavell wanted him at once. So after discussions with the Governor of Kenya about the future of the office he was vacating, he left Nairobi and arrived in Cairo on 19 January.

Mitchell had been deeply impressed by Wavell on that evening in the Turf Club – a man who had 'the serene humility of greatness'.[11] As he was to find later with the great American Admiral, Nimitz, and his senior officers in the Pacific, Wavell, was a man with whom he could work in full harmony. This appointment to a responsible post on his staff offered an exciting prospect for Mitchell, but he appreciated what it would mean for his wife, who was 'very down in the dumps. I suppose,' he reflected, 'that, if you are off to do something, you do not always realise what it is like to have the part of being left behind and waiting. She will be busy with packing and will then go home to SA and that will help.' To make the parting less hard he asked a friend to go with her at his expense.[12] Events moved fast. Lady Mitchell flew to South Africa and, much to his surprise, he arrived in Cairo as a major general. As soon as he had heard that he was to have a secretary, he had telephoned to Sir Charles Dundas, the Governor of Uganda, to ask him to release RDA Arundell of the Uganda administration. Dundas agreed at once and Arundell (later Sir Robert Arundell, Governor of Barbados) accompanied him to Cairo.

To begin with Mitchell was responsible for information and propaganda and he discovered that 'all sorts of things were being done and said, allegedly with the authority of the Foreign Office. "Missions" began to appear in the region, armed with instructions to do mutually incompatible things.[13] These things,' he wrote, 'were to plague me greatly later in Cairo when I was Chief Political Officer.'[14]

The Italian declaration of war on the Allies in June 1940 had turned the whole of North and Northeast Africa into a war zone. The Commander-in-Chief, Middle East, with his head-quarters in Cairo, had to face the Italians to the west and Italian occupied Ethiopia, the Red Sea coast and the Horn of Africa to the south east. Ethiopia was strategically a very important part of this vast area. Naturally the emperor, Haile Selassie, who had been living in England, wanted to reoccupy his country as soon as possible and he found it difficult to accept the idea that his personal position was not the most important consideration in the planning of the war. It had been thought in London that he ought to be flown out to Africa before France collapsed, as the Mediterranean might then be closed and a long circuitous journey would therefore be necessary. He landed in Alexandria on 25 June 1940 and very naturally wanted to enter a liberated Addis Ababa as soon as possible. Wavell, however, pointed out that

> Middle East was called upon to conduct no fewer than six major campaigns – in Greece, in Cyrenaica, in Crete, in Iraq, in Syria, and in Italian East Africa. During May five of these were being conducted simultaneously, and there were never less than three on hand at one time. The theatres of these operations were several hundreds of miles apart, in some cases well over a thousand.[15]

A basic necessity was to keep the Red Sea open as a safe supply route. The conquest of Italian East Africa was essential, but the timing of the campaign had to be part of the general Middle East strategy and the capture of the capital itself was not the major consideration. General Sir William Platt, the General-Officer-Commanding in Khartoum, thought the suggestion that the emperor should lead a small army against the Italians was folly, but Anthony Eden, at that time Secretary of State for War, appeared on the scene as supporter and champion of the emperor, and the GOC had to argue vehemently to prevent what he was convinced could be disastrous. A compromise was reached whereby an Ethiopian guerilla rebellion was to be fomented with the help of a small British military mission, led by Brigadier Daniel Sandford and Major Orde Wingate.

As chief political officer from the end of January 1942 Mitchell was responsible under Wavell for the administration of all reoccupied Italian colonies. It was agreed that he should have his own Department or Branch and a legal adviser. There was a frustrating delay in securing a political officer for Cyrenaica and when that appointment was made, its duration was short because on 4 April the Italians reoccupied Benghazi. 'All my Cyrenaica staff got away in good order,' Mitchell noted, 'and brought all their records with them, so except for a very wearisome experience we did not suffer there.'[16]

Wavell realized that territories freed from Italian rule would require a civil administration responsible to himself as military commander. The question was which government department in London should be in charge. He was informed by the war cabinet that the various ministers concerned agreed that one department should be responsible for the administration of occupied enemy territories and that the right department to undertake that task was the War Office. Such administration was outside the experience of the Foreign Office and, although the Colonial Office had the experience and the officers equipped to undertake the task, if the Colonial Office were given the administration of any territories captured from the Italians, Britain would be suspected of trying to incorporate them into the empire, which would cause great harm in the world, and especially African opinion. The War Office, then, was put in

charge, but a Standing Departmental Committee on the Administration of Enemy Occupied Territories was formed under the
chairmanship of Richard Law, MP, the finance member of the
Army Council. Sir Philip Mitchell, with the honorary rank of
major-general, was seconded by the Colonial Office to the War
Office but continued to be carried on the consolidated fund as a
colonial governor. In November 1941 when he was wondering
what the future had in store for him, Mitchell was told by the
Colonial Office that he was 'a Colonial Governor with as much,
but no more, claim than any other to further employment, if he
was no longer wanted by the Army'.[17]

The recognized rules of war placed the responsibility for the
government of enemy occupied territory on the shoulders of the
military commander until a settlement was made at the end of
the war and Wavell looked to experience in the Middle East in
the 1914–18 war for guidance. The War Office agreed with his
suggestion that the form of military government as applied there
by Allenby in Palestine should be followed. That meant government by the C-in-C through his political advisers, which would
in fact mean government by Mitchell. The War Office sent a
telegram about 'a Financial Adviser which looks,' Mitchell
wrote, 'as if they thought they were going to run the show and
treat it like a piece of Army accounting'. Wavell called for
Mitchell and told him that there would be nothing of that sort
and that he himself would deal with the War Office about the
matter.[18] London then agreed that 'the finance of Civil Administration should be kept separate from military accounts',[19] and
the Hon Francis Rodd (who was soon to succeed his father as
Lord Rennell of Rodd), was sent as controller of finance and
accounts with the honorary rank of brigadier.

At the end of January 1941 Wavell telegraphed his plan to
the War Office and, as no reply was sent from London, assumed
that his proposals had the approval of the cabinet.[20] He assumed
that Ethiopia, when it was liberated from the Italians, would be
under British military occupation until an agreement had been
made with the emperor enabling the country to be handed over
to him on such terms as the responsibilities of the War Office

temporarily required. In the meantime the C-in-C would be responsible for the maintenance of law and order, the safe evacuation of the Italian population, and the safeguarding of Italian property, both government and private. The C-in-C would also be responsible for the Italian colonies in East Africa and, as Mitchell told a conference in Cairo in February, he, as chief political officer, and his department were 'in effect the Court brokers in possession to look after the property pending judgement'.[21]

In Italian Somaliland there would be no complications, but Ethiopia was very different. The C-in-C could not be responsible without retaining the necessary powers and, to quote Lord Rennell, 'It was therefore thought most inadvisable to restore the Emperor's civil administration immediately although he would receive every consideration and be fully consulted.'[22] In February it did not seem that this problem would have to be faced in the very near future, but by the middle of March events had moved so fast that Mitchell was worried because he saw that they were 'not nearly ready for the collapse of Italian East Africa, which seemed to be imminent'.[23] Wavell later wrote that he realized that the capture of Addis Ababa would confront him 'with an embarrasment of very large numbers of Italian civilians and would have no very great strategical object'.[24]

The appointment of staff to the Political Branch, mainly from the Colonial Service, went on, but in the middle of April the Political Branch of General Headquarters, Middle East, had still only nine officers, three other ranks and six stenographers or clerks, but 'vast tracts of Africa and millions of inhabitants were almost daily being showered on the back of the Political Branch.'[25] It was a frightening prospect: large territories under military occupation with no civil administration until the chief political officer and his branch were able to provide it. The War Office saw the pattern as similar to colonial government, although it would be carried on under the ultimate responsibility of the commander-in-chief and in line with local military requirements; and Wavell agreed with Mitchell that the overall arrangement should be a sort of high commission with each territory having a self-contained administration. The C-in-C, as Mitchell saw, was 'plainly very worried', but he agreed that the chief political officer 'must have carte blanche, referring only in matters of major policy; and that to get the civilians away was the main business'.[26]

On 21 February Anthony Eden, then the Secretary of State for Foreign Affairs, and General (later Field Marshal) Sir John Dill, the Chief of the Imperial General Staff, had visited Cairo and discussed the Ethiopian situation with Mitchell. 'The outcome of these discussions was the rejection of any idea of a protectorate, or the provision of a strong western administration, in the country',[27] but law and order would have to be maintained, the Italian civilians would have to be evacuated and military requirements would have to be met. Mitchell had then drawn up a memorandum for his political officers, which started by saying that the policy of His Majesty's Government was that it 'would welcome the reappearance of an independent Ethiopian State and will recognise the claim of the Emperor Haile Selassie to the throne'. All too quickly the forces of General Platt, sweeping south from Eritrea, and of General Cunningham, advancing from Kenya by way of Somalia, entered Ethiopia, and Addis Ababa was surrendered on 6 April. Mitchell had already drafted armistice terms, but he was alarmed at the position of what he believed to be 20,000 Italian civilians in the capital, 3,000 of them pregnant women.[28]

As it turned out, British fears for the safety of the Italians were greater than was necessary, but not to have had them and to prepare accordingly would have been grossly irresponsible. Italian rule had been harsh and recollections above all of the atrocities committed after an attempt was made to assassinate General Graziani in 1937 might have been expected to lead to fierce reprisals when the Italian forces had been defeated. However, when he entered his capital in May, the emperor asked his subjects to have no feelings of revenge or bitterness and his plea was obeyed. In fact many Italians chose to stay in Ethiopia and the Ethiopians welcomed them, especially Italian artisans. 'Once forgetful of the myths of fascism the Italian has no recital attitudes, nor does he demand a higher standard of living than his individual industry and skill can earn him.'[29] However, many Italians did in fact have to be evacuated because they did not wish to stay and because in any case it would have been impossible for so many to be integrated into Ethiopia.

When the Italian collapse seemed to be imminent Mitchell decided with Wavell's agreement to move his headquarters to Nairobi, from where communications to the Italian colonies and Ethiopia was far easier than from Cairo. He settled into new offices in Nairobi on 18 April. M.S. Lush, given the honorary rank of Brigadier, was seconded from the Sudan civil service and made deputy chief political officer in Addis Ababa, and Francis Rodd was given charge of finance.

It was found that there were more Italians in Addis Ababa than Mitchell had expected. The Evacuation Officer in Asmara wrote a report in which he estimated that at the time of the occupation there were 119,400 Italians in East Africa, 55,000 being in and around Asmara, 40,000 in Addis Ababa, 12,000 in Mogadishu and 12,400 elsewhere.[30] There were also some 40,000 Italian service personnel with 200 guns at large in Ethiopia.[31] No mean problem faced the Political Branch. They got little help from the Italians of education and wealth, who, wrote Peter Rodd, 'with very few exceptions, at a time when their countrymen had most need of assistance, leadership and organisation . . . had no thought for anything but their skins and their possessions'.[32]

Wherever they might ultimately go, the only immediate area to which the civilians could be evacuated was Kenya, where Mitchell turned to the Roman Catholic Church with its many Italian missions to house the civilians either in the mission compounds or in small camps attached to them. He stressed that he 'would have no truck with concentration camps and barbed wire and so on and hoped to work through the missions'.[33] He insisted that, except for the hard core fascists, the Italians were to be regarded as refugees. When it was seen that the Ethiopians were not seeking revenge for Italian atrocities, Italian opposition to evacuation began to appear and Axis military successes in North Africa led many Italians to hope that Cairo might be captured and that Northeast Africa might become a theatre of war. The illegality of the evacuation was stressed. Legal opinion was in fact divided, 'the weight of it being against the measure, which was, however, justified on the grounds of paramount military necessity, the security of the Italians themselves and the treatment of Allied civilian populations by the Axis belligerents';[34] and the British military authorities pressed for the expulsion of the entire Italian population from Eritrea and Ethiopia and Somaliland. The evacuation officers undertook a registration of the Italian civilians and a year later the figures of the persons registered showed that there were still 26,500 in Addis Ababa and 12,400 in other towns in Ethiopia.[35] The Italian government had earlier said that it would send ships to remove some of the civilians, but it failed to do so, probably because of hopes of Axis military successes.

On the last Sunday in April Mitchell took the day off from work and went to morning service in the Anglican cathedral in Nairobi. The next day he was pleased to hear that the War Office had suggested to Wavell that an East African command should be formed to include Italian East Africa, the Sudan and British Somaliland. Wavell asked him for his views on this proposal. As it was what he had always advocated, he replied that he heartily approved of the idea. As far as the chief political officer was concerned it would be quite a large enough area and, as it turned out, Rommel put North Africa out of the reckoning.

His free Sunday was followed by a flight to Mogadishu, Harrar and Addis Ababa. In Mogadishu he found that, although the police force had a good supply of men and arms, 30 officers were needed and he thought that it might be necessary to recruit them from South Africa. The most heartening lesson he learned from the tour was that communication between headquarters in Nairobi and these forward areas was really well established. That was necessary, because the Italian collapse had been so quick that the problem of civil administration had to be faced inconveniently early. The capture of the capital on 6 April was followed a month later by the emperor's entry into it, and

Mitchell and the commander-in-chief had no illusions about the difficulties which might follow.

Trouble was not long in coming. Four days after his arrival in the capital the emperor appointed seven ministers without telling Brigadier Sandford, his political adviser, or Brigadier Lush, Mitchell's deputy chief political officer. This was not a good augury for cooperation, but Mitchell advised the War Office and instructed Lush 'to sit back and do nothing for a bit since the Emperor has no money and will have to ask for it'.[36] Three days later Lush telegraphed to say that the emperor regretted his precipitate action and realized the financial implication. He promised to cooperate and said that the ministers were prepared to function only as ministers designate.[37] Richard Greenfield, writing 20 years later, thought the appointment of the seven ministers was 'a shrewd move' because 'it served to emphasise the Emperor's anxiety to take over the administration of the country which the military had set up'. It was too soon, however, for Britain to give up control. The country was not yet fully liberated from the Italians. The emperor did not seem to appreciate the full reality of the situation. He had been 'shooting his cuffs over his future plans for Ethiopia – education, agriculture, suffrage, parliaments and the Lord knows what. Utterly childish and irresponsible,' wrote Mitchell, 'with the war still not won and 40,000 Italians with 200 guns at large in his country. He really shows no signs of being an adult.'[38]

The British presence in Ethiopia was fundamentally a military one and the War Office saw Ethiopia still under Italian sovereignty till a peace treaty had been signed, but the emperor could hardly be expected to accept that legal fiction and in London there was some discord between the War Office and the Foreign Office. Nevertheless General Weatherall, the senior Commonwealth officer present in Addis Ababa on 6 April when the emperor's standard was raised on the palace of the Emperor Menelik II, said to the assembled people, 'This is a proud day for me – to have come and reconquered Addis Ababa for you,' thus stating the position 'in terms which denied any suspicion of a new colonialism.'[39] But for the War Office, which had to think above all about the strategic position, a stable Ethiopia was supremely important, especially when Rommell was menacing Egypt. The Foreign Office looked at the situation from a different standpoint and was primarily concerned about the effect of British actions and declarations on world opinion, above all on the United States and the Africans throughout the African continent. Until the war was won and a peace treaty signed, in international law Ethiopia was an 'ex-enemy country', for which Britain was responsible. However, as Mitchell saw, whatever international law said, Britain could not be regarded as administering an occupied enemy territory in Ethiopia, the enemy having been replaced by the Ethiopians whom they had conquered four years earlier. In a telegram to the War Office on 8 August he made a very practical point. 'Consideration,' he wrote, 'should also be given to Ethiopian point of view that Emperor never submitted to or recognised Italian conquest and that some areas of Ethiopia were never conquered by Italy.'[40] But British responsibility was clear and the policy had to be decided by the Cabinet in London.

In May the War Office telegraphed to Mitchell that opinion in England was anxious lest slavery should revive in Ethiopia and that they hoped he had in mind plans to cope with this possibility. Mitchell replied that 'slavery was only one of the internal conditions which were continuously in my anxious thoughts'.[41] If people in England were concerned about the standards of civilization in the newly independent Ethiopia, they would have to agree that some measure of control would have to be exercised in the early stages; but Mitchell was anxious to avoid any suspicion of a protectorate. At the same time he saw the danger of the establishment of a traditional feudalism in a world where dictatorships were anathema, and he wrote a note declaring that 'if there is to be a free and independent Ethiopia it can only come about by the genuine collaboration of all men of goodwill in Ethiopia [including the Rases] and not by the establishment by the Emperor of an irresponsible dictatorship'.[42]

Unfortunately the Ethiopian forces of law and order were unable to prevent abuses. The GOC, General Platt, sent a telegram to the War Office saying, 'From all sides appearance of Emperor's officials is reported by Politicals as following at once by looting and disorder. Danger is that, while Emperor is trying to build up at centre an instrument capable of governing maladministration in provinces will bring about his downfall. Present period of uncertainty is aggravating this.'[43] He went on to say that, unless the British Government was thinking of changing its policy and establishing a protectorate, the signature of the agreement which was being negotiated with the emperor was urgently necessary before disorder became more general.

The discord between the War Office and the Foreign Office seemed to be personalized in suspicion of Mitchell in the Foreign Office and hostile criticism of his work. Plans for the adminis-tration of Italian-occupied territories, when they were con-quered, had been considered by Wavell a month before Mitchell became chief political officer and so the C-in-C's chief civil planner. 'I had begun preparations,' Wavell wrote in a later despatch

> for the administration of enemy-occupied territory in IEA [Italian East Africa] as early as December 1940 and a nucleus organisation was in existence at the time the operations began. So rapidly, however, did the advance proceed, especially in the south, that it was almost impossible for administration to keep pace. In the circumstances it reflects the greatest credit on Sir Philip Mitchell, Brigadier Lush and the Hon FR Rodd and others that so much was accomplished and that there was no general breakdown of administration or of law and order.[44]

In the middle of May the War Office sent a cable giving 'their formula for Ethiopia as approved by the Cabinet'. As it was almost word for word what Mitchell had proposed to them, he found it 'most satisfactory'. British authority was to maintain occupation in areas to be specified by the C-in-C, but elsewhere the emperor was to administer under the guidance and control of the civil arm of Middle East Command. The cabinet formula laid down that the emperor must undertake to follow advice and it recognized that he was dependent on Britain for finance. He was free to legislate provided that his laws were acceptable to the British Government. The political officers were recognized as the executive instrument, and administrative and departmental control on behalf of the War Office and the British Government were to be exercised by Mitchell as chief political officer. The channel of communication was HMG–C-in-C–CPO–emperor.[45] Wavell was in full agreement with these proposals and asked Mitchell to go to London to discuss them.

In London Anthony Eden, the Foreign Secretary, agreed that Mitchell should be called High Commissioner for the Italian Colonies and Somaliland and Agent General for Ethiopia. This distinction in wording was regarded as of great importance and, as Mitchell wrote, he was 'governing 3 colonies and controlling an Emperor'.[46] This was no overstatement. General Sir Claude Auchinleck, who succeeded Wavell as Commander-in-Chief, Middle East, signed a proclamation [Eritrea Proclamation No. 26 of 20 July 1941] vesting in the CPO 'all the legislative, executive, political and administrative functions now vesting in the General Officer Commanding HM Forces in the said territory'.[47] It was the same throughout the ex-Italian colonies. As civil administration became established, Mitchell's control was supreme. With regard to Ethiopia he had to explain to the political officers that they were under the emperor and, if any objected to this, he would have to let them resign. He immediately drafted a directive for them. There could be no British administration in Ethiopia. They were to be advisers, not administrators, and he emphasized in his instructions to them that 'it is an Ethiopian Government we want to establish and that the Emperor and his Ministers must have real authority; the need for patient tact and good manners; and the limits of an adviser's responsibility, especially the difference between what ought not to happen and what is intolerable, which are two different things.'[48]

Duncan Sandys, Financial Secretary to the War Office, expressed complete agreement with Mitchell's ideas. The War

Office realized a point which the Foreign Office seemed to overlook. The war was still being fought and, where necessary, the Emperor would have to declare martial law in particular areas and give the C-in-C 'the necessary powers which would accrue to him under Martial Law'. On the political side the British Government would do all it could to re-establish the Ethiopian Government 'as may be practical at this stage'.[49]

There was complete accord between the War Office in London and Mitchell, the chief political officer, in East Africa; but officials in the Foreign Office still seemed unable to understand the realities of the situation in Ethiopia. A stable and civilized government had to be established in a country barely yet liberated from the Italians with a police force inadequately staffed in the officer grades, with no money except what Britain supplied, and with an emperor impatient to be free from restrictions on his actions. In August the Colonial Office wrote to the Foreign Office that they would welcome the reappearance of an independent Ethiopian State, but saying that 'Any arrangement that was tantamount to the establishment of a Protectorate or protected State – *and that, I understand, is how the Foreign Office view Mitchell's present proposals* – would certainly have unfortunate repercussions in several parts of the Colonial Empire.'[50] It is astonishing that officials in the Colonial Office were unaware that the proposals submitted by the War Office were almost verbatim what Mitchell had advocated and that he continued to negotiate with the emperor according to instructions received from the cabinet.

These instructions were given to Mitchell when he was summoned to a cabinet meeting on 9 June and his negotiations with the emperor to reach an agreement were conducted according to these instructions. He later discovered that the source of the suspicions held about him in the Foreign Office was G Mackereth, an official who had at one time been a consul in Ethiopia, 'who had invented a fantastic and entirely unreal picture of the country'.[51] He was probably influenced by Brigadier Sandford, who had been appointed Principal Military and Political Adviser to the Emperor and Adviser to the Ministry of the Interior. Sandford had been seconded to the British Legation in Addis Ababa in 1914 and had lived in Ethiopia up to the time of the Italian conquest. He was a great admirer and personal friend of Haile Selassie and Mitchell sometimes wondered whether, 'in his devotion to the Emperor's interest, he was going to break off relations with Great Britain'.[52] In September 1941 Sandford was in London and Mackereth at the Foreign Office minuted that he was 'decidedly less pessimistic than Sir P Mitchell of the Abyssinians' ability to govern themselves to their satisfaction'.[53]

Mitchell had been struggling for several months to get the emperor to accept an agreement which followed the instructions given by the cabinet, but right up to the time when the agreement was finally signed the emperor procrastinated and postponed decision. Greenfield believes that 'Sandford did his duty in warning the Emperor',[54] but one might ask, warning the emperor of what? Mitchell wanted to achieve an agreement in accordance with the instructions of the cabinet, and the cabinet wanted a free and independent Ethiopia, although temporarily retaining such control as was necessary for the strategic needs of the war. Throughout 1941 Rommel in North Africa made it impossible for the War Office to agree a relaxation of British control. Britain was fighting a world war, which in 1941 was in a very critical stage, but to the emperor and his 'entourage' the predominant fact was that Ethiopia had been freed from the Italian yoke. What to the British Cabinet was a valuable step in the prosecution of a global war was to the Ethiopians the attainment of their goal.

The decision of the British Cabinet, which Mitchell had to convey to the emperor, that the emperor should 'agree to abide in all matters touching the govenment of Ethiopia by the advice of His Majesty's Government' seemed to Greenfield to show that 'Clearly the British Cabinet was then still obsessed with the concept of colonialism as a civilising medium of benefit to the backward peoples'.[55] In fact it showed that at that time of critical warfare a stable Ethiopia seemed to the cabinet, and to the War Office, to be a necessary military security; and after such an astonishingly quick reconquest of the country from the Italians by the armies of General Platt and General Cunningham the emperor had neither the organization nor the Ethiopian personnel to provide it. The danger of an Axis success in North Africa was great until after the battle of El Alamein in November 1942. Then it was possible for a new agreement with very different terms to be signed.

In the later months of 1941 inter-departmental ill-will in London seriously increased. The War Office knew that at one point the emperor had refused to instruct his officials in the provinces to cooperate with British officers.[56] Neither the Foreign Office nor the emperor's well-wishers had knowledge of current facts such as that, and supported the emperor in his obdurate refusal to compromise and to look at the situation of Ethiopia in the wider setting of the global war. David Margesson, the Secretary of State for War wrote to Anthony Eden, the Foreign Secretary, claiming that the draft agreement with the emperor sent to London by Mitchell 'followed faithfully the lines laid down by the War Cabinet on 9th June',[57] but the Foreign Office continued to be suspicious of what Mitchell was doing.[58]

Articles appeared in *The Times* in London 'from our special correspondent' in September 1941. 'So long as the agreement remains unconcluded,' the correspondent wrote, 'he [the emperor] feels that he is being kept in leading strings and is inclined to resent it. For their part, many of the British officials who are due to enter Ethiopian service are uncomfortable because they too have no formal standing. They are the emperor's servants without being appointed by him and can only make a moral appeal to his authority.' On the following day the correspondent wrote that the emperor 'is naturally somewhat jealous of his new-found sovereignty and apprehensive of his country becoming a mere protectorate'.[59]

At the end of August Noel Baker, Eleanor Rathbone and Geoffrey Mander asked to see Anthony Eden, the Foreign Secretary, because, as Miss Rathbone wrote, there were 'several questions relating to the present and future position of the

Emperor there and the Government's intentions with regard to the country's future about which we feel anxious'. Richard Law, the Financial Secretary at the War Office, explained to them that 'as long as Ethiopia was a zone of military operations, it was not possible to accord full recognition and that to have reciprocal Legations in Addis Ababa and London was out of the question and would doubtless lead to the establishment of Spanish and Japanese Legations in Addis Ababa', a point which had not occurred to them. They then asked whether the emperor would be granted a loan and have his landed property restored to him. At that point Eden joined the meeting and told them that the British Government was already giving him about £5,000,000 a year and that his revenue had been restored to him. Then another question was raised. Why did Britain not define the frontiers of Ethiopia? Was the British Government, they asked, 'contemplating some future deal with the Italians at the expense of the Ethiop?' The secretary of state 'assured them that this was nonsense', but, when the Ogaden was mentioned, they surprisingly said that they would like it to be 'part of an independent Somalia'.[60] Much well-wishing with little knowledge or realistic thought in London no doubt encouraged the emperor in his procrastination and lack of any spirit of compromise.

At the same time as Margesson wrote to Eden, Mitchell sent a cypher telegram to Oliver Lyttelton, the minister of state at the Colonial Office, who was in Cairo. He said that reports sent by eyewitnesses, mostly responsible British military officers, showed that on all sides serious abuses, murder, rape and looting had resulted from the appearance in rural areas of men sent by the emperor as governors and other officials, who were 'accompanied by bands of undisciplined armed followers whose acts must be called atrocities'. Mitchell suggested that a preliminary to an agreement should be a written communication to the emperor that, because such a situation existed, Ethiopian administrative officials, police force and regular army must be trained 'according to advice and under supervision of British Political Mission whose advice provincial officials must follow'.[61] In the same week William Temple, Archbishop of York, sent to Eden a letter which he had received from Miss Pankhurst, which expressed the hope that Ethiopia would be 're-established as a genuinely independent State which we may support but at any rate when the war is over do not seek to control'.[62] The War Office, the commander-in-chief, and the chief political officer would have agreed entirely with that, because it showed an awareness that the questions of wartime security and strategy could not be overlooked, but that a genuinely independent Ethiopia was the ultimate aim.

Mitchell had been given the cabinet's instructions in London on 9 June. On 1 July he went with Lush and Sandford to the palace to explain the cabinet's plans to the emperor who, he wrote, 'expressed great gratitude for himself and his people' to the prime minister and His Majesty's Government' and his wish to help them to the utmost 'without prejudice to sovereign rights'. He asked for a financial adviser and Mitchell promised to supply a high grade officer immediately. The Secretary of State for War was satisfied that Mitchell had 'followed faithfully the lines laid down by the War Cabinet' and Mitchell emphasized that it was an Ethiopian Government they wanted to establish.[63]

It has been suggested that Mitchell's previous service as a colonial governor must have given him an outlook unsuitable for anyone negotiating with the emperor. For instance, 'one suspects that his past dealings with the Monarchs of Uganda were scarcely preparation for such negotiations'.[64] The Kabaka of Buganda was the only 'monarch' even remotely comparable and although other governors regarded the administration of Buganda as an example of indirect rule, Mitchell declared Buganda to be a 'protected state', turned the provincial commissioner into a resident and required that the Kabaka should have the utmost freedom of action compatible with his position in the wider context of Uganda. His instructions to his political officers in Ethiopia and his correspondence with London show that he regarded Ethiopia certainly not as a protectorate, not even as a 'protected state', but as an independent state, which

1. Family group: l to r: Back row, Kenneth, Captain Hugh Mitchell, R. E. Centre row, Alan, Katherine, Hugh. Front row, Amyot, Edmund, Philip. 2. PM as Governor of Fiji and High Commissioner of the Western Pacific (US Army Signal Corps)

3. PM as Governor
of Uganda

4. PM as Governor
of Kenya

5. Kenya: PM presenting medals (Kenya Information Office)

6. Kenya: PM talking to tribal chiefs

7. Kenya: with Princess Elizabeth at Sagana Lodge

8. PM fishing

for military reasons had temporarily to be carefully controlled. His 'dealings with the Monarchs of Uganda' and his intimate knowledge of indirect rule, far from being a handicap, provided him with practical experience of the difference between a protectorate and independence.

British supervision of the expenditure of funds provided by the British Government was attacked 20 years later as having been unreasonable. 'It is too simple to say,' wrote Greenfield about the British military administration,

> that the measure of control over expenditure they envisaged was due only to their knowledge of colonial custom and their failure to comprehend the fierce independent spirit of Ethiopians. They were also schooled in the concept of responsibility to the taxpayer, British or Ethiopian, for the expenditure of public funds and did not comprehend that this is very anathema of feudalism.[65]

Could it, however, have been expected that the British Treasury would agree to a grant of £1 million given for the purpose of establishing a stable Ethiopian administration, being handed over to the emperor to be used as he liked without the responsibility of accounting for it?

Mitchell went again to London in October and on the way he read papers in Cairo which 'disclosed the milk in the coconut' in letters from Eden to Lyttelton saying that he had come to the conclusion that Mitchell wanted a protectorate and ought not to be allowed, nor should any of his officers be allowed, to have anything more to do with Ethiopia. Mitchell was naturally disturbed and angry and he reflected: 'So they propose a neat little intrigue whereby my Cabinet instructions are scrapped, the dear Emp. is given a million and asked to appoint British advisers who are to be under his orders and we are to have the millenium.' They wanted to hand things over to a diplomat, who, 'by waving the magic wand, will produce paradise'.[66] In London he 'got more light on the conspiracy by the FO, but also

Enigmatic Proconsul

learned that the WO are stiffening' and then he recorded with
obvious anger and pain:

> I now find that Eden has put a report in to the Cabinet
> accusing me (me!) of intending to set up a Protectorate and
> an Administration on the 'Italian or Colonial model' and
> urging a new Agreement of which he submits a draft: the
> draft is my Agreement word for word, with one or two
> omissions and the insertion of Borana as a reserved area and
> the addition of an undertaking to act on advice, which the
> Emp. had rejected! He also reprinted the scurrilous letter
> about Wavell, Platt and Cunningham, etc. which he has got
> from somewhere. Dirty work.[67]

Mitchell has said plainly that he was against the idea of a
protectorate and the retention in Ethiopia of British troops and
that therefore the only alternative was a stable Ethiopian government, 'for which the Emperor with discreetly camouflaged support and our money is much the best bet'.[68] The battle of
Whitehall lasted throughout November. On 11 November
Mitchell and General Platt, who was also in London, were
summoned to the cabinet. They found that the cabinet completely
reversed their previous decisions, rejected the proposed agreement and decided (i) to remove all Italians in four months, (ii) to
give the emperor a small subsidy and walk out, and (iii) to open
diplomatic relations at once. To this Mitchell's comments were,

> (i) is of course impossible; (ii) is a breach of faith, and (iii) is
> premature, but so we are governed . . . The really insoluble
> one is the Police. I can see a way through the other until
> Ethiopia relapses into chaos, but in view of the position in
> Addis I see no way out of the Police problem; nor for that
> matter the Army, for officers will not engage in it.[69]

A month later, after he had returned to Nairobi, he wrote a
letter to his sister Katharine describing his difficult journey to
London and 'the four weary weeks of fruitless argument and

134

useless talk that followed.' He had been 'negotiating with the Emperor on written Cabinet instructions'. As the new cabinet plans involved 'a complete breach of faith', he resigned. The matter was passed to Sir John Anderson, the Lord president, who found out the facts and 'educated his colleagues'. In the end Eden admitted that he had 'become aware that his people have thought nothing out and have neither knowledge nor plans'. He asked Mitchell to withdraw his resignation and promised him full support. And so things were back to where they started.[70]

So Mitchell was able to go back to Nairobi and fly up to Addis Ababa to continue consultation with the emperor for an agreement on terms settled by the British Cabinet six months earlier. The main point at issue was the police force, which the emperor wanted to get into his own hands at once. A disciplined police force was essential if Ethiopia was not to relapse into chaos. Mitchell explained that, although a change of jurisdiction could be made instantaneously, 'you cannot conjure a police force out of the ground like that'. He pointed out that, when Britain handed over the Irish Free State, the Royal Irish Constabulary had to remain in office for nine months, and even Hitler after his invasions of Czechoslovakia and Austria had to keep the Czech and Austrian police going for a while. Britain, he said, must help the emperor to get a police force established and trained, composed of Ethiopians and such foreigners as were needed and would engage in it.[71] The emperor, however, was so insistent that he should be in complete control of the police force at once that Mitchell feared the negotiations might break down completely unless the cabinet insisted that he should moderate his demand.

On 9 January Mitchell received a cable from London agreeing with all his views and he went to see the emperor and told him that 'the practice whereby he said "No" to all our requests and expected "Yes" to his could not go on'.[72] The emperor still refused to agree to the proposed terms of an agreement, but he needed money and British help in several ways. Mitchell continued to discuss the points which were still at issue and it was agreed that the Government of the United Kingdom should help the emperor to obtain 'the services of British subjects (i) as advisers to himself and his administration; (ii) as Commissioners of Police, Police officers and inspectors; and (iii) as judges and magistrates' and that the emperor should not appoint advisers additional to those referred to in paragraph (i) above except after consultation with the Government of the United Kingdom.

The terms of the agreement were finally settled. London cabled that Eden wanted signature on 28 January, enabling him to make an announcement in the House of Commons on the 28th. Mitchell flew to Addis Ababa, but the emperor said he could not sign till the 31 January. Then two texts of the agreement, one in Amharic and one in English, were signed by the emperor and Mitchell, who read messages of congratulation from the C-in-C and the East African governors, then himself made a short speech, to which the emperor replied in cordial terms. There was a tea party at the British Legation in Addis Ababa and an evening reception at the palace. The Rases and other notables all greeted the agreement with applause. So ended months of negotiation in Addis Ababa and intrigue in Whitehall, which left difficulties in Ethiopia. The Foreign Office opened a Legation and sent an officer named Howe, who had recently done good service in China, as minister. He, however, seemed to think that he was the executive officer dealing with the implementation of the agreement, which was of course a matter for East Africa Command. Mitchell reported to the C-in-C that he was convinced that there was a Foreign Office '5th column about the Army: Servants' Hall gossip from Addis no doubt'.[73]

It was not pleasant to find that the intrigues in London during the previous year were likely to be followed by intrigues in Addis after the agreement had been signed. Three days later, however, Mitchell learned that he himself was soon to be far away from Ethiopia, trying to bring an end to discord among the Allied forces in the western Pacific. 'A very flattering cable' came from Lord Cranborne, the Secretary of State for the Colonies, 'pointing out the present importance of Fiji and the Western Pacific and relations with Australia, NZ and American forces' and asking him to go as governor to Fiji and High Commissioner for the western Pacific.[74]

Before he left Nairobi Mitchell wrote a report on conditions in Ethiopia, which he sent to the Ministry of State in Cairo. He feared that chaos and disorder might engulf Ethiopia unless those responsible for the future were made aware of present conditions. He wrote 'pointing out how law and order had gone to the devil'. Howe and staff had openly supported the Ethiopians on the retention business and been as openly repudiated by HMG:

> Howe, Sandford and Co. advised as they pleased agin HMG and were uncontrollable by anyone: Emp. and Ministers made no attempt to organise a Government: Chiefs, officials and soldiers and police were unpaid: two British officers had been killed in Addis and Kenya DC murdered. All this in 4 months after we had handed over a reasonably orderly country in which we were respected and in military matters obeyed. *Quo vadimus?*[75]

And lastly he said goodbye to General Platt, the commander-in-chief, 'a great man to work for, strong, straight and able'.[76]

Mitchell's 18 months as a major general in Middle East and East Africa Commands had been full of great responsibilities. He had had to deal with the problem of Italian evacuation and the establishment of a new Ethiopia state, harmonizing the demands of war with the intransigence of the emperor, and trying to safeguard the peasants, who were in danger of suffering from feudal oppression. *The Times* special correspondent had no illusions about 'the amount of ground which has to be covered before Ethiopia exchanges twelfth-century for twentieth-century habits'. The article went on to say, 'By accepting the responsibility for establishing more or less civilised conditions of government in Ethiopia after the vicissitudes of the last five years without having direct control the British Government have set themselves a harder task than most people realise.'[77] The special correspondent in this article saw the difficulties facing the British Government and the political branch of Middle East Command but failed to see how much the emperor himself delayed the signing of an agreement. 'This is not to suggest,' said another article, 'that the Emperor is unwilling to cooperate',[78] but in fact an agreement could have been finalized more quickly if he had really shown cooperation. No wonder Mitchell often felt frustrated in his efforts to get acceptance of the cabinet's terms.

Nevertheless Mitchell had set the course and had organized the administration of the former Italian colonies, and had set Ethiopia on its road to complete independence when the successes of the Allies allowed the British presence to be withdrawn. He was succeeded as chief political officer by Lord Rennell, who in a despatch to the GOC-in-C East Africa said that arrangements for the British presence in Ethiopia and the administration of Eritrea, Somalia, British Somaliland and Tripolitania were all 'set up on the general lines laid down by Major General Sir Philip Mitchell in February and March 1941'. Later, when there were two separate political branches in Cairo and Nairobi, when Lord Rennell went to Cairo and Brigadier HR Howe took the post of chief political officer in Nairobi, the danger of divergent administrative policies, wrote Lord Rennell, was only avoided

> because of the close personal relations and contact between the senior officers of the two political branches, by their determination to follow the lines originally laid down by Sir Philip Mitchell when he had unified control, and by the general remerging of the two administrative centres . . . Since Brigadier Howe and I are likely soon to end our direct association with these administrations, we think it proper to place on record that this very considerable undertaking was initiated and carried into existence by Major General Sir Philip Mitchell, whose general policy we have done no more than follow.[79]

Sir Ralph Howe knew Mitchell well, having been his attorney-general in Uganda and later serving in the political branch in

Middle East Command. Writing to *The Times* after Mitchell's death he pointed out that his 'broad plan . . . formed the general basis on which the military administrations of British Somaliland, Tripolitania, Cyrenaica, the Dodecanese Islands, Burmah, Malaya and elsewhere were subsequently established'. He had to carry many and varied responsibilities with

> results which in retrospect can truly be said to be quite remarkable, and many feel that these outstanding services did not receive the recognition that they so amply merited . . . Many of us who had the privilege to serve under him in those difficult days remember with gratitude and affection his inspiring leadership, loyal support, and warm friendship.[80]

Notes

1. MD, 14 December 1940.
2. Ibid., 15 July 1940.
3. Ibid., 25 July 1940.
4. Ibid., 3 August 1940.
5. Ibid., 9 October 1940.
6. Ibid., 1 January 1941.
7. Mitchell, *African Afterthoughts*, p. 190.
8. Ibid., p. 193.
9. MD, 4 January 1941.
10. Ibid., 4 January 1941.
11. Mitchell, *African Afterthoughts*, p. 194.
12. MD, 16 January 1941.
13. Mitchell, *African Afterthoughts*, p. 195.
14. Ibid., p. 196.
15. Supplement to *The London Gazette* (3 July 1946), p. 3443: 'Despatch submitted to the Secretary of State for War on 5 September 1941 by General Sir Archibald Wavell, GCB, CMG, C-in-C in the Middle East.'
16. MD, 12 April 1941.
17. Ibid., 19 November 1941.
18. Ibid., 16 February 1941.
19. Lord Rennell of Rodd, *British Military Administration of Occupied*

Territories in Africa During the Years 1941–1943, (London, 1948), p. 33.

20. Ibid., p. 41.
21. MD, 20 February 1941.
22. Lord Rennell, *British Military Administration*, p. 41.
23. MD, 8 March 1941.
24. Supplement to *The London Gazette*, (3 July 1946), p. 3529.
25. Lord Rennell, *British Military Administration*, p. 39.
26. MD, 8 February 1941.
27. Lord Rennell, *British Military Administration*, p. 63.
28. MD, 8 April 1941.
29. Richard Greenfield, *Ethiopia*, p. 271.
30. Major the Hon. Peter Rodd, Evacuation Officer, Asmara, *Report on the Evacuation of Italian Civilians from Italian East Africa, 1941–1942*, (Rhodes House, Oxford, Mss. British Empire 5360).
31. MD, 8 May 1941.
32. Rodd, *Report on the Evacuation*.
33. MD, 22 April 1941.
34. Rodd, *Report on the Evacuation*.
35. Ibid.
36. MD, 13 May 1941.
37. Ibid., 16 May 1941.
38. Ibid., 2 May 1941.
39. Greenfield, *Ethiopia*, p. 262.
40. FO/371/27521, Telegram from Mitchell to War Office, 8 August 1941.
41. MD, 10 May 1941.
42. Ibid., 14 May 1941.
43. FO/371/27521, Telegram from GOC East Africa to War Office, 10 October 1941.
44. Supplement to *The London Gazette* (3 July 1946).
45. MD, 19 May 1941.
46. Ibid., 4 June 1941.
47. Lord Rennell, *British Military Administration*, p. 115.
48. MD, 11 June 1941.
49. FO/371/27521, Duncan Sandys to Richard Law, 9 September 1941.
50. FO/371/27521, T.I.K. Lloyd to G Mackereth, 18 August 1941.
51. Letter from Mitchell to his sister Katharine, 17 December 1941 (in possession of a member of family).

52. Mitchell, *African Afterthoughts*, p. 205.
53. FO/371/27521, Minute by Mackereth, 17 September 1941.
54. Greenfield, *Ethiopia*, p. 274.
55. Ibid., p. 275.
56. Brigadier M.S. Lush, Deputy Chief Political Officer, *Report of the Deputy Chief Political Officer, Ethiopia, on the Administration of Ethiopia of the Period from 16 September 1941 to 28 February 1942*, (Rhodes House, Oxford, Mss. British Empire 5360).
57. FO/371/27521, Margesson to Eden, 23 September 1941.
58. Ibid., Memorandum by Mackereth, 25 September 1941.
59. *The Times*, 18 and 19 September 1941.
60. FO/371/27521, Minute by Mackereth, 29 August 1941.
61. FO/371/27521, Telegram to minister of state, 26 September 1941.
62. Ibid., Archbishop of York to Eden, 27 September 1941.
63. MD, 1 July 1941.
64. Greenfield, *Ethiopia*, p. 275.
65. Ibid., p. 275.
66. MD, 18 October 1941.
67. Ibid., 28 October 1941.
68. Ibid., 6 November 1941.
69. Ibid., 11 November 1941.
70. Letter by Mitchell to his sister Katharine, 13 December 1941 (in the possession of member of family).
71. MD, 18 December 1941.
72. Ibid., 9 January 1942.
73. Ibid., 19 May 1942.
74. Ibid., 22 May 1942.
75. Ibid., 26 May 1942.
76. Ibid., 27 May 1942.
77. *The Times*, 19 September 1941.
78. Ibid., 30 October 1941.
79. Lord Rennell, *British Military Administration*, pp. 312–13.
80. *The Times*, 19 October 1964.

XI

Southwestern Pacific

On 22 January 1942, while Mitchell was struggling to get the emperor's signature on the Ethiopia Agreement, he wrote in his diary, 'Japs are getting on much too fast and appear to be able to go where they please and do much as they like. There is obviously serious friction with Australia.'[1] Four months later he received the invitation to go as Governor of Fiji and High Commissioner Western Pacific. 'Of course I must go,' he wrote, 'but what a shake up.'[2] He sent an immediate telegram of acceptance, saying that he could start in a week's time and asking for two weeks leave in South Africa to settle his affairs there. Lady Mitchell would clearly have to stay there among her relatives and join him in Fiji later.

Mitchell's months of working as chief political officer under a military commander-in-chief were good preparation for the work to which he was going – a war zone with himself as chief of the civil administration and Governor of the British Colony but with an American supreme commander of the armed services, responsible for the prosecution of the war. All his service life had been spent in Africa and he reflected, perhaps somewhat nostalgically, that the western Pacific was 'as far from Africa as you can get but is of course the forefront of the battle'.[3]

On 31 May he left Nairobi for South Africa. After a short leave there he went to Washington, flying by way of Kano and Trinidad, and had an immediate conversation with Lord Halifax, the British ambassador. He said that the main point on which he would need guidance was the extent to which he was

142

to regard the United States general-officer-commanding as he would regard a British GOC. He himself, he said, would not allow difference of nationality to affect the matter and would behave as if the American GOC were Wavell, Auchinleck or Platt unless he was otherwise ordered.[4] He stayed in Washington for ten days, read files at the British Embassy and met leading figures, American, British, Australian and New Zealand. Lord Halifax entirely agreed with his view of his position. The Pacific was an operations area and therefore what the service chiefs wanted must be accepted. If political difficulties arose, he would have to refer them to the Foreign Office for discussion with the State Department. He saw General Marshall, the American chief of staff, who gave him an outline of the whole position in the Pacific, and he discussed with Brigadier Dykes, the chief officer on the staff of the British general, Sir John Dill, the question of an agreement which would have to be made with the Americans if they decided to occupy Fiji (they thought a leased bases agreement would be the best solution).

Mitchell attended a conference at the New Zealand Legation, where he stressed that the Pacific was an operational area and that whoever was commanding the armed forces must be supreme. He was puzzled by conflicting views expressed about the late Governor of Fiji. The American naval leaders were 'quite frank about friction there had been with Luke', but at the conference in the New Zealand Legation he was told that Luke had not annoyed the United States but 'had no grip on the native population' (which seemed to be ridiculous when the native population was less than 200,000), and that he 'did not know there was a war on'. 'It sounds,' Mitchell recorded, 'like a dirty job to me'.[5] He had suffered from intrigue when he was in Ethiopia. He did not like it there and did not like it, or the smell of it, in Washington either.

On his way to Fiji he stayed at Pearl Harbour for a few days and had a meeting with Admiral Nimitz, the Supreme Commander of the Allied Forces in the Pacific, and his chief of staff. He told them he agreed that in an operational area 'what the C-in-C wants must be done', and he would do his best to meet the

requirements of the service chiefs. Politics must be left to
Washington and London to deal with. On the following afternoon he wrote: 'With great courtesy Nimitz came and returned
my call . . . I like him greatly for his kindly sincerity and depth
of feeling and real courage: he is certainly a leader.'[6] He saw in
Nimitz a rare quality which had impressed him in Wavell when
he met him in Cairo, and two years later, when he stayed again
at Pearl Harbour, he wrote of Nimitz:

> You can always tell the few really first class men among the
> great because they always apparently have time to spare, are
> at peace with themselves and show no sign of nerves or strain.
> Winston, Wavell and Andrew Cunningham are like that; so is
> Nimitz in spite of the tremendous burden he carries.[7]

Mitchell was captivated at once by Nimitz and his senior
officers. 'They are men I can work with,' was his reaction to
them; 'we shall fully understand each other.'[8] There had
undoubtedly been friction between the Allies. A British colony,
the Kingdom of Tonga and dependent islands spread over a
wide area in an operational war zone, in which the United States
was the supreme military power, presented no problems of
principle to Mitchell and Nimitz and his senior officers but were
fertile ground for friction lower down. And there were Australian and New Zealand forces to be considered, small in
numbers compared with the Americans but no less anxious to
play their part in the battle. Suva was a central point. Holding
the two appointments of High Commissioner for the Southwestern Pacific and Governor of Fiji, he had to look north to Pearl
Harbour and South to Australia and New Zealand. He had to
consider the welfare of the Solomon Islanders to the west and of
the Gilbert and Ellis Islanders to the east. In his capacity as
Governor of Fiji he had to administer the affairs of a multiracial
colony with particular problems arising from the war, and to
see that the special position of the Kingdom of Tonga was
respected.

Up to the time of Mitchell's arrival life in Fiji had not

experienced any fundamental changes, but his dynamic personality made itself felt within a very few days. The large number
of American troops and the weight of American forces in the
prosecution of the war had relegated the Fijian people to a
subordinate position and a passive role in the crisis which faced
their country and the area of the southwestern Pacific. They
supplied labour and food for the American forces, but their new
governor announced that he had 'come to wage war' and he
immediately sought the advice of the Fijian leaders. His ready
acceptance of people irrespective of race led Mitchell to to an
early and enduring friendship with Ratu Lala (later Sir Lala)
Sukuna, the leading figure among the Fijians, who suggested the
training of Fijians as commandos. The new governor's positive
leadership was welcomed by the Fijian people, above all by the
chiefs, who appreciated a governor who told them that he had
come to fight the Japanese enemy and whose agreement with
their leader's advice that Fijian men should be organized and
trained to commando units fired their imagination and loyalty.
They accepted Sukuna's challenge that they would not be able
to claim full recognition of their national development unless
they were willing to shed their blood for the empire. Over 5,000
Fijians out of a male population of 55,500 enlisted in the army.[9]
The formation of the commando units brought them into active
participation with Europeans in the war in the Solomon Islands
and they distinguished themselves in battle at Bougainville and
Guadalcanal, and elsewhere. In the Solomon Islands the backward, primitive islanders had shown astonishing loyalty to the
empire and had exploded the Japanese claim that the war was a
racial struggle in which the Japanese were fighting to free their
coloured 'brethren' from white oppression. The Japanese failed
entirely in their efforts to ingratiate themselves with the Islanders, who from the start resisted the invaders and showed
astonishing courage and endurance.

Mitchell paid many visits to the islands and received reports
from the military authorities of their steadfast adherence to
Britain and the empire. One remarkable case was brought to his
notice concerning 'a retired Police Sgt. Major who had been

doing I [Intelligence] work for us and was caught by the Japs who tried to make him tell how many troops there were, and when he refused and was tied to a tree, bayonetted him in arms, neck, face and stomach and left for dead'. He was found by natives and was recovering. Mitchell gave instructions that when he was fit to travel he was to be sent to him in Suva to be personally commended for his loyalty and courage.[10] Recognition was due also to the British officers who had stayed behind to encourage and inspire the islanders. The administrator, WS Marchant, and a few British officers stayed on Guadalcanal when the Japanese advance had flowed over the islands, remaining 'resolutely at their posts or in the adjacent jungle and kept the flag flying in face of fearful dangers.' Marchant's health was in a sorry state, but he left the Solomons only when he was ordered to go to Fiji by Mitchell, who had received a cable from two senior American generals saying that 'his sick body can no longer carry his great heart and if he stays here he will die'. Mitchell sent a cable to him to tell him of the admiration and praise of the work done by him and his officers expressed by the Americans, which he was passing on to the secretary of state. In 1944 Mitchell found him in Kenya as chief native commissioner and was able to express his appreciation of his courageous exploits in the Pacific when he made a valedictory speech in Legislative Council in Nairobi to mark Marchant's departure to be Director of Labour in the groundnuts scheme in Tanganyika.[11]

The governor and Ratu Sukuna were in full agreement that the prosecution of the war was a task overriding everything else. Sukuna was engaged on the extremely important work of demarcating Fijian-owned lands, but Mitchell took him off this to spend his full time recruiting Fijians for military service. When his advisers were looking for someone to run the wartime Information Office and recommended Mr LG Usher, the head of a provincial school for Fijian boys, Mitchell did not hesitate. Usher was seconded from teaching to be in charge of the Information Office and an administrative officer was posted to run the school. Mitchell waived protests aside. He admitted that education would suffer but maintained that everything was secondary to the prosecution of the war.[12]

The pressure of large numbers of American troops caused great difficulties. United States Service cash payments in Fiji were nearly $2 million a month. Prices soared and the governor could not help feeling grave concern about the future. He told the secretary of state that the 'Americans had arrived in a suspicious and critical frame of mind, largely', he thought, 'due to American press attitude to British Colonies'. It was unfortunate that Sir Harry Luke, Mitchell's predecessor as governor had been 'over-excellent and uniformed for their way of life' and had been the object of some American ridicule. They were, however, 'becoming much more friendly and ready to believe that we are in the War', he wrote, 'but there is a good way to go still'.[13] It was in general an uneasy racial and international situation into which he arrived. He had shown in Africa that he was a harmonizer and all his skill would be needed to achieve the result for which he was sent as Governor of Fiji and High Commissioner for the Western Pacific.

At the swearing-in ceremony on his arrival at Suva, when to his great surprise the chief justice told him he had become a vice-admiral, he made his attitude clear. There was 'one policy', he said, 'to make war; and we owed to the US service authorities who were in command, every help and support: what they want must be done'.[14] In Middle East Command he had been referred to always as major-general, but in Fiji the office of governor seems to have been important enough to enable the address of vice-admiral to be forgotten.

The governor had to consider the welfare of the native population as well as the requirements of the armed services. He found that there was a shortage of labour for agricultural industries and that this 'was largely caused by the recruitment of men for the Fiji Military Forces and essential war work', but he saw also that large numbers of Fijians and Indians were also employed by the American forcers 'on camp duties and personal services'. He had no doubt that these amenity, rather than essential, services were of less importance than agricultural work and he was able to reduce them drastically 'with the ready cooperation of the Commanding General and his staff'.[15] The Colonial Office agreed with Mitchell that the American military authorities, who were responsible for the defence of the colony, could rightly expect the civil administration 'to see to it that labour was provided to back up in every possible way their efforts to provide the territory with a sure defence system', but that the imposition of compulsory labour might provoke internal opposition and an international scandal.[16]

He started immediately to organize the war effort through constitutional channels. The Executive Council agreed to become a war council with a war supplies and production board and at the end of August Legislative Council voted unanimously for compulsory national service.[17] By the end of September Mitchell felt that the War Council had become a machine which was really working well.[18] He offered Government House as an emergency hospital, which could 'at a pinch' provide 500 beds, but invasion did not seem to be imminent and in November, when it was suggested that there might be a general evacuation of Suva, he and the American general, Thompson, decided against such a step. In the event the tide of war turned and the danger passed.

The huge amount of money which the American troops were able to spend upset the economy and tended to cause envy on one side and a feeling of superiority on the other. Anti-American attitudes were exacerbated by the local newspaper, the *Fiji Times and Herald*, owned and edited by a certain Mr Barker (who hated Americans), and his bitterly anti-British Irish son-in-law. He was very angry about the presence of some of the American troops and objected to the very existence of black soldiers. Mitchell reasoned with him about the need to tell people 'to put up cheerfully with the little discomforts and inconveniences the War brought to them', but he doubted whether he made any impression on him,[19] and he wrote to the Colonial Office to ask permission for the government to publish a daily paper to give a good news service and counteract the anti-American, anti-British and anti-New Zealand attitude of the *Fiji Times and Herald*. The Colonial Office saw great difficulties in this and refused permission but allowed the government to print two extra pages every day for inclusion in the paper, and Barker agreed to accept them.[20]

Mitchell's earliest hopes that the Indians would be 'loyal and helpful' were not completely fulfilled. Although most of the Indians had been born in Fiji, their feelings of loyalty were apt to be towards India rather than Fiji, and news of political stresses in India was likely to cause anti-government feelings in Fiji. They were not pro-Japanese, but they were not noticeably pro-British, and it may be said that their attitude to the war was one of 'indifference rather than positive disloyalty' to the government and the Allied cause.[21] Not unnaturally the Americans were perturbed about the security aspect of the Indian attitude and the governor's main anxiety was not about Indian loyalty but the chances of an unfortunate incident with the Americans.[22] He had to be constantly on the watch for signs of trouble. In November 1942 Mitchell found a very unofficial way of helping to win the loyalty of the Indians, or at any rate elicit a more friendly response from them, by employing a retired LMS (London Missionary Society) missionary 'with a broad mind and a kind heart', who really understood the Indians and India, to be a sort of guide, philosopher and friend of the Indians.[23] There were still difficulties with the Indians, above all the sugar cane cutters' strike, but there were no anti-Indian difficulties with the Americans.

Diplomatic skill was needed also to bring about goodwill between the Americans and the New Zealanders, who naturally wanted to play an active part in the war, but some Americans felt that they had no need of the comparatively small New Zealand forces and would prefer to keep the fighting to themselves. Mitchell wanted New Zealand troops to be stationed in Fiji and used with the Americans in the reconquest of the various islands occupied by the Japanese. In October 1942 he flew to Australia and New Zealand to discuss the delicate problems of cooperation. The New Zealand authorities made it clear that their troops 'ardently want', as he noted, 'to get into the fight

149

rather than to sit by while the US reconquer our territory and they fully took my point about using leader personnel to its best advantage'.[24] The air base at Nandi was an area of friction and the American GOC tackled Mitchell about it. Mitchell told him that the root of the trouble was that the young New Zealanders 'did not like being relegated to back area duties and treated rather scornfully by US Personnel'.[25] It was strange that this treatment of allies should have been allowed to exist. It was one example of the frictions and misunderstandings which Mitchell had been appointed to overcome. General Thompson apologized sincerely for the unhappy situation at Nandi and admitted that friction at the air base was due to the American commander there. He asked Mitchell to assure the Prime Minister of New Zealand that he greatly appreciated the New Zealand Air Force and he asked the governor to smooth over other misunderstandings also with New Zealand.[26]

Mitchell always took great pains to stress that the western Pacific was a war zone, that the American supreme commander and his generals were in authority and that what they wanted must be done, but he was never ready to accept high-handed attitudes and lack of reasonable international relations. General Thompson's correct appreciation of the relationship of military and civil authority in the Pacific was not at once understood by all his officers. A glaring example occurred in the Solomon Islands. The Japanese were being pushed slowly northwards and the administration of liberated British colonies was an important matter. 'I think I may want to do without British officers altogether', the American general told Mitchell, 'I do not think your Government should try to re-establish authority now while ops are on but should leave us to do it in our own muddled American way'. 'A nasty bit of work', was Mitchell's reaction. He thought that a particular American officer was at the back of this. Marchant, who did such magnificent work in the Solomon Islands, was present during this conversation. To make such a derogatory remark in his presence was an example of the insensitivity which had so seriously soured relations. Mitchell controlled his temper and replied, 'I hope this is a misapprehension: you are the supreme authority in the Solomons and we are here to see that what you want is done';[27] but he had to insist all the time that he was in charge of civil administration. It needed more than a 'muddled American way' to cope, for instance, with such curious things as the 'Jonfrum' cult. It was but one example of the need for experience and understanding in dealing with primitive societies. Mitchell recorded that he had:

> Read an interesting report about an outbreak of the 'Jonfrum' cult on Tanna I. This time a man has declared himself to be 'Jonfrum' which is apparently a pidgin corruption of 'John Brown'; he also said he was King of America and set to work to make an airfield so that his planes could land there, and promised his followers women and beer. Nicoll, the District Agent, handled the thing very well with the help of a Defence Force patrol from Villa sent in a US ship; and a very ugly looking business – for 'Jonfrum' was arrested and his followers then collected to release him by force and kill Nicoll – was dealt with and disposed of without any bloodshed.[28]

In September 1943 Mitchell went to Pearl Harbour and stayed with Nimitz. They were in complete agreement on policy. The Solomons had been freed from the Japanese and the general there wanted as much labour as possible to deal with the loading of ships and generally to process supplies for the troops in the war zone. Everything possible had to be done to satisfy the general's needs, but Mitchell thought that conscription of labour, which seemed to the military mind to be the obvious solution, might be fatal, because it 'might put the natives to the bush, or make them unfriendly'.[29] The right decision could not be made by American military officers but only by someone who was experienced in understanding the minds and reactions of primitive peoples.

At the beginning of 1944, when more and more islands were being or would soon be reconquered from the Japanese, Walter Nash, the Foreign Minister of New Zealand, was in Fiji and told Mitchell that both New Zealand and Australia felt that 'the essential thing [was] to maintain the interest and authority of the UK in Pacific Affairs'.[30] To free the islands from the Japanese and win the war was the first task, a naval and military task with the Americans in command aided by such help as could be given by Commonwealth forces. But to restore the devastated islands and re-establish civil administration was a matter needing the skill, understanding and experience of a colonial service, and Walter Nash agreed with Mitchell that in the economic field 'the control and management of primary produce and foodstuff prices so as to give producers a fair standard of living [was] the central Colonial problem'.[31] To Mitchell's great satisfaction the Colonial Office agreed with all his plans for reconstruction in the Solomons, the Gilberts and elsewhere. He believed that planning should be 'on the basis of re-occupying as much as possible of the G. and E. Isles so as to discharge our duty to the natives and to be able to render to the US service commanders as much help as possible in various ways, e.g. intelligence and perhaps labour'.[32] He told the Colonial Office that he wanted to buy out the owners of the copra plantations in the Solomon Islands and have copra processed by the islanders themselves with government guidance. He did not foresee any financial difficulties, because the plantations had been so badly damaged during the war.[33]

He worked out a produce or war materials development board for the Solomons and advocated the appointment of a 'Custodian of Property'. In the middle of 1943 he swore in an agent and consul in Tonga, a kingdom different in status from anything else in the western Pacific. His experience with Buganda gave him a clear perception of the correct relations between himself and Tonga and he explained to the new agent 'how to handle Native Governments, especially that he should always remember that they are the Government and should be allowed to govern as they please within very wide limits – only gross oppressions or serious abuses justify interference. On the other hand,' he pointed out, 'in War matters, they *must* do what is required of them'.[34]

Relations so happily established between Mitchell and the American High Command were not always understood in Washington. Early in 1943 Mitchell heard that the US War Shipping Administration had been writing direct to shipping firms about the rate of loading ships at Suva and Mantolia and had been asking for an explanation of the alleged decline during the previous six months. 'I took the gravest exception', he wrote, 'to a US official department corresponding direct with merchants and in fact inviting them to tell tales out of school, especially when the merchants had by their inefficiency driven us to form the Labour Corps and had until recently tried to sabotage its work'. The relations in Fiji between the commercial companies and the government were not easy during the war and the governor had a difficult task in trying to produce some sort of harmony between the government and the firms, and within the commercial community itself. Interference from outside could only aggravate an already difficult situation. Mitchell reported the matter to the GOC, who was angry that service matters should be investigated except through him.[35]

Fiji presented problems different from those in the less developed islands. It was a colony with three races, legislative and executive councils and large commercial interests. The organization of manpower to meet the requirements of the war was a complicated matter and the governor made the Executive Council into a war council. It was decided that the first concern of the council was to get the Fiji Military Force up to strength. Then came the question of ordinary labour. Labour in the docks, loading and unloading ships with food and other supplies for the armed forces was of vital importance. In fact the GOC told Mitchell that he regarded unloading ships as second only in importance to combat.[36] Mitchell went into the details of lighters and tugs and wharves. Personal inspection of the docks revealed that in the labourers' mess there was no provision for the men to sit at meals and that they had to stand. Mitchell promptly told the official in charge that this situation must be put right 'and that after Monday week officers must take their meals standing also until it was: tired men off shift eating

153

standing up!'[37] He was equally concerned about the welfare of men in the Fiji Military Force. He had heard that officers and NSOs often struck men in the force and he 'wanted it to be clearly understood that it was anathema to do so and would mean Court Martial and the sack in every case, *for I will not have it*'.[38] Commerce and labour were not nationalized, but a labour corps had been formed. For the rest, commercial firms recruited their labour, because the War Council decreed that there should be no compulsion of labour for private firms, and employers and labourers would have to agree among themselves.

The internal affairs of Fiji and relations among the Allies were inevitably intertwined. The military authorities needed sugar for the troops and labour for loading and unloading ships in Fiji, and they needed labour in the various islands in the area, but the cultivation of sugar and the provision of labour depended on human beings in various stages of development. The governor would not, indeed could not, compel the growers to cultivate and cut sugar cane, or force the islanders to provide labour under coercion. One of Mitchell's officers returned to Suva from a visit of inspection to the Gilbert Islands, from which the Japanese had retreated. He reported that the Japanese had done themselves 'great harm by taking round with them their miserable Korean labour troops – for, say the natives, if that is what it means to be under Japan, the British Empire for us'.[39] Mitchell's work in getting the Americans to understand the problems was made more difficult by such people as the editor of *The Fiji Times and Herald*, who received his strongest condemnation for his anti-American publications. But Mitchell's human understanding produced a very different attitude to a European who had been spreading objectionable stories about the conduct of American troops at Lantoka. He had the man brought to him, but reprimand gave way to sympathy. 'Poor devil,' he recorded, 'his own wife has gone wrong with one of them and that being so I told him he would hear no more about it: he was pathetically grateful'.[40]

Mitchell was amused and not offended when he went with the American General to an American Memorial Day service and, because the arrangements were very muddled, was himself shown into a back pew;[41] but a few days later he took great pains to prevent any hurtful embarrassment falling on Lala Sukuna, who was about to be appointed ANA. They were going together to visit an American base. Knowing 'the odd US intransigence about colour', Mitchell made a plan in advance for use if necessary. His fears were justified, because the American commander 'would not have him in the place', and so Mitchell sent Sukuna with one of his senior European officers to the New Zealand camp on the score that the American base was so full that there was no room for them there.[42]

The serious nature of relations with the Americans is indicated by the fact that, although most British files are made available after 30 years, a Foreign Office file on 'Anglo-American Relations' was not; but during Mitchell's time as High Commissioner they steadily improved. In the middle of 1944 Nimitz invited him to visit Pearl Harbour and the Colonial Office urged him to accept the invitation. Nimitz did not want him at Supreme Headquarters for the purpose of discussing plans or delivering reports. He wanted to make clear to everyone his appreciation of the great change which Mitchell had brought about: friction had been replaced by harmony, and suspicion and distrust by international goodwill. This visit to Pearl Harbour, Mitchell wrote in his diary, 'has been most enjoyable and, more than that, has been a remarkable expression by Nimitz and all his commanders and senior officers of the warmest feelings to all things British. I am really very happy and proud that my two years mission over here should have resulted in so cloudless an allied sky'.[43] He was awarded the American Legion of Merit. There was some doubt as to whether he would be allowed to wear a foreign decoration, but a few weeks after he arrived in Kenya Mitchell recorded in his diary: 'The American Legion of Merit business is cleared up at last by a cable saying the King has given me leave to wear it, grade of Commander.'[44]

Notes

1. MD, 22 January 1942.
2. Ibid., 22 May 1942.
3. Ibid., 22 May 1942.
4. Ibid., 1 July 1942.
5. Ibid., 4 July 1942.
6. Ibid., 16 July 1942.
7. Ibid., 22 July 1944.
8. Ibid., 15 July 1942.
9. D.A. Scarr, *Ratu Sukuna: Soldier, Statesman, Man of Two Worlds: A Biography* (London, 1980), p. 130.
10. MD, 9 September 1942.
11. Kenya LCD, 3 January 1947, col. 956.
12. Note written for the author by LG Usher in January 1981. Mr Usher later became editor of *The Fiji Times and Herald.*
13. CO/83/238/85466, Telegram from Mitchell to secretary of state, 7 August 1942.
14. Ibid., 21 July 1942.
15. CO/83/235/85088, Governor to secretary of state, 30 September 1943.
16. CO/83/238/85465, Minute by FK Lloyd, 7 August 1942.
17. MD, 25 August 1942.
18. Ibid., 30 September 1942.
19. Ibid., 29 January 1943.
20. CO/83/85481, Mitchell to secretary of state, 29 April 1943.
21. KL Gillion, *The Fiji Indians: Challenge to European Dominance, 1920–1946* (Canberra, 1977), p. 176.
22. MD, 24 August 1942.
23. Ibid., 6 November 1942.
24. Ibid., 19 October 1942.
25. Ibid., 19 November 1942.
26. Ibid., 3 November 1942.
27. Ibid., 4 February 1943.
28. Ibid., 16 January 1944.
29. Ibid., 21 September 1943.
30. Ibid., 1 January 1944.
31. Ibid., 23 August 1942.
32. CO/243/85489, Mitchell to Gent, 5 August 1943.
33. MD, 26 June 1943.

34. Ibid., 17 January 1943.
35. Ibid., 4 November 1942.
36. Ibid., 22 May 1943.
37. Ibid., 8 July 1943.
38. Ibid., 6 July 1943.
39. Ibid., 7 December 1942.
40. Ibid., 30 May 1943.
41. Ibid., 4 June 1943.
42. Ibid., 29 July 1944.
43. Ibid., 3 January 1945.

XII
Fiji

When Mitchell became Governor of Fiji in 1942 the population was made up of:

Fijians	101,285
Europeans	4,188
Half castes	4,879
Rotunans	2,967
Other South Sea islanders	1,637
Indians	92,309
Chinese	1,979
Others	1,274
	210,518[1]

Mitchell arrived in Suva on 21 July and a fortnight later he sent a telegram to the secretary of state giving his impressions of the racial situation in the islands. In his autobiography he wrote that a fact of the greatest significance was the relations between the coloured and the white races: 'In the Fiji military forces there were Fijian company commanders with British subalterns and NCOs under them. In fact, in every way the Fijian or Tongan, British and half-caste population – inter-marriage was quite frequent – while recognising their differences of colour and custom, were one people and on the most cordial terms.'[2]

But he saw from the start that the Indians might cause difficulties and that race relations as a whole were uneasy. The Fijians were the landowners and looked down on the Indians, who were largely the descendants of indentured labourers. The

Indian peasants were tenant farmers, half of them tenants of Fijian landowners and half of the Colonial Sugar Refining Company, an Australian company which had acquired a considerable amount of land in Fiji. To begin with, consciousness of colour gave the Indians and Fijians a certain affinity, but, as the war went on, Indian lack of loyalty to the British Empire (to which the Fijians were happy to belong), and the influence of New Zealanders, white and Maori alike had a great influence on the relations between the Fijians and the European residents.

Mitchell started by thinking well of the Indians. 'I do not believe they are disloyal,' he told the secretary of state, 'in fact I hope for much from them. Their leaders are politically immature and prone to exaggeration and alarming language in telegrams, and are not in sufficiently close touch with the Government. In fact the Kenya Indians over again, but with little substance in their grievances. I believe they will be loyal and helpful.'[3] He was soon to find, however, that the Indian politicians were much influenced by events in India and had little in common with the loyalty felt by the Fijian leaders and the peasants of the islands.

As High Commissioner for the Western Pacific, much of Mitchell's time was spent on bringing harmony out of discord among the Allied forces in the war zone. At the same time, as Governor of Fiji he was concerned in the colony itself with colonial problems and situations complicated by the war. The long strike in the sugar industry showed how strong and lasting were the effects of the Indian indentured labour system of the past, and within the Indian community Muslim fears of Hindu dominance complicated plans for the development of representative government. He thought that greater power in government would be welcomed by the Fijians, but to his great surprise they came out strongly in favour of leaving things as they were. They pointed out that the Indians could not be excluded from an increase in political responsibility, and Lala Sukuna, the leading Fijian who became Adviser on Native Affairs, specifically said that, until the Fijians had gained much more political experience in local government they would be overtaken by the Indians in

central government circles and so they did not want constitutional changes to be introduced until later.[4] The Indians thought
that they would have more power in central government if the
post of Secretary for Indian Affairs were abolished and they had
an Indian member of Executive Council. Mitchell, however, told
them that their poor showing in the war effort made it impossible for him then to talk about an Indian member of the
Executive Council and in any case it would be very wrong to
allocate seats on the Executive Council by race rather than by
suitability for the position.[5]

Another complication was caused by Muslim fear of Hindu
dominance. Mitchell had known it in East Africa and was to
encounter it again when he returned as Governor of Kenya. The
Muslim representatives in Legislative Council in Fiji presented a
petition, which the governor passed to the secretary of state,
asking for separate representation. As the Muslims saw things,
it was clear from their speeches that the Hindus intended their
community to monopolize all six council seats which, it was
being proposed, should be reserved for the Indians.[6] But none of
Fiji's constitutional problems and none of Mitchell's proposals
were attended to in the Colonial Office before he left the colony.
A year after he sent his confidential dispatch and memorandum
on post-war reconstruction in Fiji, a senior official in the
Colonial Office wrote to the chief secretary in Suva to
apologise.[7]

The aim underlying Mitchell's plan was that Fiji should be
more firmly set on the road to self-government, but he appreciated the social difficulties which beset constitutional change. He
issued a confidential paper on the 'Problems of Post-War
Reconstruction in Fiji' over his own signature to members of
Executive and Legislative Councils and government departments, in which he said that the secretary of state was intent on
seeing that 'every post in the service of the Colony should be
open to the inhabitants of the Colony who are able to qualify
for it and that a special effort is needed to enable them to
qualify'.[8]

In East Africa he had demonstrated his belief that an adequate amount of higher education was needed to produce an African élite. In Fiji also his hope of giving greater responsibility in government and government services to the native inhabitants required improved education for a sufficient number of Fijians and, as in Uganda, where he had said that Makerere ought to be regarded as the starting point and not the apex in education, he declared that in Fiji 'school systems must be planned from the top (that is from the more advanced stages) downwards, the controlling factor for all the lower stages being the occupations open to pupils and the facilities available to qualify them for those occupations'. He thought that in countries whose economy was based on agriculture with the majority of the people a rural peasantry, purely academic education ought to be restricted to a comparatively small proportion of the population. For the majority the aim should be basic literacy accompanied by practical work on the land, because 'education must be planned to fit those who receive it to live the lives they are likely to have to lead in the circumstances peculiar to themselves.'[9]

The monopoly enjoyed by the Colonial Sugar Refining Company in the main agricultural export crop meant that the lives which the peasants were likely to lead depended almost entirely on the world sugar market. When he was Governor of Uganda, Mitchell had realized with alarm that an economy based on one crop was at the mercy of the developed countries and the great trading companies. In Fiji he thought that the uncertainty of the farmers getting an adequate price for their sugar might persuade some of them to turn to growing rice or some other remunerative food crop for export. Nevertheless, because he felt sure that in the long run the cultivation of sugar cane was of the greatest importance Mitchell urged the Colonial Office to do all it could to secure an adequate guaranteed price. At the same time training in good agricultural practices would enable the peasants to improve their own diet from their small farms.

While he wanted the peasants to have a better standard of living he wanted a Fijian élite to enable government to become more and more in the hands of the local inhabitants with development towards autonomy. He discussed his ideas with members of the administration and leading unofficials and said that he thought the aim should be to have a speaker in Legislative Council with the Executive Council exercising 'in some form second-chamber functions, members of Ex. Co. not being members of Leg. Co. There were be 4 officials – CS (Chief Secretary), AG (Attorney General), FS (Financial Secretary) and ANA (Advisers on Native Affairs) – and 4 unofficials on Ex. Co. who would be as it were members of a Cabinet. They would have an obligation to support Government or resign and this would be a very powerful weapon.'[10] He had to explain that 'an official must *do* what he is told, but may *think* what he likes; when an investigation is being held he is perfectly at liberty to say what he thinks without any reservations'.[11]

He thought that the normal Colonial Legislative Council was apt to be a farce and that the official majority should be abolished wherever possible, and he believed that the time had come when this could safely be done in Fiji. With 'a nice balance of racial representation . . . and a solid and sensible race like the Fijians' there was nothing to be afraid of. His experience of legislative councils made him feel ever more strongly that having 'a row of dummy heads of departments' who were there 'simply to vote' was absurd. It really made no difference whether the governor himself was empowered to overrule the house or merely ordered a row of officials to do it for him. 'Waxworks should do just as well' as officials. Mitchell was trying to develop the Executive Council, with two unofficials on it, into some sort of second chamber and, in any case, he thought it was much better to face postwar difficulties 'with a Council, proceedings in which had the reality which comes from an elected majority, than with a Council packed with automatic votes for the Government'. Then, having got an efficient and partly unofficial executive council, he wanted the secretary of state to 'put on an official footing' his practice of using members of the Executive Council as if they were ministers. Many people were concerned about the administrative ineffectiveness, which resulted from the bottleneck created by the practice of using the secretariat for work which could be done by quasi-ministers.

However, Mitchell thought that, unless the secretary of state gave *his* authority to the proposals, 'the next Governor might reverse the process and go back to the centralised Secretariat system' and be in great difficulties in trying to undo Mitchell's reforms.[12] Gent replied that the Colonial Office liked his proposals,[13] but his term of office in Fiji was not long enough for him to carry his plans to fruition. But for him personally they were a valuable blueprint from which to start on his plans for reconstruction of the administration in Kenya.

During most of his time in Fiji Mitchell was burdened by a strike by the sugar growers. In any case the strike, so largely backed by Indian politicians, would have been difficult to deal with. It was made more difficult by the dilatoriness of the Colonial Office and the requirements of the war. The production of sugar in Fiji was of great concern to the fighting services: the more that could be grown in the war zone the less would have to come from elsewhere. As was the case with other tropical products the price of sugar was regulated by a worldwide system of control of the market in the prosperous industrial West. During the war the British Ministry of Food bought the whole Fiji crop from the Colonial Sugar Refining Company, which was the only company in Fiji buying sugar from the growers. As Mitchell pointed out to the secretary of state, the Company was therefore in effect the agent of the Ministry of Food for procuring, manufacturing and exporting sugar.

In July 1943 the sugar farmers were on strike everywhere, refusing to cut their crop unless the company raised the price. The dispute which flared up into a strike by cane growers was about the price paid for cane by the company, but, as sugar was an essential item of food for the American forces in the Pacific, the government could not be unconcerned about its supply. Indian politicians in Fiji urged the growers to refuse to cut their cane, but the governor could not compel the company to pay more without the agreement of the Colonial Office. Machinery for fixing prices could only have been instituted with the permission of the secretary of state after a visit by an expert, on whose report decisions could have been based. Mitchell asked the Colonial Office to send an expert but his request was not acted on with speed.

In the absence of authority the governor had to rely on persuasion and on 17 November 1943 he sent a despatch in an attempt to describe the situation. He was afraid that the Indian politicians might try to persuade the farmers to turn to other crops. They might succeed in doing this because 'in the absence of any guarantee for the purchase of the crop at a remunerative price' rice or some other food stuff might pay more. Nevertheless he went on to say that the cultivation of sugar cane was of the greatest importance and he therefore asked for authority to give a guarantee in respect of the 1944 crop. Even a promise to buy at the current Ministry of Food prices would be enough. Definite action was needed because he suspected that the farmers' leaders wanted 'to drive the CSR [Colonial Sugar Refinery] out of business and for it to be replaced by an Indian Company financed by Indian capital'.[14] It is probable that at that time financiers in India would not have been interested in establishing an Indian sugar company in Fiji, but Mitchell must have had grounds for suspecting that that was what the Indians in Fiji would have liked.

The Colonial Office found the despatch 'very pessimistic' and 'purely descriptive', and one official minuted: 'The Indian long-term aim of driving the CSR Company out of business seems to me to be somewhat conjectural'. It seems strange that an official in the Colonial Office should think that he could know better than the governor in Suva about the wishes of the farmers' leaders in Fiji. Another minute complained that 'it appears that all endeavours to persuade the Governor that sugar is and is likely to remain an urgently wanted commodity and not a surplus have been in vain', while another official pompously wrote, 'I think it is important to do all we can to convince the Governor that, when we allude to the need for the maintenance of production, we mean what we say'.[15] If the governor had seen this minute, he might have replied that attention to his request for a visit and report by an expert and agreement to his wish for the institution of price fixing machinery would have been the way for the Colonial Office to show that it meant what it said about the need for maintaining production.

A few months later Mitchell was able to send a telegram in which he said:

> Government, after declining to be coerced into panicky or opportunist courses, has emerged with European or Fijian opinion solidly behind it, with much Indian opinion impressed by its strength of purpose, and with even extremist elements aware of the need to devise some means of getting under its wing. All my advisers are agreed that Patel and Swami should now be left to sink in the quicksands that are forming round them, and that our line for the present should be to concentrate on assurances that you are giving urgent and careful consideration to the whole problem, and that your decisions, which will safeguard farmers' interests to the fullest possible extent, may be awaited with perfect confidence.[16]

On this an official in the Colonial Office minuted: 'The long telegram . . . indicates that the dispute is taking a more favourable turn, and in paragraph 5 the Governor attempts to take some credit for this'.[17] Disputes do not take more favourable turns of their own volition and the patronising complacency of this minute lets in a little light on the difficulties which Mitchell faced when he expected some understanding of colonial problems and asked for decision on important issues.

The farmers were basing their case on standards of living, but Mitchell saw that the company and the Colonial Office assumed that 'world price was uncontrollable and profit took preference over standards of living'. Although he entirely disagreed with this and advocated a very different outlook, he saw that ability to fix prices was a temporary necessity. The Colonial Office next sent a telegram saying that they thought the best course to take in the dispute was to have a statutory price fixing machinery 'as soon as it can be set up' and there ought to be a visit by an expert. 'What did Mitchell think about this?' they asked. As he had been urging this course for some months, his exasperation with the Colonial Office became even greater,[18] although he added 'the fact has to be faced that the "world price" may not give a local price on which the farmers can live'.[19]

In January, however, the Colonial Office sent a cable saying that they thought it would be unwise to initiate price fixing machinery and the company then felt able to do as it pleased and decided to refuse to buy any cane from farmers who had refused to sell – a decision which Mitchell thought might cause a revival of the strike. The company had not only told 56 tenant farmers that, because they had refused to sell cane in 1943, the company would not buy cane from them in future, but had also served notice on 46 of their tenants that their leases would be terminated. Mitchell was furious and cabled to the secretary of state on 28 February saying, 'You should know that I do not propose to permit eviction of tenants during war time'.[20] And he repeated what he had often stressed:

> What is awaited here is the decision of the Secretary of State and not that of the Government of Fiji . . . I have no objection to taking full responsibility in matters in which I decide policy. As the Secretary of State must himself in fact decide in this case, it is right that decision should be announced as his, with all the added weight which that will give it.[21]

At last the Colonial Office understood that, however much they wanted the production of sugar to prosper, the governor was powerless to coerce the company, to fix the current price paid for cane or to guarantee future prices. The permanent undersecretary himself sent a telegram on 2 March: 'I quite understand your conclusion that nothing short of announcement by HMG is likely to remedy situation and restore goodwill and full production'.[22] At last in March 1944 it was announced that Professor CE Shepherd of the Imperial College of Tropical Agriculture in Trinidad was coming to Fiji to investigate and issue a report.

For Mitchell much more was involved than the settlement of the strike. When he went to Uganda as governor one of his first acts was to ask the treasurer to make an enquiry into the incidence of taxation on the peasants. He felt strongly that taxation there should on no account injure the peasants' ability to have essential foodstuffs and other things necessary for a simple but adequate, standard of living. In Fiji he thought that the sugar farmer ought to be able to earn an income sufficient to maintain a similar standard and he did not see how this could be achieved unless the developed countries paid a higher price for sugar. During the war the British Ministry of Food brought all the sugar grown and processed in Fiji and he saw what was going on at that level when he sent a telegram to the secretary of state saying, 'It is not surprising, as things are, that it is not sugar the Ministry wants, but cheap sugar'.[23]

Mitchell discussed the future with Walter Nash, the New Zealand Foreign Minister, and convinced him that 'the control and management of primary produce and foodstuff prices so as to give producers a fair standard of living [was] the central Colonial problem'. Adequate world prices were the basic essential, but local conditions had to be taken into consideration in particular cases, and subsidies given by the imperial power might perhaps be necessary, because, as he saw, the fact had to be faced that the 'world price' might not give a local price on which the farmers could live. He sent a 'Private and Personal telegram to Oliver Stanley, in which he said, 'I hold also very strongly that it is a vital Colonial interest that produce prices be related to Colonial costs and living standards instead of, as at present, to lowest price which world surpluses can be used to create . . . Our Colonial future turns on this above all else.'[24] He felt that he was living in a time of revolution when the standards and complacencies of the past would be overthrown. '. . . it may be a dangerous will o' the wisp to follow,' he wrote, 'to seek for a stable remunerative price for sugar – so was the abolition of slavery, of child labour in mines and factories, of slums and all sorts of other things.' But if the Colonial Office thought that colonial people were 'going to live again in poverty and misery to keep Lever Bros, and the like going they were living in a fool's paradise'.[25]

Alas, the colonial peoples, now for the most part the new nations of the developing world, are still living in poverty. The markets of the industrialized nations still control their standards of living. Child labour in mines and factories was not done away with overnight and the abolition of slavery was an arduous business. Materialism and human selfishness hold sway, but 'where there is no vision the people perish'.

His two years in Fiji were not the happiest period of Mitchell's life. He found the climate of Suva debilitating and the many air journeys he had to make very tiring. Although he really knew that he had been sent to the Pacific because the job which needed doing was of exceptional difficulty and delicacy, in moments of depression he feared he had been relegated to a backwater. He was overworked and suffering from a severe and painful infection in one of his ears. This was finally cured in the hospital at Suva, but only after many weeks of pain. He was physically tired and mentally depressed, but the problems which crowded in on him in 1943 must have shown him that he was without doubt engaged in work of prime importance in the prosecution of the war. Then in 1944, when he felt that he had successfully accomplished the task for which he had been sent to the Pacific, he wrote to Sir George Gater at the Colonial Office to tell him that, when it became possible, he would like to be moved. Some months earlier the secretary of state had written personally to tell him that his success in the western Pacific did not mean that he would be kept indefinitely there and Mitchell had replied that any sacrifice in going to that area was of no importance. During the war he would willingly go anywhere in any capacity. He was horrified when the Colonial Office wrote to say that they wished accumulated leave to be taken, because they said that 'the majority of Governors have represented that the Service will resent the cut, morale will suffer and so on'. On reading this he concluded that the 'Service must be in a rotten state if it is true that alone in the Empire it is going to haggle over privileges and refuse to make even this sacrifice'.[26]

Looking further ahead, he had to say that his heart was in

168

East Africa. Some critics have accused him to being proud, but personal ambition took second place to his desire to serve East Africa where he hoped the territories would be welded into some form of union, and he assured Oliver Stanley that he would go to a united East Africa as an executive councillor under any first class man he sent as governor. On no occasion did he ask for that most senior position for himself. When he wrote to Gater, he said that he had done the job for which he had been sent to the Pacific and reminded him of the undertaking made by Stanley and Lord Cranborne, his predecessor as secretary of state, that he would not be left for long in Fiji and said that he would like to become Governor of Tanganyika if that post became vacant. He then repeated what he had written to Stanley that he would be willing to 'revert to the status of an Ex. Councillor for NA [Native Affairs] in a united EA'.[27] There was no immediate response, but he must have remembered that in the previous May Francis Rennell had written to tell him that Stanley had asked him to tell Mitchell that he was 'a white haired dog and not likely to be left [in Fiji] for long'.[28] It was fitting that on his return from Pearl Harbour in July 1944, when Nimitz had acknowledged the success of his work of bringing harmony and friendly cooperation out of discord between American and Commonwealth forces in the Pacific, he found waiting for him a cable offering him the Governorship of Kenya.

His service in Middle East Command and the Pacific had been very arduous and overwork produced bouts of depression, but he realized that he was engaged in work of great importance and he managed to enjoy relaxation from time to time. Lady Mitchell had been able to join him in Suva and his life had been enriched by the visits of people of all kinds, for whom Fiji was a centre in the war area and a convenient stopping place between Australia and New Zealand, and Supreme Headquarters at Pearl Harbour. His guests ranged from Admiral Nimitz, who paid several visits, to 'two young US fighter pilots', whom he 'took sailing in the afternoon in a harbour full of big ships',[29] and a young New Zealander, 'a very charming young man whom it was great fun to have in the house'.[30] There was a US Minister, 'a flamboyant Southerner, very talkative and refreshing', who told Mitchell that 'his family owned a canyon in Mexico, the entrance to which was so narrow they had had to teach their dogs to wag their tails up and down and not across!'[31]

The strangest visit was that of an uninvited guest who was discovered by Lady Mitchell [M for Margery in the diaries] in the bathroom. Mitchell's reaction was unusual for a governor, but it showed the human and understanding traits in his character, which underlay so much of his official work:

> At about 1 a.m. M woke me up with some indignation to say that there was a man in her bathroom. I went along and found a very drunk young officer from Lantala Bay, apparently RNZAF. He had walked out of the dance into the pouring rain and got soaked. Now he had shed his shoes in the passage and got his clothes off and was swathed in a bath towel: he just stood there saying gently, 'I don't know where I am.' I thought we had no empty bedroom and so took him down to the morning room, lent him a change of dry clothes and told him to sleep it off on the sofa. In the morning Singh gave him some tea and Prayad drove him home: he sent very contrite messages.[32]

His sympathetic attitude to the young people he met during the war was not new. His reaction to the young New Zealander's befuddled appearance in that bathroom in Government House was not what might usually have been expected in a governor, but not many governors had had to leave Oxford for daubing the noses of statues there with red paint and for committing what he described in retrospect as other undergraduate pranks. Although Mitchell was very critical, he was always ready to listen to young people's views and discuss the issues of the day with them on a level. His nephew Michael, later Sir Michael Crosswell, British Ambassador in the Argentine, remembers how, when he was an undergraduate at New College, Uncle Phil, when home on leave, would visit him in Oxford and go for long walks with him discussing the problems of foreign policy – discussing different points of view, not pontificating from the heights of successful Colonial service.

At times in his career Mitchell suffered from overwork and strain and he was always ready to understand the effects of strain on others. A certain Donald Kennedy, who had spent many months commanding a private war against the Japanese in New Georgia, was called to headquarters to meet the governor, who was his commander-in-chief. An appointment was made, but Kennedy was too drunk at the time to keep it. The governor understood what the effects of relief from a long period of great strain might be and merely postponed the meeting and invited Kennedy to stay at Government House while he was on leave, and then took no notice when Kennedy fell asleep one night at dinner.[33]

Eight years earlier, when he was Governor of Uganda, he reacted in an equally ungubernatorial way to a letter from a schoolboy at King's College, Budo, who wrote to him saying that he had no money with which to pay his school fees and asking for work in the holidays. The governor went over to Budo to see him and, thinking that 'he looked genuine enough', told him to report for work at Government House in the middle of April.[34] He was very much a proconsul, but that was what governors were expected to be; at the same time he was very human. He enjoyed the results of the expertise of the cooks at Government House, but he got great satisfaction from cooking breakfast on his boat, *Bluebell*, on Lake Victoria. He enjoyed the pomp of official occasions with the governor's uniform and plumes, but he wrote ecstatically of the pleasures of an early morning hike in the uplands of Mount Elgon. He was able to be a proconsul when the occasion required him to be so but to ignore protocol and formality when the human factor seemed to him to outweigh other considerations. The young New Zealand pilot had broken into Government House but, like Donald Kennedy, was to Mitchell first and foremost a young man reacting to months of strain in active warfare; and this sympathetic understanding was fully inter-racial. When he was Governor of Kenya it was put to the test during an agricultural show in

171

the Nandi District. The governor was attending the Nyanza Provincial Agricultural Show at Kapsabet and to quote his account: 'Had a rest in a cottage put aside for me. Just before 2 a heavy storm broke and large numbers of people took refuge in my cottage – including one old Gentleman and his stark naked daughter of about 14 or 15! They were smelly but cheerful and friendly.'[35]

Great mental ability, devotion to duty, at times over-confidence in his own judgement but willingness to listen to advice, although not always to take it, arrogance at some times and sympathetic understanding at others were among the ingredients making up his character. A few days before he left Fiji he said in reply to speeches of appreciation in Legislative Council that, if he had achieved anything, it was due to his 'firm faith in human nature and interest in all things human'.[36] Race, as such, meant nothing to him, but racial characteristics and present capacity were basic to his aims and planning. He was fervently British and anxious to hand on to the less developed people for whom he worked the best of British culture. The welfare of the Solomon Islanders, recently liberated from the Japanese, racial harmony and a stable economy in Fiji, and the affairs of the western Pacific in general had his full attention while he was Governor of Fiji, but his heart really lay in East Africa to whose inhabitants he felt he owed a lifelong debt.

Notes

1. CO83/238/85450, Colonial Office minute, February 1942.
2. Mitchell, *African Afterthoughts*, p. 211.
3. CO83/238/85466, Telegram from governor to secretary of state, 7 August 1942.
4. CO83/235/85038, Mitchell to Gent, 29 November 1943.
5. CO83/235/85038, Governor to secretary of state, Confidential No. 69, 23 September 1943.
6. CO83/235/85038, Governor to secretary of state, 4 September 1943.
7. CO83/243/85489, JB Sidebotham to JF Nicoll, 2 December 1944.

8. CO83/243/85489, Reconstruction Paper No. 1, 4 August 1943.
9. CO83/235/85090, Note by Mitchell.
10. MD, 1 October 1943.
11. Ibid., 7 October 1943.
12. CO83/243/85489, Mitchell to Gent, 5 October 1943.
13. Ibid., Gent to Mitchell, 27 October 1943.
14. CO83/238/85460, Governor's despatch, 17 November 1943.
15. Ibid., minutes by Trafford Smith and BY Carstairs.
16. CO83/242/85460/1/1944, Telegram governor to secretary of state, 5 January 1944.
17. Ibid., minute by Trafford Smith.
18. MD, 14 December 1943.
19. MD, 1 January 1944.
20. CO83/242/85460/1/1944, Telegram Mitchell to secretary of state, 28 February 1944.
21. Ibid., Telegram Mitchell to secretary of state, 28 February 1944.
22. Ibid., Telegram from permanent undersecretary of state to governor, 2 March 1944.
23. Ibid., Telegram Mitchell to secretary of state, 30 December 1943.
24. CO83/242/85460/1/1944, Private and personal telegram, Mitchell to Stanley, 4 March 1944.
25. MD, 29 November 1943.
26. Ibid., 5 September 1943.
27. Ibid., 5 January 1944.
28. Ibid., 8 May 1943.
29. Ibid., 22 December 1942.
30. Ibid., 10 February 1943.
31. Ibid., 19 August 1942.
32. Ibid., 1 October 1944.
33. Note written for the author by LG Usher, January 1981.
34. MD, 22 February 1936.
35. Ibid., 15 December 1948.
36. Ibid., 27 September 1944.

XIII

'If I Cannot Retire'

On several occasions while Mitchell was serving as Secretary for Native Affairs in Tanganyika it was hinted in London that he ought to go to Kenya as chief native commissioner. Rumours of this reached him in Dar es Salaam and horrified him. He had trouble enough with the comparatively small settler community in Tanganyika and he felt sure that his inter-racial feelings would meet strong opposition from the politically powerful Europeans of Kenya. In December 1928 it seemed that he really might be posted to Kenya. He was appalled and wrote in his diary, 'I should not last long in Kenya before being thrown to the wolves'.[1] In 1931 on his way to London to give evidence to the Joint Parliamentary Committee on closer union he met CV Maxwell, who had just vacated the post of chief native commissioner in Kenya and was leaving the Colonial Service altogether. He told Mitchell that the Kenya Government was 'hopelessly dishonest and no kind of square deal for natives is possible'. Grigg, the governor, Maxwell said, had 'emasculated his Annual Report and cut out whole pages'. Maxwell was going to London to give evidence to the Joint Committee and was taking the missing pages with him. He told Mitchell that attempts were being 'made by his Government and by the unofficial members to muzzle him before he goes to the JC, but he refused to be muzzled. He says no honest man with any self respect can hold the office of CNC in Kenya as things are now'.[2] In London Mitchell met Sir Donald Cameron, who told him that he was in grave risk of having to follow Maxwell in Kenya.[3] The post *was* in fact offered to him, but he refused it.[4]

That seems to have settled the danger of his having to become chief native commissioner in Kenya, but a year after he became Governor of Uganda Sir Philip Sasoon, the British Undersecretary of State for Air, visited him at Entebbe after staying with Sir Joseph Byrne, the Governor of Kenya, in Nairobi. He told Mitchell that Kenya was in a bad state and that Byrne was unable to cope with the problems there, and that he was going to tell Orsmby-Gore, the Secretary of State for the Colonies, that Mitchell should be appointed Governor of Kenya. 'God forbid', said Mitchell, but he felt that he was 'in some peril of it'.[5] Then in 1939 he received a curious telegram from London saying that the secretary of state, Malcolm MacDonald, wanted to inform him that Sir Henry Moore had been appointed Governor of Kenya in place of Air Chief-Marshal Sir Robert Brooke Popham, who had been recalled for duty in the Royal Air Force, and to assure Mitchell that he had been very carefully considered but that it was felt that he could not be moved so early in the war. With the following year's moves in mind he proposed giving Mitchell another governorship. 'Very good of him,' Mitchell commented, 'but I was not a candidate for Kenya and do not want to move until I have finished my commission'.[6]

It was unusual, to say the least, for the secretary of state to send an apologetic message to a colonial governor explaining why he was not being offered another governorship. There must have been wire-pulling to get Mitchell moved to Kenya and MacDonald must have imagined that Mitchell knew about this. He did not know about it and he would have stamped on it if he had been aware of it. He wrote to Malcolm MacDonald thanking him for his telegram but saying he thought the Colonial Office knew that he 'was not a candidate for much the same reasons as led [him] to refuse the post of CNC in 1931'. He felt, as he put it, that 'greatly as I like Kenya and many of the people in it the prevailing attitude to Asians and Africans is one I cannot stand or rather could not *qua* Governor'. He went on to tell the secretary of state that he wanted to stay in Uganda, where he had projects not yet resolved, either for three or four years, followed by retirement, or for two years and then to succeed Sir Mark Young as Governor of Tanganyika. He reminded Malcolm MacDonald that he had been offered that post in 1937, but that he felt then that his duty lay in Uganda, although the Governorship of Tanganyika was what he most desired.[7] The one post which he definitely did not want and would have refused, unless pressed, was the governorship of Kenya.

The territory which became Kenya had been occupied by Britain not for its own sake but because it lay between Uganda and the sea. The safety of the Christian missions in Uganda, the development of trade and, above all, Britain's strategic interest in controlling the headwaters of the Nile required a more efficient means of transport than human porterage. The construction of the railway led to the introduction and encouragement of European settlement in order to provide freight to produce some revenue to support the line. Indians had traded on the coast for centuries and enterprising Indians followed the railway and set up trading centres throughout its length. The conditions of the indigenous Africans, the enterprise of the Indians and the capital and agricultural initiative of the Europeans had together produced the plural society of the new colony. After the Second World War race relations became in some ways more difficult when the expansion of European commercial enterprises brought a large addition of junior European staff and the urban European population outnumbered the farmers. The newcomers lacked experience in living among people of another race. Mitchell had no doubt that in the complex society of Kenya the improvement of race relations was vital for economic and political progress. That was a challenge to be faced all the time, but there were administrative and constitutional changes which he thought were necessary to enable government to meet the requirements of the Kenya which was taking shape after the war.

When Mitchell accepted the governorship in 1944 he felt that his long experience of East Africa could enable him to make a contribution to the solution of some of Kenya's problems. He had no doubt that it was 'the most difficult task in the

176

continent',[8] and he knew that his wartime exertions had affected his health. He had already been thinking of retiring from active service before he was offered the governorship, but a sense of duty and a response to a challenge led him to accept the post, which he said he would most like to have, 'if I cannot retire'.[9] Exactly a year after he became governor he was so tired, so near to breaking point, that he had to take a quick decision and go on leave to South Africa, and, as the years passed, his health deteriorated. Early in 1948 the question of the renewal of his commission for a second term had to be discussed and he told Sir Alfred Vincent, a member of the Executive Council, that he 'wanted to retire and would certainly not take another job and only very reluctantly would remain in office here', but that he 'would not absolutely decline'.[10] A month later he wrote, 'feeling very run down and rather depressed. I cannot yet get the Members – or many of the Kenya Government – to get on with their jobs and stop bickering with each other.'[11]

In the following January, when he was in London, the secretary of state offered him a peerage and asked him to accept reappointment. He expressed his appreciation of the offer of a peerage and said he would accept it, but about the question of reappointment he said that he would be glad to retire but would undertake further service in East Africa if he was wanted.[12] The extension of Mitchell's governorship was announced on 11 April. His sense of duty had overcome his fears of failing health and energy. 'I hope,' he wrote in his diary, 'I have decided rightly, but I often feel very tired and doubtful whether I am up to the job; certainly I have not the drive I used to have'.[13]

Before the end of the tour which he had reluctantly agreed to, the visit of Princess Elizabeth was planned to take place at the beginning of February 1952. A change of governors so soon before that would have caused many difficulties and his term of office was extended for six months more. In keeping him for so long in his arduous post the Colonial Office made a cruel mistake. In June 1951 he admitted to 'a sort of weary feeling' and recorded in his diary that his horse, Ewhurst, had died. He added, 'He was a dear little horse and it is sad that he has gone

– but old horses like old men must be glad to be at peace.'[14] He was not an old man. He was only 61, but he had had an arduous career and his reserves of energy were becoming exhausted. He no longer rode and played golf and took other exercise, and the resulting lethargy kept him too much in Nairobi.

He and Lady Mitchell arrived in Nairobi on 11 December 1944. He was happy to be back in the Kenya he loved so dearly and he wrote that night of the 'soft evening of the kind which only the Kenya Highlands can produce'.[15] On the following morning he took the governor's oath of office. On 12 December 19 years later, Kenya became an independent nation. If anyone had prophesied in 1944 that in 1963 Kenya would become independent with a preponderantly black government under which a great majority of the European population would declare their willingness to live and work, he would have been accused of living in cloud-cuckoo land, but so it happened. That it did happen was the result of a remarkable change in race relations, without which the story might have been very different. Many people, black, white and brown, worked to bring that change about, but perhaps the greatest influence of all was that of the governor who believed that 'the great, the overwhelmingly great, problem overshadowing all else, is the human problem'.[16] There were many economic and political questions to be tackled, but everything was complicated by the racial outlook of almost everybody. Little was examined from an unbiased Kenya viewpoint; emotion conflicted with reason and the communal structure of society bedevilled important issues. The problem which faced him as Governor of Kenya was how to use the skills and talents of the European minority and the inherited values of Britain for the general development of what he hoped would ultimately be an independent multiracial country founded on the civilization of Britain. 'We are all indispensable to each other,' he told the United Kenya Club in 1950, 'if the attempt to found a civilised and prosperous State within the Commonwealth . . . is to be successful.'[17]

Mitchell did not like the great disparity of representation of the races in Legislative Council, but in the late 1940s there were but a handful of Africans capable of meeting the requirements of membership of the council. It was his reorganization of Makerere as a college of higher education to produce an African élite which raised the standard of African education in general and enabled Africans to fill responsible posts in government and in the universities of East Africa. From his early days in Tanganyika he had disliked European monopoly of areas of land, but the Elgin Pledge and the authority of the Highlands Board in Kenya prevented him from having Africans even as tenants on Crown Lane in the 'White Highlands'. As in Tanganyika and Uganda he was anxious in Kenya to give Africans opportunities for training in political responsibility. He thought that local government could provide the best training; but no governor with any sense of realism could have supported the demands of the nationalist politicians for political independence. Sympathy for African political aspirations was very different from acceptance of demands for political independence, for which he was not alone in thinking there were at that time no realistic foundations.

Any thought of getting rid of the immigrant communities would in any case have been completely unrealistic, because both the Labour and Conservative parties in Britain were fully in favour of a multiracial Kenya. Oliver Littelton, the Secretary of State for the Colonies in the Conservative Government, cited the bipartisan agreement in a debate in the House of Commons a fortnight after Mitchell left Nairobi on retirement leave. He quoted from the Journal of the Fabian Colonial Bureau: 'Europeans who have settled in the Highlands were deliberately encouraged to go there. They have been allowed to acquire land on the guarantee that it would be theirs. They bring up their children as citizens of Kenya and they cannot settle elsewhere in land reserved for Africans'. 'That,' said the secretary of state, 'is a very forthright statement with which I agree.'[18] And in July 1952 in a written answer he said:

The broad lines about European settlement in Kenya have not changed and remain as follows. Her Majesty's Government fully recognise the values of European settlement to Kenya, and the important part that the European community has taken and will continue to take in developing the resources of the country and in helping to raise the standard of living of the African population. In short, European settlement is regarded as an essential and permanent part of Kenya's development.[19]

In the East Africa to which Mitchell went in 1913 the vast majority of Africans were illiterate, burdened with the superstitions of the past, economically on a bare subsistence level and quite unable on their own to face the modern Western world which had intruded into their lives and, when he became governor of Kenya, the condition of the peasants was still one largely of poverty.

First, then, he saw that the Africans would have to be rescued from poverty by a programme of agricultural development and improvement of urban life. The agricultural and business activities of the Europeans in Kenya were needed to produce finance to sustain the budget, great through the African contribution was, and the Europeans would not have remained in Kenya unless they could have maintained a standard of life at least equal to that enjoyed by their friends and relations in Britain. Sadly however, their superiority in education, in financial status and experience in the techniques of administration in the modern world produced a sense of racial arrogance which made many of them unwilling to recognize the few but increasing examples of African cultural attainments. Mitchell had no doubt that no real progress could be made in the economic or political fields unless race relations could be improved and the Europeans be shown the advance being made by other races. It was no fleeting whim that made him declare that a vital necessity was to 'get on to the job [of improving agriculture in the reserves] on a really large scale with determination and consistency' and at the same time to say that the project for building a national theatre and cultural centre in Nairobi was one of the most important with which he had ever been associated.

Mitchell has been criticized for what George Bennett called 'the gradualism implicit in his own doctrine of trusteeship'.[20] To criticize that, however, is to criticize the accepted opinion of most responsible people of the period. It was the opinion of the Hailey Committee, and was accepted by both the Labour and Conservative parties in Britain. Few would have dared to prophesy at that time that an African government could take its place in an international assembly within a hundred years. Even the most liberal of scholars could do no more than suggest a few years later that the Gold Coast elections of 1951 made it possible to think that the African colonies might perhaps become independent before the end of the century.[21]

The shock and revelation of 1951 came six years after Mitchell became Governor of Kenya. The duties of a trustee were ever-present in his thinking and what to African politicians seemed to be a reactionary attitude was in fact caution, due to his sense of responsibility to his wards. During the first year of his governorship of Kenya he spelt out his belief:

> If, as I profoundly believe there is, there is any substance in the doctrine of Trusteeship, it must include a guardian with the moral courage as well as the capacity to be a guardian, and to resist the temptation of giving to an immature ward an excessive degree of freedom from control before he is ready for that freedom. Guardians and wards habitually disagree as to when the time for the next step in relaxation has arrived, and that is inherent in the relationship, but cannot absolve the guardian from his duty.[22]

In opposing the idea of 'one man one vote' for Africans Mitchell was in keeping with traditions in Britain where universal suffrage had not been granted until there was universal education. However, he was aware of changes in outlook and capacity in all the racial communities, and in 1952 he was thinking of a multiracial Kenya with a prime minister within the life span of existing politicians; a Kenya in which it was clear that the African voters would in time outnumber the Europeans. Carl

Rosberg and John Nottingham have pointed out that to believe, as Mitchell did, that 'all human beings are inherently capable of civilization' was 'to place oneself on the liberal wing of European thought at this time'.[23]

A criticism which can legitimately be made is that the administration failed to understand the new spirit which resulted from the experiences of the war. Young men were acquiring influence and chafed at the lack of political opportunity offered to them. The paternalistic and too static attitude of the administration denied them a share in government, because the implications of the increase in education were not recognized. Many young men had a certain amount of education. 'A little learning is a dangerous thing',[24] and practical experience was all the more necessary. Mitchell's appointment of seven Africans to be African assistant administrators in 1946 was a valuable innovation. More were appointed in the following years, but it would have been wise to give a larger number of posts in local government to the new, better educated Africans also. Failure to recognize the growing frustration of these younger Africans and unwillingness to take risks in giving them responsibility in public affairs was one of the factors which encouraged the militant organizers of Kikuyu revolt.[25]

Notes

1. MD, 18 December 1928.
2. Ibid., 2 February 1931.
3. Ibid., 4 May 1931.
4. Ibid., referred to on 6 November 1939.
5. Ibid., 12 October 1936.
6. Ibid., 27 October 1939.
7. Ibid., 6 November 1939.
8. Ibid., 30 August 1944
9. Ibid., 30 August 1944.
10. Ibid., 10 February 1948.
11. Ibid., 13 March 1948.
12. Ibid., 11 January 1949.
13. Ibid., 7 April 1949.

14. Ibid., 27 June 1951.
15. Ibid., 11 December 1944.
16. Sir Philip Mitchell, 'Africa and the West in Historical Perspective', in Charles Grove Haines (ed.), *Africa Today* (Baltimore, 1955).
17. EAS, 14 October 1964, quoted in obituary notice.
18. HCD, Vol. 503, col. 2377, 17 July 1952.
19. HCD, Vol. 504, cols. 129–30, 29 July 1952.
20. W. George Bennett in DA Low and Alison Smith (eds.), *History of East Africa*, Vol. III (Oxford, 1976), p. 113.
21. Margery Perham, *The British Problem in Africa Foreign Affairs*, Vol. 29, No. 4 (June 1951), p. 637.
22. CO533/537/9501, Mitchell to Gerald Creasey, 29 August 1945.
23. Carl G Rosberg and John Nottingham, *The Myth of Mau Mau* (New York, 1966), p. 199.
24. Alexander Pope, *Essay on Criticism*.
25. Richard Frost, *Race Against Time* (London, 1978), pp. 142–3.

XIV

Administrative and Constitutional Changes in Kenya

Reorganization of the Government

During the war a third of the officers of the administration were serving in the armed forces and the government welcomed the help given by those of the settlers and urban Europeans who remained in Kenya. Many farmers' wives ran the farms while their husbands were away and many farmers and businessmen served on the various boards and committees, which became increasingly important as agricultural production grew to meet wartime requirements. The result was that, although Africans as well as Europeans profited from the growth of agriculture, the Europeans acquired a position of power and influence greater than they had occupied before. Their eyes were set on the vision of a European-dominated dominion and, when Mitchell became governor, he found them aiming at 'a form of self-government based on a legislature in which the European as such is to be entrenched in power by the terms of the constitution and has a majority over all other races combined'.[1]

The problem of European power had always been a nettle which the Imperial Government had been afraid to grasp. Early in the war senior officers at the Colonial Office admitted that the policy of the home authorities had always been one of appeasement and conciliation[2] and, as Mitchell wrote later, 'No Secretary of State would ever force a row with settlers.'[3] One of the problems which he discussed with Oliver Stanley on his way from Fiji to Kenya was how to lessen European power, which had grown so greatly, without a head-on collision. African

184

educational development and social welfare depended to a great extent on the wealth of the Europeans and the richer members of the Indian communities and to have declared open war on European power would have been political folly.

Among matters which Mitchell discussed with the secretary of state were his plans for the reorganization of the Government of Kenya with the introduction of a speaker into the Legislative Council, the membership system, and the creation of an East African Central Assembly. Senior officials at the Colonial Office had experienced Mitchell's drive and determination in the past and were afraid of what he might do in the future, although, however much he might argue with Whitehall he accepted the fact that in the end a colonial governor had to yield to the instructions of the secretary of state. A few days before he arrived in Kenya a leading official wrote a revealing minute: 'I feel that Sir P. Mitchell will try to move pretty fast and for this reason I think the instructions given to him by the S of S should be drawn as tightly as possible.'[4]

Mitchell's plans for reorganizing the government began with the introduction of a speaker into the Legislative Council. To have a speaker presiding over sessions of the council would not only save the governor from spending many unprofitable hours there but, as Mitchell wrote to the Colonial Office, it would 'greatly strengthen the Governor's hand in composing racial rumpuses if he does not have to be in the ring while the free-for-all is going on',[5] and 'it would give a greater independence to Leg. Co.'[6] This change was willingly accepted by everybody, but another innovation was not so harmoniously received.

Government policy was discussed in Executive Council under the chairmanship of the governor and then presented to Legislative Council for debate. The official members of Legislative Council, the chief secretary and heads of departments, were of course bound to support the government, and at the time of voting they were the dummy waxworks whose individual votes had seemed to Mitchell in Fiji to be so unnecessary in a council with an official majority. But some unofficial members of Legislative Council were also members of Executive Council and

Mitchell thought it entirely wrong that, having taken part in discussions in Executive Council and shared the secrets of the government, they were free to attack government proposals in Legislative Council. They 'ought to support Government or resign'. He proposed that analagous departments should be grouped together and put under a member of Executive Council who would have to support the government and be in effect an official member of Legislative Council whether he was a member of the colonial administration or elected to Legislative Council. The proposal had been approved by the secretary of state, but, when it was announced in Kenya, it was greeted by a storm of opposition from Indians and Africans.

It was clear that the members having responsibility for different subjects such as education and agriculture would at that time all be European. This was regarded with horror because it was thought that they would all discriminate against Africans and Indians in favour of the European community. That, it was felt, was bad enough, but when it was announced that the agricultural portfolio was to be given to Major (later Sir) Ferdinand Cavendish-Bentinck, the outcry was great indeed. He was not a farmer, but a man with great influence in the commercial, and particularly agricultural, life of the colony. He was a member of the East African Production and Supply Council, East African timber controller, chairman of the Kenya Agricultural Production and Settlement Board, and active in other boards and committees. He was regarded as the epitome of Europeanism who, it was feared, would undoubtedly use his new power to favour European agriculture and discriminate against African agriculture. One Kikuyu newspaper wrote:

When Sir Philip Mitchell chose a European Member for Agriculture and Animal Husbandry he chose a European Settler so that he may finish off our cattle and goats and so that he may control squatters and enforce agricultural rules in the reserves which compelled people to do as he liked with their own crops.[7]

186

When Mitchell appointed Cavendish-Bentinck as Member for Agriculture in Kenya he made it clear to him that 'He must be a member of the Government and if he did not agree with the Government he must resign before he could recover his freedom of action'.[8] Both he and C-B understood the principles of British politics and five years later A. B. Patel, the Leader of the Indian Elected Members, admitted that fears of the member being influenced by his European friends had proved to be groundless. The departmental members had shown that 'they are immediately within the fold of the Government benches and are not likely to be influenced as we had anticipated then by the unofficial side'.[9]

Cavendish-Bentinck worked enthusiastically for the agricultural policy advocated by Mitchell and supported by Creech Jones, then the assistant secretary of state. When C-B was in England in September 1946 he saw a lot of Creech Jones and reported him 'full of determination to help us tackle our agrarian problem in every way and really believing in us and what we hope to do'.[10]

A year later Mitchell wrote with great satisfaction to Creech Jones, who had become secretary of state, to tell him that C-B had got six Africans on the African Settlement Board, including Jomo Kenyatta, and that he hoped that good results would come from that.[11] When the measure was introduced and debated in Legislative Council, Mitchell stressed that the proposals involved 'no such thing as the establishment of Ministries'. He explained that 'a Minister is a person who discharges a responsibility by virtue of the authority of his office. What is proposed here is the appointment of members of Executive Council who will have duties to perform by virtue of the authority of the Governor', who under the constitution is 'the sole responsible authority on whom personally rests the whole responsibility and authority for the government of the country'.[12]

Criticism that 'the constitutional changes which Mitchell initiated' showed his inability to 'adopt an unbiased attitude towards the three races'[13] fails to appreciate the current situation and the responsibilities of a governor. The appointment of

187

Cavendish-Bentinck was useful in two ways. It gave to agriculture, both African and European, a member of great ability and knowledge, while at the same time depriving the Europeans of one of their most influential political champions. If Mitchell had withdrawn his plan, which had been accepted by the secretary of state, to establish the membership system because Africans and Indians opposed it, he would have been giving in to opposition, based on lack of understanding. His responsibility as governor required him to pursue what he believed to be in the best interests of Kenya. He saw also that in time to come, with the advance of education among Africans and the consequent establishment of election for the African members of Legislative Council, these departmental members would not all be European. 'If African Members of Legislative Council could be directly elected,' he said in 1947, 'nobody would be better pleased than I would be'.[14] But there was need for more education before that would be possible.

The questions of the speaker and the membership system were set out in Sessional Paper No. 3 of 1945. The third innovation explained in this paper was the establishment of a Development and Reconstruction Authority, which would have to administer large sums of money, mainly coming from Britain. It seems that Mitchell did not discuss the financial organization which would be needed to administer these funds with Oliver Stanley and the Colonial Office when he was in London. It may be that the basic point, which was opposed by the Colonial Office, had not been in his mind until he reached Kenya and discussed plans with Gilbert Rennie, the chief secretary, and other senior officers of the administration. He wrote that he had been studying for a long time 'in consultation with Rennie and other advisers' plans for putting postwar reconstruction and development into execution. He was anxious that development funds should be kept separate from the ordinary colony budget and safe from interference by the European elected members of Legislative Council, and be allotted for specific purposes on long-term rather than annual budgeting.

Mitchell's campaign to get the organization and authority he wanted began with a telegram he sent to the secretary of state on 28 February 1945.[15] He proposed that the budget should be divided into two parts, (i) normal revenue and expenditure, and (ii) reconstruction and development projects and finance. He also suggested that all Colonial Development and Welfare Fund grants and loans, votes from revenue and allocations from special funds earmarked for development should be allotted to the latter and spent without the need for an annual vote. He proposed that a reconstruction and development authority should be set up to administer these funds. It should not be concerned with planning but with execution and the chief secretary should be its chairman. Mitchell wanted to avoid the danger of creating a special department and adding 'a fifth wheel to the coach', and 'the awkward question of authority over other departments'.[16]

His idea was that the chief secretary should be relieved of other work and so be able to 'organise and supervise the carrying out of plans and the spending of Development funds by appropriate Departments';[17] but he would still be the chief secretary, the chief officer of the government, ultimately responsible for both the ordinary work of the government and the special work of development. In Mitchell's view development and reconstruction were inextricably mixed up with, and spread over the whole field of administration and formed part of departmental activities. He maintained that to secure the necessary authority for the implementation of development plans, all special development funds should reach the spending departments through a Development Authority. He felt that the Development Authority and the chief executive officer of the government could not be separated.[18] Mitchell had to fight hard to get his plan accepted by the Colonial Office and he finally wrote a personal letter to Oliver Stanley.[19]

His persistence was rewarded and the opposition with which his first telegram was received was replaced by complete agreement with his plan. After the publication of the sessional paper, the Development and Reconstruction Authority was set up with the chief secretary at its head. Within a year of being offered the governorship of Kenya Mitchell had formulated his plans for the reorganization of the government and the administration of postwar development, and had received permission from the secretary of state to implement them. That he was a man of action was evident from the beginning of his governorship and was remarked on by all races in the speeches of welcome made when he opened his first session of Legislative Council.

In July 1945 Britain was in the throes of a general election and on the 25th Oliver Stanley wrote to Mitchell: 'I am just off to my constituency to learn my fate and that of the Government. I only hope that I shall be given an opportunity of seeing through to the end some of the many reforms that you have initiated since you went to Kenya.'[20] He was, however, not elected. The government was defeated and Labour was returned to power at Westminster.

The new Secretary of State for the Colonies, George Hall, had a high opinion of Mitchell and supported him as his predecessor had done. He knew that Mitchell was anxious to involve Africans in national as well as local administration, but he was realistic and aware of African educational limits and experience in public affairs. When he was asked by a left wing member of Parliament in London whether it was 'proposed to reconsider this so as to ensure a larger share of administration by Africans', Hall replied that the reorganization of the administration of government in Kenya was not a constitutional change but was designed to increase efficiency; above all in the execution of the development programme and the coordination of the departments dealing with agriculture, animal husbandry and natural resources. Hall went on to say he was anxious that Africans should 'play their part in the administration to the full extent that they are qualified to do so' and that he knew that the Government of Kenya was entirely of the same opinion'.[21]

There was always the problem that idealism in certain quarters in Britain and the aims of African nationalism were often unrelated to reality and oblivious of facts and possibilities. It was fortunate that Mitchell was supported by all his secretaries of state; Oliver Stanley, George Hall, Arthur Creech Jones,

James Griffiths, and Alan Lennox-Boyd, when they were apprised of the realities of a situation.

Legislative Council

Mitchell's proposals for reorganization of the Government of Kenya were administrative, but he soon turned to the consideration of constitutional changes. The European Electors' Union announced in 1949 that their 'undeviating purpose' was the control of their own affairs,[22] and irresponsible European politicians might shout that the time had come to stop 'this fooling about by the Colonial Office'. Yet Mitchell saw that after the war, Europeans in general were beginning to accept the fact that self-government under European dominance was no longer a possibility. In 1950 he wrote to the Colonial Office, 'It can be assumed that all responsible opinion out here accepts the proposition that the Colonial status must continue in Kenya indefinitely'.[23] Eliud Mathu, representing African interests in Legislative Council, had said in 1945 that, until Africans had advanced sufficiently to be able to hold their own in a multiracial society 'self-government would be premature'.[24] Mitchell agreed, but he was anxious to bring Africans into public affairs of all kinds as quickly as he thought their capacity made it possible to do so. Less than a year after he became governor he recommended that Mathu should be a member of the Standing Finance Committee, replacing Archdeacon Beecher while he was on leave in England,[25] but Mathu was educationally almost unique at that time.

Mitchell would have liked to increase the number of Africans in Legislative Council, but he could not find men with the educational standard needed and, when he and Creech Jones discussed the matter in 1946, they decided that they would like five Africans but were doubtful of finding as many able to meet the requirements.[26] He thought that the Representatives of African Interests, as Beecher and Mathu were designated, would more properly be called trustees, his point being, as he told Cohen in London, that educated Africans were beginning to say that Europeans, or Africans nominated by governments to represent them, were not really their representatives. His aim was that as many as possible should be Africans, but if enough suitable Africans could not be found at once to fill the seats, whether in Legislative Council or the East African Assembly, the idea of trustees would be more appropriate than representatives.[27]

The governor and the Colonial Office agreed that it was necessary to give a sense of security to all communities and that *for that* the ultimate authority of the secretary of state was essential. 'As long as the spectre of becoming a minority hangs over the Europeans and the Asians,' wrote Mitchell, 'and the temptation of securing a majority lies in the way of the Africans, I do not believe we shall ever escape from politics founded primarily on hate and fear.'[28] 'He was most anxious also not to create in East Africa a class of African professional politicians out of touch with the people themselves.'[29] In 1947 a leading article in the *East African Standard* saw what was bound to happen in the end. As the Africans advanced educationally and economically, their progress would 'require an ever increasing ratio of representation' and at last the European community would become 'constitutionally a racial minority'.[30]

Mitchell was becoming more convinced every year that one of the great defects of Kenya was that the executive civil service was so continuously embroiled in politics. The attorney-general and the chief native commissioner would have to remain Colonial Office appointments, although it was generally accepted that the CNC would one day be an African. For this, however, two things were needed – a man completely adequate for the job and a lessening of tribalism. Mathu, he thought, might in a while meet the requirement but, as things were, tribalism would see to it that no Luo or Nandi or Kamba had any confidence in a Kikuyu CNC.[31] Mitchell wanted to get 'some Indians, Africans and maybe Arabs on the Government benches' and suggested nominating members of Legislative Council to be like government back-benchers at Westminster, holding posts like those of undersecretaries of departments in London but not being members of the Executive Council or cabinet. The Executive Council itself might be divided into two parts; the Executive Council proper and a sort of privy council containing elder statesmen including Africans and Indians. [32]

In 1950 James Griffiths replaced Creech Jones as secretary of state. He was greatly concerned about the question of parity, the European insistence that the number of European seats should be not less than the number of seats held by the members of all other races. Griffiths was insisting that more Africans should be nominated to Legislative Council without any increase in European membership. Mitchell believed that this would cause all the Europeans to resign and force a general election, which would be full of bitterness and do great harm to race relations. Mitchell was so insistent that it was decided the secretary of state should visit Kenya and examine the problem himself, on the spot. He arrived on 17 May 1951.

On the day before he arrived Mitchell told Sir Alfred Vincent, the leader of the European elected members, that the European elected members 'had isolated themselves' from everybody else and that except for Blundell and 'perhaps Cooke' they had shown themselves to be 'rigid as bars of iron' and would have 'nothing at all in common with the S of S'.[33] In 1947 Vincent had said bluntly in Legislative Council that the Europeans did 'not accept any principle of equal representation between races'.[34] They had changed considerably since then and Blundell's liberal and realistic views were splitting the European ranks, but the die-hards still had great influence.

In 1951 Mitchell saw that he had two tasks ahead of him. He would have to persuade the European elected members to show at least some small signs of cooperation in discussions with the secretary of state, and he would have to use the ten days of the visit to show Griffiths the extent and nature of the political problems which had to be solved. Griffiths, a Labour Party politician, whose approach to colonial problems was naturally affected by his party's traditional concern with the condition of the British working class, was ready to consider evidence with an open and impartial mind. Mitchell poured what oil he could on the troubled waters of European intransigence and he found much help from 'Blundell's contribution in the closing stages' of the visit.[35] The secretary of state told Mitchell that he liked and respected Blundell but would not put up any of the other elected members he had met as a parliamentary candidate.[36] Mitchell fully agreed with the secretary of state's opinion. He thought that most of the European elected members were neither intellectually of a high calibre nor imbued with the human sympathies which he regarded as so important in the multiracial society of Kenya. On one occasion he was so much exasperated by them that he described them as 'little, frightened, narrow, heathen men with nothing to offer but words, tricks, schemes and spite',[37] but on the whole his feeling was best expressed when someone asked why there were statues of puffed-up bull frogs at the entrance of the Legislative Council building in Nairobi. 'Oh,' he said, 'those represent two typical European Elected Members.' There were a few, particularly Ernest Vasey, Michael Blundell and Derek Erskine, of whom he thought differently, but near to the end of his governorship he confided to his diary that Archdeacon (later Archbishop) Beecher was 'the man whose views I really trust and value'.[38]

Griffiths appreciated the arguments which the governor had submitted in correspondence now that he was able to study the situation at first hand. While saying that parity was 'not acceptable as a part of the constitution', he agreed that it should be maintained 'as a temporary concession'[39] and Mitchell recorded that all had been 'settled in an atmosphere of sober responsibility and good will in the manner I had hoped by the personal influence of this remarkable man who has spread good will wherever he has been'.[40] On his return to London Griffiths announced his decisions in the House of Commons. There would be no major change till after the election in 1952, but then a constitutional conference would be held. In the meantime all Mitchell's proposals were accepted: European parity for the time being, an African member of Executive Council, six Africans in Legislative Council with Asians and Arabs each having

194

one more seat and the European membership being increased from 11 to 14.[41]

When Mitchell became governor, Legislative Council had a majority of official members. It would have been possible to force through the council measures of a liberal character, to which most Europeans in Kenya would have been opposed, by throwing the official votes into the battle. That would probably have caused wholesale European resignation, a general election and great racial bitterness, and would certainly have been no way to train the members and their constituents for parliamentary government. But to give way to European opposition would make the Africans and Asians feel that their aspirations and development were being disregarded. As the Westminster model of parliamentary government was the goal of colonial policy, official pressure had to be withheld and as much responsibility as possible given to the unofficial members. In order to achieve the next step in development, Mitchell sought and obtained the secretary of state's premission to have an unofficial majority. The powers which he gave to Legislative Council were a necessary step in his strategy of working towards responsible government. Training in the use of responsibility requires the exercise of responsibility, but by giving to Legislative Council the power of the purse and the control of legislation Mitchell hampered his own freedom of action.

A month after new powers and new responsibilities were given to the unofficial majority Mitchell had to point out to the Colonial Office what the new arrangements meant and he had to write about 'financial devolution from London to Colonial Governments'.

He agreed that the CO made some quite sensible suggestions but spoilt them all by proposing that they should have an advance look at the budget and should be able to 'make suggestions' in time for them to become effective when the budget is debated. Of course no council in a place larger than the Seychelles would stand for that and here, with an unoffi-

195

cial majority, it would lead at once to deadlock if it became a reality.[42]

Until the number of well educated Africans had greatly increased Mitchell had no doubt that colonial government would have to be retained and the principles of trusteeship required that the Africans should be regarded as wards in trust. His view was the general view of the Western world towards Africa; a view held by the British Colonial Office and the Imperial Parliament. No one foresaw the speed with which the African élite of Kenya would advance in education and competence nor the profit they would gain from the service given to them by British educationalists and administrators. At the same time relations between the races were improving, not by chance, but because much conscious effort was being exerted to make it so. Mitchell saw that race relations were improving and there was evidence of an unexpectedly quick increase in African education. At the end of his governorship he thought that some form of multiracial self-government with an electoral college system of election for Africans could be expected within the lifetime of the present generation of politicians and that 'Ernest Vasey, a móst able and valuable Minister ... will certainly be the first "premier" of Kenya.'[43]

Having given to Legislative Council the power of the purse he had to do what he could to make the European politicians understand their position in a plural society. He had to walk warily and felt like a man on a tightrope. If he turned too much to the Europeans, he would be accused of racial discrimination by the Africans and, if he seemed to the Europeans to be favouring the Africans, he would be in danger of provoking one of the racial dog fights which he sought so hard to avoid.[44] On more than one occasion he had to point out to the European politicians that the fact that he was British did not affect the impartiality of his decisions.

The Electors' Union was a European political party, quite legitimately a racial party, but within a fortnight of his arrival as governor he was pressed to allow civil servants to join it. Of course he refused and 'gave them some of the obvious reasons';[45] but the need for impartiality in governors and civil servants in plural societies was apparently not understood even then, because a few months later he was asked to help to write the Electors' Union's statement of policy. 'I had of course to say,' he wrote in his diary, 'that it was a political document and I could have no part or share in it, nor responsibility for it; for *ex hypothesi* I am entirely impartial and unconnected with any party and my "policy" was embodied in my oath of office.'[46]

Early in his governorship he gave the Colonial Office a picture of the background to Kenya politics. Many of the settlers were colonial Colonel Blimps, living 'in complete mental isolation', while among the European business community in Nairobi there were a number who were not very reputable. The standard of political leadership was poor, willing to acquiesce in supporting bad European policies rather than run the risk of being thrown out from leading positions in European circles. And there was a general and pretty deep dislike of the Indians, sadly only too frequently justified. They were often 'receivers of stolen goods and the principle purveyors of illicit liquor', and at the back of many dirty pieces of work. Of course there were 'many very decent characters among them but it did explain the European attitude to them'.[47]

The East African Central Assembly

Throughout his years of service in East Africa Mitchell had seen the value of interterritorial organization for common services. He thought that the Governors' Conference did not provide adequate machinery for administering the interterritorial activities of East Africa and that it, like the Government of Kenya, needed reorganization. Before he left Fiji he started work on plans for creating an East African community.

When he was in London Mitchell discussed his ideas with Oliver Stanley and the Duke of Devonshire, the parliamentary undersecretary, both of whom were in favour of his plan, and Colonel Stanley later told the House of Commons that he accepted responsibility for the main lines of Mitchell's proposals.[48] Before a white paper could be issued the Conservative Government in London had been replaced by a Labour Government. Mitchell told Sir George Gayter, the permanent secretary of the Colonial Office that, because the war with Japan had ended so abruptly (leaving attention free to focus on peacetime plans), the matter was so urgent that, if the new secretary of state did not like his proposals the Colonial Office would have 'to produce something in their place, for the Governors' Conference must really be given some constitutional and juridicial standing and some means of contact with public opinion'. He said that he expected that 'Equal representation for Africans, Indians and Europeans as such will probably be disliked by the Europeans. It will no doubt be ascribed to the wickedness of the Labour Government by some of the people in these parts, 'but,' he promised, 'I will take an opportunity of letting it be known here that the proposal was mine, and made irrespective of any political question in the United Kingdom, and that I think it is right'.[49]

Mitchell had told the Colonial Office in March 1945 that the new arrangements which were being discussed would have to 'come into force on 1 January next if we are not to have a shocking mess here',[50] but the influence of the Europeans of Kenya was highly suspect in the other territories. In February the Governor of Uganda had written to the secretary of state that it was feared in Uganda that, 'despite all safeguards that could be devised, the European settlers of Kenya would in practice control policy and its application. The whole dog would in fact be wagged by its tail'.[51]

By the end of 1944 a sort of central administration had grown up round the secretariat of the Governors' Conference. It was incomplete, as railways and customs were not included, and it had no judicial or constitutional existence or authority and could only proceed by consultation and agreement, even in quite unimportant matters. The need, as Mitchell saw it when he became Governor of Kenya, was for a body with the power of legislation binding on all the territories on common subjects.

Legislation required a legislative assembly, and at that time the composition of the assembly would have to be by nomination by the governors. Mitchell had suggested that each territory should send six representatives: two European, two Asian and two African, and that the Resident of Zanzibar should nominate an Arab. He had come to the conclusion that 'where there was a problem of several communities with political capacity in more or less inverse ratio to number, the only workable solution was the equal representation of them all without any regard to numbers'.[52]

The other governors agreed with Mitchell's proposals which appeared in the form of an official paper, issued in London – 'Colonial 191', but there was immediate opposition from the politically active Europeans in Kenya. They thought that parity with Asians and Africans might be dangerous and they felt that at best it was degrading. Many intemperate statements were made. One letter in *The East African Standard* went so far as to call the proposal 'The most dangerous and insidious attempt that has ever been made to liquidate white settlement in this country'.[53] Another advocated union with South Africa: 'I would rather be under General Smuts than under the people in London.'[54]

The European elected members in Kenya proposed an alternative plan under which in fact no powers at all were to be transferred to a central legislative body. It was an absurd document, but it showed the strength of European political feeling. As an article in *East Africa and Rhodesia* explained, they felt they had always to be on their guard 'lest the greater good of the territories as a group unfairly prejudices their own community.'[55]

Six months after the publication of 'Colonial 191' most Europeans had forgotten the initial outcry and had become immersed in the affairs of their farms and businesses, but the politicians were intransigent. '. . . in fact,' Mitchell wrote in his diary, 'everyone agrees except Vincent and Co: but we cannot have an Assembly if all do not cooperate nor can we concede a specially privileged position to a small group of Kenya farmers and politicians'.[56] Arthur Creech Jones, at that time the Under-secretary of State for the Colonies in the Labour Government, visited East Africa in 1946. Just before his arrival Vincent and some Elected Members in Tanganyika and Uganda wrote a letter to the secretary of state with copies to the three governors saying that they would not 'at any price agree to equal representation with Indians'. Mitchell thought this letter would do great harm and was 'calculated to ensure that Creech's visit becomes a racial dog fight'.[57] He wrote to Vincent asking him to reconsider publication, but European political racialism was too strong. In spite of disappointments he continued to work for racial harmony and not long afterwards Dr Rana, the Indian Elected Member for the Eastern Area, remarked that the absence of racial issues in the debate on the report of the Development Committee was due to the governor's lead in 'cooperation and toleration among all races',[58] but he failed to soften the Europeans over 'Colonial 191'. European politicians in Kenya were always fighting to maintain their predominant position and they thought 'Colonial 191' set a dangerous precedent for its erosion.

Creech Jones arrived in East Africa during the storm of European political opposition to 'Colonial 191'. In August he met the three governors, Sir William Battershill of Tanganyika, Sir John Haythorn Hall of Uganda and Mitchell, and discussed the problem. 'Colonial 191' had been approved in principle by a Conservative secretary of state and was welcomed by the Africans. Creech Jones and the governors decided that it would be unwise to disregard European opposition and they discussed a suggestion made to Creech Jones. This proposed that membership of the East African Central Assembly should be one European, one Indian and one African nominated by each governor, and one member from each territory elected by all the unofficial members of its Legislative Council voting together, with one nominated Arab for the whole of East Africa, and a nominated speaker.

Creech Jones and the governors felt that, with further political development in mind, it would be wise to placate the Europeans by withdrawing 'Colonial 191' and issuing a new plan, 'Colonial

210', with which they hoped all would agree. There was a significant change in the method of electing the fourth member of the territorial groups. In the original scheme proposed by Creech Jones the electors were to be the *unofficial* members of each Legislative Council;[59] in the final plan they were to be *all* the members. It was hoped that the *official* members would help to secure impartiality and attention to merit. But, even so, 'Colonial 210' raised an outcry among the Africans even more violent than European opposition had been to 'Colonial 191'. At that time the members elected by the legislative councils would undoubtedly be Europeans, and African politicians saw in the arrangement a scheme to give the Europeans a permanent majority in the East African Assembly. The Europeans were jubilant, but the African politicians were furious and despondent. They could not see that in time African representation in Legislative Council would increase and the extra members would be chosen by African majorities. 'Two ten' became a rallying cry for discontent and provided ammunition for the Kikuyu organizers of Mau Mau. Mitchell and the Colonial Office failed to appreciate the strength of the Kikuyu movement of militant opposition to the government which was growing underground, but it would probably have been impossible to find a scheme which, if satisfying one race, would not have been bitterly opposed by the others. In any case Mitchell was the architect of East African interterritorial cooperation, of the East African High Commission, which achieved so much before independence and, in essence, of its successor, the East African Community, which so sadly drifted to disintegration.

National Registration

Another crisis was not long in coming. To a man like Mitchell the registration of individuals by methods which were different for different races was unacceptable and he aimed at a method applicable to all. For many years Africans, above all the better educated Africans who were coming out from school after the war, had found the *Kipande*, the registration card which had to be carried by all Africans outside the reserves, increasingly irksome. It was a *sine qua non* for employment which gave a prospective employer an account of the applicant's past work, but unscrupulous employers could abuse it by writing on it adverse comments which the illiterate Africans could not read. If an African domestic servant even walked a short distance down the road to see a friend in a nearby house and was challenged by the police, he could be arrested and taken off to the police station cells if he had not got it on him. It was of course strongly resented by the educated Africans who, like the illiterate, had to carry it at all times, just as the Jews in Nazi Germany had to wear the Star of David. Eliud Mathu fought for its abolition and in 1947 Legislative Council agreed that it should be replaced by a registration card, for which members of every race should give their fingerprints. The Asian members opposed the measure, but all the Europeans voted for it and Mathu was warmly congratulated on his success.

The government decided that in a country with a large proportion of illiterates registration by fingerprinting was the only method applicable to all. Although in Britain fingerprinting was used only for compiling a criminal register, in itself there was nothing degrading in it if applied in the completely different circumstances of a plural society for the purpose of compiling a national register. The chief native commissioner told legislative council that 'if the registration is non-racial the identification must be non-racial',[60] and, although the Indian members opposed, all the European members voted for it.

There were, however, some Europeans all over the country with minds too small and vision too obtuse to appreciate the simple facts and, when a Nairobi lawyer, a certain W.T. Shapley, founded The Society for Civil Liberties to oppose national registration by fingerprinting, they hastened to join it. Public meetings and letters to the press showed a racial and ignorant hysteria. One postwar immigrant wrote to *The East African Standard* prophesying that Europeans would be hauled off to police stations and subjected to treatment made infamous in Europe by the Nazi Gestapo[61] and equally astonishing speeches were made at public meetings. A few weeks later a 'Not so New Settler' wrote to the paper to point out that this violent new settler should remember that there were differences between Kenya and Britain and that he ought not to forget that he had come to 'a colony of mixed races' and that he should set himself to learn something about 'the background of registration in the country to which he had chosen to come';[62] However, the European Members had their eyes on their electorates and the next election; and something had to be done to lessen the violence and bitterness of the wrangle.

Mitchell has been accused of giving way to European pressure and disregarding the wishes of the Africans, but closer study shows that his tactical skill enabled him to safeguard African interests without causing a violent quarrel with more than the racial extremists among the Europeans. Before the ordinance was translated into a bill, European opposition was placated by government agreement to institute a commission of enquiry into the whole question of registration, if all the unofficial members wished it to do so. All of every race did in fact vote for a commission. Sir Bertrand Glancy was appointed commissioner and reported that, although fingerprinting was the best method of identification, ability to write one's name unaided and to supply photographs was an alternative method, though a far less efficient one. There was general satisfaction among the Europeans that the commissioner had suggested an alternative, although he said it was far less efficient than universal finger-printing. The Africans, however, objected strongly because they saw that all Europeans would be exempt, but most Africans would have to give their fingerprints.

Mitchell wanted the ordinance of 1947 on universal finger-printing to become law but, as all the unofficial members of Legislative Council had asked for the appointment of a commission of enquiry, the government introduced a measure in favour of the amendment recommended by the commissioner, Sir Bertrand Glancy. This would enable them to find out the views of the unofficial members, which turned out to be ten in favour of the amendment and ten against (the opposition being composed of Africans, Arabs, Asians and one European, Derek Erskine). The official members had of course to vote for the measure which the government had introduced, but the government then took no further action and did not initiate legislation to enforce the amendment. The government was in a difficult position and Mitchell called a meeting of his principal officers to consider tactics on the motion Major Keyser was moving condemning the government for having moved a motion in favour of Glancy's alternative to fingerprinting and then taking no further action.

In fact, Mitchell had no intention of giving way to European pressure but, as it was not possible to dissuade the European leader from initiating a debate, government tactics in opposing his motion had to be very carefully worked out. During the debate Colin Thornley, the deputy chief secretary, referred to the equality of the unofficial votes and asked, 'What more logical or natural attitude can possibly be imagined, Sir, in such circumstances than that the Government having found the Unofficial side of the Council completely divided should decide to maintain the status quo in a law which had been passed as recently as 1947 without a division at all?' He went on to say that the country-wide enquiries made in 1950 'showed conclusively that the vast majority of the people inhabiting this land, and I include in that majority a large number of the European element of the population, prefer the law as it stands in this respect to the alternative provision recommended by Sir Bertrand Glancy'.[63] The next day the chief secretary explained to the council that 'in any case the final question of whether the law should be amended is one to be decided by the Council if and when an amending Bill is presented to it'.[64]

The most die-hard among the Europeans were furious and perhaps the most galling point was Thornley's reference to 'the vast majority of the people of this land'. There were many Europeans to whom 'the people of Kenya' meant the European residents unless otherwise qualified. The Electors' Union passed a resolution, with which the elected members agreed, that the Government of Kenya by its action in overriding the decision of Legislative Council expressed by a clear majority in regard to the Glancy Report on the Registration of Persons Ordinance has proved to all people of good will and sincerity that the present system of Government is neither workable, tenable nor acceptable and is one in which no fair-minded person can retain any confidence.[65]

Mitchell saw clearly, as he wrote in his diary, that 'all there is to it is indignation that the Government should have turned down the European Elected Group'.[66] He understood the Africans' objection to any amendment of the ordinance and adopted the tactics of delay to achieve his aims without causing a further damaging racial contest. Quite naturally the Africans were unable to see what he was doing and accused him of giving in to European pressure. In fact he had no intention of introducing an amending bill. His tactics of inactivity succeeded. The general situation in Kenya was becoming more uneasy and it was possible to persuade the European elected members that the most efficient method of national registration should be adopted.

On 6 March 1951 a bill was passed legalizing the ordinance of 1947 without any amendment, but the governor wisely refrained from prosecuting any Europeans who still refused to give their fingerprints. So many Europeans had in fact registered by fingerprinting and so many continued daily to visit the registration offices for the purpose that it seemed wise to turn a blind eye to the dwindling number of defaulters. A year later the Emergency made it necessary for new measures to be introduced.

The story of national registration by fingerprinting showed how essential it was that positive action should be taken to make the Europeans realize that Africans different from the farm workers, domestic servants and office boys, whom they knew, were coming on the scene; but the farmers had little opportunity of meeting any of them, while in the towns economic disparity was an insuperable barrier. Face to face meeting with the educated 'new Africans' was the greatest need and

Mitchell did his utmost to help those who were working to provide it.

Notes

1. Mitchell, *African Afterthoughts*, p. 217.
2. CO967/37/46709, NY Dawe to Sir George Gayter, 27 July 1942.
3. MD, 16 June 1956.
4. CO822/114/46523, 4 December 1944.
5. CO533/532/38032, Mitchell to Creasy, 24 December 1944.
6. MD, 4 September 1944.
7. CO535/560/4 (38760), Quoted by Mitchell in a speech opening the 17th Conference of Chairmen of District Production Committees, 16 June 1949.
8. MD, 19 January 1945.
9. LCD, 10 January 1950, col. 741.
10. MD, 27 September 1946.
11. CO533/549/38238/15, Mitchell to secretary of state, 14 April 1947.
12. LCD, 18 July 1945, col. 67.
13. Fay Carter, 'Sir Philip Mitchell' in Kenneth King and Ahmed Salim (eds), *Kenya Historical Biographies*, (Nairobi, 1971), p. 32.
14. Sir Philip Mitchell, 'Current Affairs in East Africa', an address to the African Affairs Study Group of the Empire Parliamentary Association, 25 June 1947.
15. CO533/537/38646, Telegram from Mitchell to secretary of state, 28 February 1945.
16. Ibid.
17. Ibid.
18. Ibid., Telegram, Mitchell to secretary of state, 7 March 1945.
19. CO522/114/46523/1945, Mitchell to Stanley, 15 March 1945.
20. CO533/537/38646, Letter from Stanley to Mitchell 25 July 1945.
21. HCD, Vol. 413, col. 636, 22 August 1945.
22. The Electors' Union, Kenya Plan, (Nairobi, 1949), p. 4.
23. Remark made at the Electors' Union conference, supplement to the EAS, 1 February 1946.
24. CO537/5847 (38032), Mitchell to Cohen, 17 April 1950.
25. LCD, 20 July 1945, col. 131.
26. MD, 21 July 1946.

27. CO822/114/46523/1945, Minute by Cohen describing discussion with Mitchell, 6 November 1945.
28. CO537/5847 (38032), Mitchell to Cohen, 17 April 1950.
29. CO822/114/46523/1945, Note by Cohen on discussion with Mitchell, 30 October 1945.
30. EAS, 4 April 1947.
31. CO537/5847 (38032), Mitchell to Cohen, 17 April 1950.
32. CO537/540/38032/1949, Creech Jones to Mitchell, approving proposals put forward to him by Mitchell, 18 March 1949.
33. MD, 16 May 1951.
34. LCD, 17 April 1947, col. 97.
35. MD, 29 May 1951.
36. Ibid., 21 May 1951.
37. Ibid., 31 December 1951.
38. Ibid., 25 February 1952.
39. Ibid., 23 May 1951.
40. Ibid., 26 May 1951.
41. HCD, vol. 488, cols 406–10, 31 May 1951.
42. MD, 27 July 1948.
43. Ibid., 9 February 1952.
44. Conversation with the author shortly before retirement.
45. MD, 22 December 1944.
46. Ibid., 25 July 1945. This question is discussed in CO/533/557/3.
47. CO822/44/46523 Part 1, 1946, Mitchell to Gayter, 19 March 1946.
48. HCD, Vol. 425, col. 267, 9 July 1946.
49. CO822/188/46794, Mitchell to Gayter, 3 September 1945.
50. CO822/114/46523, Mitchell to Creasy, 3 March 1945.
51. Ibid., Sir John Haythorn Hall to Secretary of State, 8 February 1945.
52. Sir Philip Mitchell: *African Afterthoughts*, p. 219.
53. EAS, 25 January 1946.
54. Ibid., 25 January 1946.
55. *East Africa and Rhodesia*, 30 May 1946.
56. MD, 21 August 1946.
57. Ibid., 10 July 1946.
58. LCD, 21 November 1946, col. 324.
59. MD, 11 August 1946.
60. LCD, 24 July 1947, col. 122.
61. *East African Standard*, 11 March 1949.

62. Ibid., 1 April 1949.
63. LCD, 15 February 1951, col. 80.
64. Ibid., 16 February 1951, col. 139.
65. European Elected Members Organisation: Minutes of Meeting on 9 February 1951. There is a copy in Rhodes House, Oxford, in Blundell 14/1.
66. MD, 16 February 1951.

XV
Race Relations

The war greatly affected the thinking of many Africans and Europeans. Africans serving in the forces overseas saw societies where there was not a colour bar like that which they had grown up with in Kenya. The British officers and NCOs, under whom they served, were in the main free from the racial prejudices to which they had too often been accustomed at home. Many Kenyan Europeans serving as officers grew to admire the qualities of the African soldiers and returned to their farms and businesses with a new and more liberal outlook little known before the war. The new governor had always believed that human relations, which in Kenya meant primarily race relations, were the most important factor underlying progress and development and, while he was wrestling with the problems of administration and constitutional change, he was thinking of ways of increasing interracial understanding and goodwill. He appreciated that, as some Africans became better educated, racial discrimination became increasingly painful and that the social aspects of the colour bar caused understandably bitter feelings among the educated and prosperous members of the Asian communities. But Mitchell was a realist with great experience of East Africa, which told him what could be done and what was impossible in the circumstances of the time.

The Europeans had come to Kenya from economic and social backgrounds totally different from anything known in Kenya, and few Europeans were brought into contact with Africans who were rising above the general level. '. . . to pretend,' wrote

Mitchell, 'that a stark naked Karamoja savage is in all respects the same person as a twentieth-century European is just nonsense. In the long run it is only in the spiritual and cultural field that these age-old tough and lasting differences can be gradually resolved.'[1]

In the early years of Mitchell's governorship there were a few people of all races who were actively working for the improvement of race relations and trying to bring people of the different races in touch with each other. The United Kenya Club was a pioneer organization which was steadily increasing its membership among all races. They demonstrated the value of doing things together and their combined work in repairing and decorating the original clubhouse, an old wooden building in Whitehouse Road (later called Haile Selassie Avenue), broke down many barriers between them. Mitchell had a high opinion of the club, but he wanted something more. He wanted a cultural centre or institute, including a theatre, and when at his request the British Council agreed to start work in East Africa, Creech Jones told the representative before he left England that he hoped the greatest stress would be laid on the improvement of race relations.

Mitchell did his utmost to help any sound work for the improvement of race relations, and of the plans to establish a cultural centre he wrote, '. . . the project is one of the most important with which I have ever been associated'.[2] The European National Theatre Movement Trustees were raising money for building a theatre. This would no doubt have been for white audiences only and the Indians would probably have started to follow suit, while the Africans would have been excluded altogether. To his great surprise the British Council representative found that, provided their internal affairs were not in question, one society after another agreed to support a common enterprise and send representatives to a common board of management. There was no objection to the proposed theatre and centre being open to all on a basis of cultural standards alone. As early as December 1947 it was possible to ask the governor to appoint an inter-racial committee 'to make definite plans for the project' and the chairmanship was given to Sir Godfrey Rhodes, a liberal-minded man with long experience of Kenya.[3]

In the following year the representative was called to London for consultations with council headquarters and the Colonial Office. His knowledge of Kenya made Mitchell certain that to raise money on an idea was impossible but that, if a theatre were built and seen to be useful, it would be possible to raise money from voluntary subscriptions in Kenya for a cultural centre or institute. The absolute necessity, therefore, was to get money from Britain for a theatre. The British Council's representative made this point to the Colonial Office and to Creech Jones himself, who said, 'It's a time of financial stringency in Britain but, if necessary, I'll go myself to the Chancellor of the Exchequer to get the £50,000 you need.'[4] After his return to Nairobi the representative announced this undertaking at the next meeting of the committee and it became public knowledge. No one doubted that Creech Jones would keep his word and plans for organization and building were put in train. Creech Jones did have to go to the chancellor, and the governor had to write several despatches, but the grant of £50,000 was given and the project was brought to a successful conclusion. Creech Jones wrote to the British Council representative, 'At one moment because of stringencies I had doubts',[5] but he never wavered from the promise he had given that day in July 1948.

The Mau Mau Emergency prevented money being raised from voluntary sources for some years but the theatre, which was opened in 1952, immediately proved its value. It was used for the annual inter-racial competitions of the East African Conservatoire of Music; for drama festivals and schools drama festivals, which were all inter-racial; for concerts by world famous artists, the first being a pianist, Andor Foldes; for lectures and film shows to pupils of schools of all races around Nairobi; and for lectures by visiting academics and performances by local dramatic societies.

The Charter of the Cultural Centre, which was written by Mitchell, showed very clearly his views of race relations. He never suggested that a 'stark naked Karamoja savage' should be regarded as the intellectual or cultural equal of a twentieth-century European, but he did insist on the inherent human value of all men and women. The Charter of the Cultural Centre laid down that any society or institution, which was not political, could be affiliated and have a representative on the board of management, if the governing council considered it to be of sufficiently high standard. Membership of societies could be non-racial or confined to a single race. Quality alone was the requisite for affiliation to the centre. As he put it, it was as if the centre were the top of a mountain. Anyone who could reach it was welcome there, but no one could join who could not reach the top.[6]

In 1947, in an address to the Nairobi Rotary Club Mitchell said that in general anyone of any race 'if he wants to join others on the hilltops ... should be capable of the climb involved, instead of deluding himself and others that the road is flat and he has only to stroll easily along it without effort'.[7] The standard should be set by the civilization and values of Britain and his aim was to establish 'a civilized state in which the values and standards are to be the values and standards of Britain, in which everyone, whatever his origin, has an interest and a part'.[8]

It was natural that the Indians should feel aggrieved by anything that might seem to discriminate against them or deny them a privilege enjoyed by the Europeans. One such complaint arose over the question of trial by jury. Mitchell made a point which had not occurred to the Hindus who demanded that trial by jury should be extended to the Asians. Historically from the European point of view trial by jury seemed to be logical. It was a right enjoyed by the people of Britain for centuries, a right which they felt they took with them to their new home in Kenya, but Mitchell saw how impossible it would be to extend it to the Asians who were divided by deep and often fanatical communal divisions and religious strife. 'On the question of trial by jury of Indians,' he wrote, 'Patel was asked to discuss with the Congress and to ask them to be more explicit; did they really mean that a Hindu, for instance, might be tried by a jury of Moslems – it would be a matter of chance if they were Moslems or not – a jury of Moslems for killing a Moslem?'[9]

Great ill-will was caused by the racial discrimination in the law concerned with sexual relationships between people of different races. An African found cohabiting with a white woman could be sentenced to hanging, but a white man was not subject to any penalty for having intercourse with an African woman. Mitchell was glad when the Colonial Office instructed him to abolish the penalty of hanging. Constitutionally he had to refer the matter to Legislative Council, where it divided the members in heated debate. Blundell and his supporters were in favour of repeal and after much discussion they managed to persuade the opponents to agree to repeal, provided a repeal clause were included in a bill containing many other clauses so it would be less prominent than if it stood alone. Mitchell saw a weakness in the anti-repealers' case and said, 'I have at the present time two cases of cohabitation on my desk. What are you to do if in such cases the white girl says, "Oh, but I love this African"?'.[10]

Particularly hurtful to the better educated Africans who were coming on the scene after the war, albeit in small numbers, and to the educated and economically prosperous Asians was their exclusion from all good hotels and restaurants. In a study of Mitchell's governorship written 19 years after his retirement he is censured because 'he did not even end the colour bar in hotels, the segregation in schools and hospitals'.[11] Historical judgements are likely to be false if the writer relates the events concerned to the conditions of the time of writing rather than of the time which is being written about. When Mitchell became governor there were only two African University graduates and scarcely any others with an educational standard equal to a sixth form in Britain. Due to Mitchell's reorganization of Makerere when he was Governor of Uganda a great educational advance began in Kenya immediately after the war. At the same time the first Africans reached the standards of a university of high quality when a few began to take with success the examination for the external BA degree of the University of London.

African educational and economic advance and the growing number of advanced Asians made the colour bar in hotels and restaurants out of date and what would have been impossible in 1945 became reasonable in 1953.

Kenya was a British colony and its social as well as its constitutional life was accordingly being developed along Western lines. At the time of Mitchell's governorship only a handful of Africans were at an economic level which allowed them to pay the prices charged at Kenya's hotels, but there were Asians who were able to meet the cost but who were conversant with Eastern rather than with Western manners and customs. The hotel proprietors, some of them Asians, were afraid that they would offend their European customers if they relaxed the 'Europeans only' rule so the 'Westernized' Asians and the few Africans who could have met the hotel charges suffered accordingly. Mitchell deplored the existence of a ban based solely on race, but he was not a dictator. In Kenya, as in Britain, a race relations act which made a colour bar illegal would have been a matter for the Legislature. Mitchell appreciated that to force a measure through Legislative Council by using the official votes would not only have disregarded the power he gave to the unofficial element by making an unofficial majority but would have created such European bitterness that race relations would have been seriously harmed by public incidents.

The inter-racially minded realists, including the governor, thought that the right course was to change the outlook of the European community. Then, as they saw the economic and educational advance being made by Africans and the increasing Westernization of the leading Asians, they would see that their prejudices and fears were no longer reasonable. This proved to be a wise strategy. By 1953 there had been a sufficient increase in liberalism to enable Michael Blundell, then leader of the European Elected Members of Legislative Council, and some of his colleagues to convene a meeting of the Hotel Keepers' Association and to ask them to bring the colour bar to an end. Then, because the move came from European leaders, hotels could be opened to all without any racial incidents and ill will.

In the case of schools the economic impediment to integration was even more clear and Mitchell and those people who were working towards the abolition of racial discrimination saw that until economic and social conditions had greatly changed inter-racial schools could not be established. In the 1940s economic disparity and differences in diet and home backgrounds were so great, and ability to learn in English was so unequal that inter-racial entrance at primary level would not have been practical. Even at sixth form level insurmountable problems would have arisen. Mitchell himself was in favour of racially mixed schools if conditions made them possible. Six months after he arrived as governor he called the European Elected Members of Legislative Council together and told them that it seemed to him to be wrong to exclude from European schools children who were 'near white' and came from homes of European standards. Yet the European elected members were adamant against the admit-tance of children of mixed race to European schools and Mitchell saw that, if he overruled them and the school com-mittees, such unpleasantness would result that the children themselves would suffer.[12]

In 1950 an opportunity for racial integration arose which he seized gladly. John Karmali, a Moslem of the Ismaili community, and his English wife faced the problem of the education of their own children and decided to found a small non-racial infant school. They made a start with six Asians and four Europeans and then went to see the governor. Economically and socially these ten children could meet on equal terms and Mitchell of course supported the project. He interested the Colonial Office in the school and soon after his retirement the Kenya Govern-ment provided land and simple buildings on Hospital Hill in the grounds of Government House. The school received a govern-ment grant-in-aid in accordance with the rules applicable to all non-African aided schools, and a Board of Governors was appointed by the Director of Education. A few Africans from suitable backgrounds were enrolled and ultimately Hospital Hill School became a school of high repute.

In 1960, when conditions made it possible, the admission of

Asian and African girls to the Kenya High School, to be followed by the opening of the principal boys' schools to non-Europeans, was due to Mitchell's skill as Chairman of the Board of Governors of the Kenya High School.

The change in race relations made during the years following the Second World War was remarkable and the knowledge that the governor was fully behind their efforts was a great inspiration to those individuals and groups who were working to improve them. The chief native commissioner, P. Wyn Harris (later Sir Percy Wyn Harris, Governor of the Gambia), was a great advocate in Legislative Council of the policies of the governor, who from his earlier years in Tanganyika and Uganda had striven to create an African élite. He saw, as Mitchell saw, the need to bring these new, young educated Africans into contact with the liberal element among the Europeans. He told his colleagues in Legislative Council that 'men of goodwill of the three races must resolutely, by example, cultivate good race relations'. He stressed that Africans would study in Britain, would 'receive a university education' and, unless there was a change from the situation they found themselves in at that time, would be 'debarred from the very civilisation we have taught them to admire and share', and that would create 'great hatred between the races, hatred for which we will be responsible'.[13]

The most surprising development was that two years later the African Affairs Committee of the European Electors' Union said the same thing. Some members of the Union like Major Frank Sprott, who had a farm at Karen, near Nairobi, and John Riddoch, the leading businessman in Kisumu, had already got into contact with progressive African farmers and the 'new Africans', who had received education and experience in East Africa or overseas. Indeed, Lord Francis Scott, the prewar Leader of the Electors' Members, had deplored the lack of interest shown by his colleagues in African development. However, the Electors' Union had never before appealed to its members to give time and friendship to the new class of educated Africans. If an African who had been to Britain for education, they asked, 'is to have no further contacts with Europeans on his return from England, what is he going to do for his cultural progress?'[14]

This plea for establishing social relations with the new African élite was made only five years after the end of the war. Before the war it would have been unthinkable. Africans with such education did not then exist and, even if they had existed, it is extremely unlikely that any Europeans would have asked them into their homes. But in 1950 it was possible for the Europeans' political organization to ask its members to dispense with the colour bar where cultural interests made social meeting possible without being artificial. There can be no doubt that the campaign to improve race relations would not have been so successful without the revolutionary change in Government House which occurred after Mitchell became governor. He made friends with many of the leading Asians whose economic status made social mixing an easy matter and did what he could to recognize in a social and not merely official way the emerging African élite.[15]

When Mitchell was on leave in England in August 1947 he received an envelope forwarded by the Colonial Office. It contained an explosive device, addressed to 'Sir Philip Mitchell, Governor of Kenya. Private and Confidential'. Letter bombs were rare in those days. Fortunately they were not as sophisticated as they became 30 years later and Mitchell merely recorded that the envelope sent to him 'had been damaged in the post and did not go off'. He does not seem to have been greatly perturbed. He buried the package in the garden of the house in which he was staying, took the envelope to Cohen and asked him to warn Rennie by telegram.[16] No serious attempt seems to have been made to find out who had tried to murder him. He had sailed from Kenya soon after the outcry which greeted the acceptance of 'Two ten'. A fortnight before the letter was delivered Mathu had succeeded in securing the abolition of the Kipande. National registration by fingerprinting had been generally accepted: open opposition to the ordinance did not come till later. There was nothing to indicate whether the attack on his life was racial or personal and the intended victim showed little concern.

Notes

1. CO533/553/38557/12, Mitchell to AH Poynton, Colonial Office, 14 June 1949.
2. Ibid.
3. Richard A. Frost, *The British Council in East Africa 1947–1948*, talk broadcast.
4. Creech Jones in conversation with the author.
5. CO533/553/38557/12, Creech Jones to RA Frost.
6. A copy of the charter is in the archives of the National Theatre.
7. Sir Philip Mitchell, Address to Nairobi Rotary Club, 24 October 1947.
8. Mitchell, *African Afterthoughts*, p. 275. The inscription on a plaque at the entrance of the cultural centre is curiously inaccurate. It reads 'In 1949 it was decided to bring together in one centre all those societies which were interested in music, drama and the arts and which contributed to the cultural life of Kenya. The inspiration behind this idea was the then Governor of Kenya, Sir Philip Mitchell, GCMG, MC. In 1952 the National Theatre was opened by Sir Ralph Richardson as the first part of the Kenya Cultural Centre.' The credit for the idea must certainly go to Sir Philip Mitchell. In 1947 he asked that it should be put into effect and £50,000 for the building of the theatre was promised by the secretary of state in 1948.
9. MD, 16 July 1948.
10. Interview with Sir Michael Blundell, 16 February 1982.
11. Carter, 'Sir Philip Mitchell', p. 43.
12. MD, 7 August 1947.
13. LCD, 18 March 1948, cols 224–5.
14. EAS, 16 June 1950.
15. Frost, *Race Against Time*, especially chapters 3 and 4 for details of the efforts made to improve personal relations between the races.
16. MD, 7 August 1947.

XVI
Kenya: Agriculture

In Tanganyika Mitchell had been largely concerned with the establishment of native administration. The problems of peasant agriculture, although of keen interest to him, were outside the scope of his authority; but, when he became Governor of Uganda, he was directly concerned with peasant farming and the dangers of a one-crop economy. In Fiji the sugar industry, monopolized by an outside company, was the basis of the whole economy of the colony, and, when he went to Kenya, he became governor of a colony which depended to a very great extent on the agriculture of the European settled areas. The view is often expressed that during most of the period before the Second World War government assistance was given generously to European farming while comparatively little was spent on African agriculture. Much money was certainly poured into European farms. A survey undertaken by the Royal Institute of International Affairs, published in 1937, estimated that in Kenya and Uganda up to 1934 some £27 million had been unwillingly supplied by the British Government, while £28 million had been invested by individual European farmers, and specialist services, such as coffee research, were financed by crop taxation on the European estates. The development of European farming was financed by private and commercial capital more than by government funds and depended on the hard work and skill of the majority of European farmers, who courageously experimented on land, much of which was not the most fertile or well watered in Kenya, and who lost much of their capital in the process.

219

Kenya was a poor colony and in the Depression of the 1930s staff in all departments of government had to be cut, just as was the case in Uganda, where inadequacy of staff prevented Mitchell from carrying out some of his plans there. Even so, much devoted work was done in the African districts by agricultural officers, and crops both for food and cash sale, like beans, pulses, cotton and wattle, were introduced. What the government spent was not enough but was all it could afford in those years of world depression. Mitchell arrived in Kenya with years of experience in different agricultural situations, intent on improving and developing farming in the African reserves. His great contribution was to show how two major problems which had baffled previous administrators could in the long term be solved, given a wide and imaginative vision – overstocking in some districts, overcrowding and bad farming in others.

Professor Sorrensen has accused him of being 'unsympathetic towards peasant agriculture'.[1] This accusation, however, is not supported by the facts. He had shown throughout his career that he was dedicated to helping the peasants to improve their standard of living. What he was unsympathetic towards was the continuation of low standards. A man with a hoe could do no more than keep his family alive and Mitchell wanted to make it possible for Africans to engage in 'economic agriculture' giving a surplus above the mere subsistence needs of the family. As things were, the peasant could not increase his income: 'no amount of agricultural instruction will help him to overcome the limitations imposed by his present circumstances' he told the Colonial Study Group of the Empire Parliamentary Association in 1947. 'We have simply got to break out of this state of affairs,' he continued, 'either by collective farming or by cooperative farming'[2] or at any rate, as he said at other times, by regarding the individual as 'the tenant of the tribe' and supervised by tribal authority. He was emphatic that preservation of the land was fundamental and that it was therefore essential 'to legislate and take powers to protect the land from destruction, a power overriding all rights of whatever kind', and overstocking and erosion must be primary concerns.[3]

Within a week of his arrival as governor he toured the Kamba District of Machakos. This was one of the areas with the worst conditions of soil erosion, but Mitchell was glad to see that the work done by the agricultural officers during the previous few years had had some encouraging results and that there was some good terracing and 'signs that the people were now receptive and soil conscious'. But there was much to be done and he and the district staff who went with him

> formed certain basic conclusions which might be summarised as (i) the position is bad but not desperate, but it is a salvage job and the use of the land will have to be adjusted to the salvage and not the other way round, (ii) relief from pressure of people and stock must be afforded, (iii) it is not now sufficient just to be a Mkamba and entitled to land in Ukambani; you have got to be a Mkamba who used the land reasonably.

In spite of good work done and a sound five year plan already devised, more study was needed. He lost no time. He decided that two agricultural officers should go at once 'to Basutoland and Transkei to get wider experience, have leave, get plant, staff and finance and set 1/1/46 as D. Day'.[4] Then two days after Christmas he gave a broadcast talk and announced this date for the opening of the campaign for the attack on soil erosion and the other agricultural problems of Machakos.

The problems of Machakos were not isolated. They were problems over which he had pondered for years, and study of agriculture in Kenya at first hand enabled him in 1946 to complete 'thankfully', as he wrote, 'the draft despatch I have been working on for years about the basic problems of economic agriculture and agrarian policy in the Colonies'.[5] He thought that in Kenya, as he wrote in his diary, the government 'had simply not begun to tackle its agrarian problem until a few months ago, and even now they know very little about it'.[6] His chief secretary reported to him that the provinical commissioners 'showed a very limited understanding of the agrarian

221

problem we have to face and of the fact that overcrowding and overstocking occur whether there is settlement of Europeans or not'.[7] He expressed his concern in a letter to Colonel Stanley. Unless action on a large scale was taken quickly, he believed that 'a shocking disaster' was inevitable and he asked the secretary of state to ensure that his opinion of the gravity of the situation was placed on record: 'I am afraid,' he wrote,

> that as far as the real problem of Kenya is concerned – that is to say the use of the native reserves by their inhabitants – there is no policy here at all, and moreover no organisation for giving effect to a policy once it has been formulated. I can't think how they can have existed all these years without having thought out their land administration at all, and without any attempt at getting the Administration and the Departments to shoot at the same target.[8]

To improve African agriculture would need money and first of all he had to be sure of the necessary funds. He therefore fought for the divided budget and the plans which formed the third part of Sessional Paper No. 3 of 1945. Early in 1944 the government had begun to give serious thought to postwar problems and a development committee was suggested but was not appointed till January 1945. A year later it issued a report which was adopted as the Ten Year Development Plan 1946–55. Out of a total of £15 million which the plan envisaged, £8.1 million was earmarked for crops, livestock, land and water and was split up among the appropriate departments – agriculture, veterinary, forestry and water development. Having won his battle over the divided budget, Mitchell was able to insist that these funds should be kept separate from the colony budget.

The Development Committee under the chief secretary saw that a great deal of money would be needed but that it was impossible to say how the difficult job could best be done, so a block amounting to £3 million – far larger than any other allocation in the Ten Year Plan – was entrusted to a new Board, the African Settlement and Land Utilization Board (ASLUB), which later became the African Land Development Board, always known as ALDEV. It was safe from interference by the unofficial members of Legislative Council and became a sort of financial corporation making grants to approved schemes for African agricultural betterment, submitted through the District and Provincial Agricultural Committees, of which the district or provincial commissioners were the chairmen. 'The original block allocation of £3 million came mainly from Kenya funds'.[9]

Mitchell and his advisers said that, although the money was secure under the DARA arrangements, the implementation of government plans would need legal powers applying equally to the European settled areas and the African reserves. The European areas had suffered extensive damage from bad agricultural and pastoral practices and, said Mitchell, they were 'still deteriorating owing to the lethargy, ignorance or greed for money profits of some farmers or to absentee ownership'. But he believed that by 1947 European public opinion had been at last aroused and was 'ready to support authority in dealing with those who persist in objectionable practices'.[10] District committees in the settled areas accepted responsibility for maintaining standards even to the length of confiscating farms for sale at public auction, while in African areas the chain of command ran through the district and provincial agricultural committees to the member.

By the end of 1948 plans were sufficiently advanced to make it possible for Mitchell in his speech opening a new session of Legislative Council to tell the members that a bill would be introduced based on the principle

> that not only has no man the right to ruin agricultural land, but that all users of such land have a duty towards the community as a whole to develop the land which they are using by means of sound farming practice, which must include adequate capital investment.
>
> It would be recognised in the Bill that the State must provide the means, both in the form of advisory services and finance on reasonable terms, if the owners of agricultural land

who were reluctant or financially unable to conserve and develop their lands were to be compelled to do so.[11]

There was a regrettable lack of cooperation in some areas between the agricultural and veterinary departments. At times their rivalry had been really absurd, as when the Director of Veterinary Services in Nyanza Province refused to allow veterinary schoolboys 'to be contaminated by associating with any other schoolboys, while the native employees of the Veterinary and Agricultural Departments will have nothing to do with each other and shout insults at each other when they meet'.[12] Better coordination of both central planning and execution in the field was fostered under the membership system by the setting up in the African areas of district and provincial teams made up of departmental officers under the chairmanship of the district and provincial commissioners, which later became the District and Provincial Agricultural Committees, already mentioned, which were responsible for the coordination and execution of approved projects in the field.

Mitchell's great contribution was to show that there *was* a way out of the agricultural impasse, which had come to be regarded as insoluble. British administration had stopped inter-tribal warfare and produced a machinery for the distribution of food to areas afflicted by famine, while medical services had vastly lessened the death rate. All this resulted in a great increase in population, and many districts, especially the Kikuyu land units, Machakos and parts of Nyanza, were suffering from excessive pressure of population and stock. Some African politicians were declaring that to take land from the scheduled areas would solve the problem but, as the secretary of state forcefully said in the House of Commons, the scheduled areas were the European reserve, safeguarded by imperial policy, and Mitchell had come to the conclusion that permanent solutions could be found only in better use of the land and urbanization of some of the population; a development which presented a host of other difficulties. There would have to be old age pensions, decent urban housing, schemes of superannuation – in general security in old age, making it unnecessary for everyone to have a piece of land.[13]

He set the details of agricultural policy in a wide framework. 'I want to emphasise,' he wrote, 'that first and foremost this is a human problem, the problem of man in Africa in relation to the land and to the new forms and pressures which the opening of these countries to external social and economic influence has introduced'.[14] For many years he had believed that East Africa ought to be looked at as a whole. Only so could people from overpopulated areas be given land in districts with unused resources.

His views were set out in detail in a memorandum dated 16 November 1951, which he wrote for the secretary of state asking for a royal commission to be sent to investigate the problems of land and population in East Africa and 'not only point the way to the solution of our problems but bring a clearer understanding of them to those who at present advocate facile solutions divorced from reality'.[15] He had always thought that some form of closer union of the East African territories was needed. As time passed, his experience led him to think that 'excessive overheads could only be cured by a single unitary Government, at least of Kenya and Uganda.'[16] This idea had to be abandoned and the East Africa Central Assembly took its place; but with machinery on an East African scale. He pointed out that in spite of 'areas of local congestion, whether of people or stock or both together, the greater part of the region is under-populated and under-developed'. But traditionally Africans looked only as far as the next piece of uncultivated land, which they would overwork and overpopulate and therefore 'the addition of more land with no change of methods of farming is in fact no solution at all'.[17]

The East African governments had the task of trying to change the outlook and methods of African farmers and persuading them to accept the idea, 'altogether revolutionary to the African mind', that cattle are an integral part of farming, that forms of rotation are needed to prevent ruining the land, that land cannot for ever provide security for an ever-increasing population and

225

that 'a long term solution can be found only in the full development of the economic resources of East Africa'.[18] He continued to press for a Royal Commission on Land and Population, but it was not till eight months after his retirement that the Royal Commission, for which he had pleaded, arrived in East Africa.

Many Africans were employed on agricultural work, on European farms, on the Indian sugar plantations and by the tea, coffee and sisal companies. There was also an increasing amount of employment by Africans, mainly in the Central Province of Kenya, where for a number of years rich Kikuyu had been buying land and employing labourers to work on it, and a landless class was coming into existence. As in many other ways, elements in the history of Britain were repeated later in Africa. British industry grew up in the tradition of low wages, and in East Africa it had been thought that cheapness of production must be the overriding consideration in the case of tropical raw materials and that it could only be achieved by low wages. The result, Mitchell wrote, 'has been a wasteful use of unskilled, often undernourished and generally unhealthy labourers, of whom the majority were temporary immigrants from some distant tribal area, and from whom nothing but an excessively low standard of industry was expected.'[19] He had deplored such a situation in the western Pacific, but the North/South dialogue of the 1980s and 1990s stresses that it is an international problem which is still unsolved.

Another facet of the problem was the lack of African craftsmen in both towns and rural areas. In all kinds of crafts the Indians excelled and the Africans, whose work was so inferior to theirs, could only be employed on cheaper rates. The development by Africans of small industries and crafts and trading could have been greatly helped by the Indians if they had been willing to teach and support African artisans, and to smooth the path of African traders. Not unnaturally however, they were not willing to train Africans to become their competitors. By their skill and hard work they had taken possession of the artisan trade and through their family ramifications they controlled the

226

wholesale supply of goods needed by the retail traders, the small shopkeepers in the towns and country markets.

African bitterness at their exclusion from the retail trade continued throughout the colonial period. The municipal welfare officer at Nakuru reported what was a general complaint by Africans, 'that they are cheated at every possible opportunity and they experience great difficulty when buying in small quantities', which forced them to buy at almost retail prices from Asian shopkeepers, who acted as wholesalers when small quantities were concerned.[20] The government appreciated the problem but refused to contemplate discriminatory legislation against the Asians. Mitchell, who had seen the need for an African intellectual élite and had reorganized Makerere to supply it, saw the need for technical education also and founded the Royal Technical College in Nairobi, the Mombasa Institute of Muslim Education and three trades schools.

An understanding of the basic principles of farming and conservation of the land, training in technical skills and simple crafts, sympathetic attention to the needs of the landless population, which was bound to increase and required security in retirement – all these things were essential; but in Mitchell's view they were not enough. While he always balanced idealism with realism, he never thought that material success alone would solve such fundamental problems, and at the end of his long memorandum, dated 16 November 1951, he wrote:

Finally, it is imperative to keep clearly in mind that the problem is a human problem, compounded of the needs, hopes and fears of a great mass of people, most of whom are at the present time sadly handicapped by ignorance, ill health, poverty and inexperience for the world which has rushed upon them with a bewildering suddenness. It is a spiritual problem, too, for the superstitions and sorceries of the past, the worship of ancestors and the propitiation of spirits are in ever-increasing measure being seen for what they are by the people concerned and being abandoned through incredulity. There is a grave danger that their place may be taken, for a time at least, by the delusion that material things suffice as the basis of human society; there is in consequence a task of ever-increasing urgency for the Christian Churches.[21]

From a Kenya point of view he believed that much could be done through settlement schemes in marginal areas with low rainfall or other impediments. These settlement areas were to be inside the ordinary African districts, many of which contained areas which were used very little or even not at all because of shortage of water, infestation by tsetse fly and in some cases the presence of hundreds of rhinos and elephants, which made farming impossible. The Makueni settlement scheme in the Machakos District was his pioneer scheme. Work started on it as early as 1945, and it was regarded as of crucial importance, because so much of East Africa consists of similar land. It covered approximately 50,000 acres with a rainfall of between 20 and 30 inches a year. It was a pioneer scheme showing all the problems which settlement in the districts would face and its success or failure would therefore be of far-reaching consequence. The low rainfall, lack of water and presence of tsetse fly had kept it uninhabited except by wild animals and nearly 1,000 rhinos had to be shot before it could be used for settlement. Only the most careful management and strict control could make settlement there succeed. At first the rules were resented, but despite setbacks the settlers came to realize that success in this difficult country depended on their strict observance. The tsetse fly was eliminated, dams constructed for conservation of water and the experiment succeeded in the end and was a valuable precedent for further settlement schemes.

Mitchell's thinking about the agrarian problem was based on the fact that there was plenty of viable land lying unused in the African districts, which could be developed by bush clearing, the elimination of tsetse fly, the provision of roads and control of game. Andrew Cohen had written in a minute in a Colonial Office file in July 1945 that there 'is no doubt that Sir P Mitchell means business' and that 'it was only when Sir P Mitchell arrived in Kenya that really vigorous attention was given to the

228

problems of resettling Africans and rehabilitating the Reserves.'[22] Another scheme at Olenguruone, where 3,600 acres had been excised from the Masai Land Unit in 1941 for settling some of the Kikuyus who had infiltrated into Masailand, failed because the settlers refused to comply with the simple rules of good husbandry and recognize government authority. 'Their resistance became a major political issue, and eventually they all had to be repatriated to their districts of origin in 1949.'[23]

By the time Mitchell became governor there was great ill will at Olenguruone and the militant Kikuyu politicians found it a useful issue in their campaign of creating hatred against the immigrant races and the colonial government. Mitchell's plans for solving the agrarian problem depended on proper agricultural practices and their observance in future settlement schemes. The colonial Office saw that, if Olenguruone was allowed to be a precedent for disregard of government regulations, 'the Government's whole policy of land betterment and African settlement would be jeopardised – and indeed the good work so far done would be ruined'.[24] The government had proof that the banned Kikuyu Central Association had 'fostered defiance of Government at Olenguruone'.[25] The Colonial Office and the Kenya Government thought it essential to take a firm line. The repatriation of the settlers to the overcrowded and overworked Kikuyu reserves was effectively used by the militants in their campaign which led to the Mau Mau revolt. But to have allowed disregard of government agricultural regulations at Olenguruone would have been a precedent which neither the government nor the Colonial Office felt it possible to allow.

Mitchell did not expect quick results. As he thought that the Kenya Government had never understood the agrarian problem and his own provincial commissioners 'showed a very limited understanding of it', he had to start with a programme of reorganization and the laying of new foundations. 'Foundations, in any case', he said in 1947, 'are seldom spectacular, and we have been mainly occupied with laying foundations. We are indeed tackling a problem which, as far as I know, no Colonial

229

Government has ever before attempted on such a scale, and have encountered many new and baffling things.'[26] Although in the decades before the Second World War the emphasis had been on European agriculture, the great volume of scientific research carried out in government laboratories and the private experiments made and financed by European farmers had amassed a stock of knowledge and expertise. This was of great use to the Department of Agriculture when Mitchell from the very beginning of his time as governor directed his energy to the task of reclamation, preservation and development of the land and agriculture of the reserves.

Opposition was many-sided. There were Europeans who feared that, if Africans were allowed to grow cash crops such as coffee, the loss of their monopoly would harm their income. They were convinced that Africans' involvement in their own coffee *shambas* should adversely affect the supply of labour for European plantations during the picking season. There were African politicians who set out to hinder the government by opposing measures such as the construction of terraces to combat soil erosion. The poorer the peasants the more they would cast envious eyes on the European farms: the greater their grievances the more easily they could be drawn into the movement of discontent and hatred which was to come into the open in 1952.

Human selfishness also had to be faced. In parts of the Kikuyu reserves, for instance, the wattle bark trade brought much money to Kikuyu owners, but to stop soil erosion in wattle plantations it was necessary to uproot some of the trees to make room for conservation terraces. The administration and the agricultural officers worked together to stop soil erosion, but greed for present profit caused the wattle tree owners to resist the thinning of their trees and the politicians found other ways also of opposing terracing.

Elsewhere in the districts, however, the administration had some success in its encouragement of young farmers' clubs at the schools, smallholdings, care of springs, better breeding of grade cattle and AI. Leaders like Chief Muhoya at Nyeri

230

and Chief Magugu at Komothai had exemplary holdings. It was the same in neighbouring Embu, where the district commissioner and his staff, working with the agricultural officers, had success in some places but had to fight against African suspicion in others. Everywhere conservatism and suspicion had to be shown to be groundless. In the Kamba Reserves it was rumoured that the belts of trees which had to be planted for conservation purposes were really the boundaries of future European farms. In some areas, when Africans were allowed to plant coffee, they had to be urged to grow it, because they feared that, if they did grow it, their land would be given to European coffee farmers. To overcome these suspicions and to explain the reasons behind government policy really strong information and community development services were needed. However, in the campaign to develop the agriculture of the reserves at a most critical stage the European elected members cut much of the vote for community development out of the budget.

In the Kikuyu Reserves many holdings were composed of scattered fragments and land consolidation would have to be a preliminary to any real improvement in agriculture. Here again Kikuyu politicians stood in the way and at the same time through the action of the European politicians the District Administration and Agricultural Department were denied the information and community development services which were needed to combat adverse propaganda. The detention of the political leaders at the beginning of the Emergency enabled the District Administration to tackle the issue of land consolidation vigorously and in Nyeri the district commissioner recorded in 1953 that it was not possible to 'keep pace with the desire of the tribe to bring about a complete land revolution'.[27] It was hampering to have to work within the limits of a settlement which Mitchell himself thought bad in many respects. He regarded the Carter Commission's report as 'a bad and wrong settlement',[28] but he could not disregard it and he wrote that 'for the practical purpose of tackling the agrarian problem now it must be accepted'.[29]

For some years individual tenure of land had been increasing

231

among the Kikuyu but under traditional tribal law all transfers of land rights were subject to the approval of the traditional authorities. The Colonial Office and virtually every administration was against trying to impose change on this traditional system or interfering with the statutory duties of the Native Lands Trust Board. The chief native commissioner and other senior officers in Kenya agreed with this view and even the registrar of cooperative societies, who was in favour of individual titles, thought that title should not be granted 'until the most important agrarian reform of all had been achieved, i.e. the consolidation of holdings into economic units'.[30]

Mitchell agreed with the opinion of the Hailey Committee and his own officers who had worked on the problem of land and thought that the individual farmer ought at that stage in agricultural development to be 'a tenant of the tribe'. Although his view was in keeping with the policy of the Colonial Office, it was not in accord with the current trend in the Kikuyu Reserves and was used by the politicians as an example of what they regarded as his wish to retard African progress. In fact he wanted to foster African progress, but he was anxious to ensure that it developed along lines of good farming and respect for the land. Supervision by administrative and agricultural officers, even though backed by local bylaws passed by African district councils, caused resentments which were grist to the agitator's mill. They had greatly hindered the improvement of agriculture in the Kikuyu Reserves where, according to the Provincial Agricultural Officer of the Central Province, in 1952–3 the percentage of land well farmed was in Kiambu District 2.4 per cent (6,750 acres), in Fort Hall District 5.75 per cent (13,911 acres) and in Nyeri District 6.93 per cent (11,522 acres).[31]

Mathu and other Kikuyus pointed out that in the Central Province well-to-do Kikuyus had for many years been buying land from their poorer neighbours, but, without individual titles registered with the Land Office, they were unable to obtain agricultural credit. The provincial commissioner reported that many of these landowners employed landless peasants and exploited the land, the protection of which was to Mitchell the most important responsibility of all. Moreover the granting of individual titles presupposed the consolidation of holdings into economic units. In his Despatch, 'Kenya 98', of 2 June 1950, Mitchell reviewed the obstacles to sound development: 'Local systems of land tenure probably constitute at present the greatest single obstacle in the way of achieving our objective. Land holdings are often small and scattered, bearing no relation to the contours of the land.'[32]

Good progress was made in Kericho District, which was developed along lines of exemplary crop and stock rotation. In Maragoli and other parts of western Kenya fragmentation was bad, but there was not the same political opposition to improvement as in the Kikuyu Reserves. Even so, individualism and conservatism retarded progress and as late as 1965 Tom Mboya, then Minister of Economic Planning, who had earlier said that it was foolish to clamour for European farms while land in African ownership remained so unproductive, pointed out that of 30 million available acres only 3 million had been consolidated and then he went on to say that 'it was not enough to consolidate and register land – the land must also be worked'.[33]

Overcropping, overstocking and problems of the conservation of water were plain for all to see, but before Mitchell's governorship there had not been a coordinated effort with the necessary administrative machinery to attack them. He gave a great boost to the morale of the officers concerned, agricultural, veterinary, community development and others, who were engaged in the attack. His speeches and writings like *The Agrarian Problem in Kenya* described the problems and gave his suggestions for their solution. He maintained that there was enough land available – good land, at present badly farmed, and marginal land, which could be profitably settled under good, but firm, management. The development of industry, small scale though it must needs be, must be correlated with agriculture in a development plan and legislation to preserve the land must apply to Africans and Europeans alike. For the Africans cash crops and increased production of traditional crops providing surpluses for sale

233

above the needs of the family must be the goal. But Mitchell saw a danger which the agricultural officers would have to keep in mind. The production of cash crops was a goal to be aimed at, but the production of food for the family was fundamental. 'Fortunately,' he stated, 'most Kenya Africans look after their food crops.' Nevertheless a lesson could be learned from the mistake made by some of the Kikuyu of Kiambu, who had planted such large acreages of vegetables and flowers for the Nairobi market and had neglected the production of food for themselves that, when there was a bad general harvest, they had had to be fed for a time on subsidized Australian wheat. Such dangers had to be watched, but they did not affect the general aim.[34] 'It is an idle dream,' he wrote, 'to suppose that a liberal modern civilisation and a high standard of living can be created on a basis of production and a system of agriculture and animal husbandry which have been evolved to enable primitive tribes to subsist in a primitive way.'[35]

Ways had to be found of overcoming poverty and of creating 'new wealth, because poverty and civilisation simply do not go together'.[36] When he was Governor of Uganda he had seen how extreme poverty impeded good husbandry. He thought that few people realized that 'erosion is a sign – and consequence – of poverty. Over-stocking, paradoxically, is a result of poverty: it is not true that natives hoard and will not sell stock, but it is true that they are too poor to buy and eat meat and that none can run dairies or sell ghee for the same reasons.'[37] They felt that to eat their stock themselves was to eat their capital; but he wrote later, 'either they eat their surplus stock or their surplus stock will eat them'.[38]

When he was Secretary for Native Affairs in Tanganyika, Mitchell disliked the idea of purely white farming areas and was glad when some Africans bought 285 hectares of farming land near Moshi from 'Kilimanjaro Smith'. When he was Governor of Kenya he was opposed to any thought of compulsory purchase of European farms but wanted to be able to have African farmers as tenants on unused crown land in the 'White Highlands' under careful supervision. As African progress was so promising, he told the Royal Commission on Land and Population, for which he had asked, that he would like Africans to be able to buy land from Europeans on a 'willing seller, willing buyer' basis if their standards of farming and financial competence were approved by a board established for the purpose. A year after his arrival he managed to get Alfred Vincent to agree to try to persuade the Highlands Board to sanction leases of unused land in the 'White Highlands' for African occupation; but nothing came of that.[39]

A few years later the case of the Ithanga Hills showed that, although he was governor, Mitchell was constitutionally powerless to override the Highlands Board. The Ithanga Hills were on the edge of the 'White Highlands', adjacent to the Kamba Reserve. They were unoccupied by Europeans but much wanted by the Kamba for settlement. Great efforts were made to persuade the Highlands Board to allow them to be used by the Kamba. As Mitchell wrote to Creech Jones, 'The CNC (Mr Wyn Harris) has exercised his powers of persuasion, as have the Chief Secretary and the Member for Health and Local Government, but this Board, as it is in law empowered to do, has refused to sanction the use of the land for Kamba Settlement'. It would only have provided land for a few hundred families, but 'it would have been a triumph of good will between the Highlands Board and the Local Native Land Unit'.[40] He believed that much ill will could have been averted and one of the causes of the Mau Mau revolt could have been removed if the secretary of state had issued a new order-in-council reconstituting the Highlands Board and issuing new instructions for it to follow in place of the 'Elgin Pledge'.[41]

During the last year of Mitchell's governorship two new posts for assistant directors of agriculture were created, one to take charge of research services and one for field services. T Webster was appointed to fill the first and R.J.M. (later Sir Roger) Swynnerton the second. He was in the Agricultural Department in Tanganyika and had been working with the Chagga, who were successfully growing coffee on the lower slopes of Kilimanjaro, and marketing it through an efficient cooperative society

235

in Moshi. It was a wise appointment. He was a man of great ability and brought to Kenya experience of work with one of the agriculturally most successful tribes in East Africa to add to the development projects which had been embarked upon since the adoption of the Ten Year Development Plan in 1945. It is sometimes thought that the Mau Mau insurrection forced the Kenya Government to do something for African agriculture which it had hitherto neglected. This view is far from true, as Swynnerton showed when he was entrusted with the task of supplying a detailed development project to accompany an application to the British Government for development funds for African agriculture. His *Plan to Intensify the Development of African Agriculture*, which came to be known as the Swynnerton Plan, was published in February 1954, and was rightly received with acclamation. It was a brilliant synthesis of knowledge gained from experience, and of ideas and projects begun since the end of the war. Swynnerton himself made that very clear in his memorandum.

'Plans for the development of African agriculture,' he wrote,

are no new concept. In 1946 the Government of Kenya initiated a ten-year development plan which covered all aspects of development including natural resources, social services, communication and so forth, augmenting the very substantial sums expended directly by the Colony. Having regard to development to date and the experience gained in the first eight years, the Planning Committee now has under consideration a three year phase to cover the years 1954–6. In preparing a plan for the intensified development of African agriculture, we have the advantage of the sound foundation laid during the last eight years, covering soil conservation, livestock improvement, construction of water supplies and investigation and experimentation into farming systems, cash crops, methods of cultivation, fertilizers and pasture research. It is on the knowledge so gained and the work already done that the next phase of intensification can be built.[42]

236

This was a generous acknowledgement but no more than a straightforward statement of the truth, which showed that concern for African farming was a major government interest in the immediate postwar period. These were the years when Mitchell was governor – a governor who showed in the very first week of his governorship that the preservation of the land and the welfare of the peasants were at the heart of his endeavours. He had written despatches to the secretary of state and semi-official letters to officials in the Colonial Office, and had given addresses to many organizations on the agrarian problem in Kenya. The Swynnerton Plan spelled out in detail the thinking which lay behind Mitchell's writings and speeches, the conviction that Kenya had a great agricultural potential awaiting development, not least in the African areas, and that in this development lay the long-term answer to the agrarian problem.

Notes

1. MPK Sorrenson, *Land Reform in Kikuyu Country: A Study in Government Policy*, (Nairobi, 1967), p. 55.
2. Mitchell, 'Current Affairs in East Africa'.
3. MD, 14 December 1946.
4. Ibid., 19 December 1944.
5. Ibid., 30 March 1946.
6. Ibid., 6 October 1945.
7. Ibid., 17 October 1945.
8. CO822/114/46523/1945, Letter from Mitchell to Stanley, 15 March 1945.
9. R.O. Hennings in L. Winston Cone and J.F. Lipscomb (eds), *The History of Kenya Agriculture*, p. 92.
10. Sir Philip Mitchell, *The Agrarian Problem in Kenya*, para. 3.
11. Legislative Council Debates (LCD), 23 November 1948, col. 7.
12. CO537/38046/1945, Mitchell to Creasy, 5 June 1945.
13. *Land and Population in East Africa*, Exchange of Correspondence between the Secretary of State for the Colonies and the Government of Kenya on the appointment of a royal commission, 'Colonial 290', HMSO 1952.

14. Mitchell, *The Agrarian Problem in Kenya*, para. 88.
15. *Land and Population in East Africa*, para. 58 (i).
16. Mitchell, *The Agrarian Problem in Kenya*.
17. *Land and Population in East Africa*, para. 2 (ii).
18. Ibid., para. 23.
19. Ibid., para. 40.
20. Letter to Michael Blundell, 22 July 1953, in Rhodes House, Oxford.
21. *Land and Population in East Africa*, para. 58 (ii).
22. CO533/537/38646, Minute by Cohen, 10 August 1945.
23. *African Land Development in Kenya, 1946–1962*, (Ministry of Agriculture, Animal Husbandry and Water Resources, Nairobi, 1962), p. 165.
24. CO533/557/38678/1, Minute by ID Robertson, 28 November 1949.
25. CO533/543/38086/38/1949, Governor to secretary of state, 28 February 1949.
26. Mitchell, *The Agrarian Problem in Kenya*, para. 47.
27. O.E.B. Hughes, *Nyeri District, 1949–1952*, p. 11.
28. MD, 14 December 1952.
29. Mitchell, *The Agrarian Problem in Kenya*, para. 32.
30. Quoted in Sorrensen, *Land Reform in Kikuyu Country*, p. 62.
31. EAS, 17 April 1953, Letter from provincial agricultural officer.
32. Despatch No. 98, 2 June 1950, para. 14.
33. EAS, 7 October 1965.
34. Despatch No. 98, 2 June 1950.
35. Sir Philip Mitchell, *General Aspect of the Agrarian Situation in Kenya*, Despatch No. 44 of 1946 from the governor to the Secretary of State for the Colonies, para. 15.
36. Mitchell, *Current Affairs in East Africa*.
37. MD, 13 March 1949.
38. Despatch No. 44, para. 16.
39. MD, 27 November 1945.
40. CO533/558/38678, Mitchell to Creech Jones, 7 September 1949.
41. Conversation with the author, 16 February 1955.
42. R.J. Swynnerton, OBE, MC, assistant director of agriculture, *A Plan to Intensify the Development of African Agriculture in Kenya*, (Nairobi, 1954).

XVII
Last Months as Governor

Although during his last year, Mitchell saw that in general relations between the races were better than they had been formerly, he was depressed by the quality and attitudes of many of the European Elected Members of Legislative Council. At the end of December 1951 the budget session showed them in a bad light. The governor deplored the way in which 'Leg. Co. drags on its weary way with the European Members making quite deplorable exhibitions of themselves and daily becoming more completely discredited'.[1] And the next day he wrote: 'The budget through, new taxes passed, including export taxes against the votes of the European Members who showed up very badly against the Africans who agreed to taxes on themselves.'[2] Then on New Year's Eve he wrote in a state of great depression: 'Here the country could have made great progress in politics and relations between communities had there been anyone among the European Elected Members able and willing to lead and to see further than narrow self interest, largely governed by fear.'[3]

During the month of January 1952 Mitchell was concerned with arrangements for the visit of Princess Elizabeth and Prince Philip at the beginning of February. They arrived in Nairobi on the 1st and it was planned that after staying at Government House with a busy programme they should go to Nyeri and take possession of Royal Lodge, the colony's wedding present to them, spend a night at Treetops, watching big game, and then fly to Mombasa to board the liner in which they would travel to Australia. On 4 February, before driving through Nairobi, the

239

princess greeted school children who were gathered in the grounds of Government House. She drove up and down along the lines of cheering children of all races in an atmosphere of harmonious rejoicing as warm as the sunshine of that happy day. On 6 February Mitchell left by train for Mombasa, where he was to meet the royal visitors on their arrival from Nyeri and say goodbye to them on the liner which was moored in the harbour there. He and Lady Mitchell left Nairobi in the afternoon and at Kilima Kiu, about 60 miles down the line, he was given a message that the king had died. He returned to Nairobi and went to Government House, where Thornley and the members of Executive Council were waiting for him. Instructions were immediately given for Wing Commander Francombe to fly to Nanyuki and take the new queen to Entebbe, from where she would be flown to London. Francombe had already been warned to be on the alert. After having lunch in Nairobi he had gone to have his hair cut. While he was at the hairdresser's a messenger from East African Airways found him and gave him a message instructing him to gather his crew together and wait for further orders.

The small airport at Nanyuki had a good and quite adequate grass airstrip, but it was late afternoon before arrangements were completed and nearly dark when the queen arrived and boarded the aircraft. A flare path had been prepared, but Francombe would not allow it to be used, because the grass was rather long and very dry and he took off with only the aircraft landing lights. That was a hazardous undertaking but less dangerous than the risk of having the airfield in flames. The KAR mess had hurriedly provided an excellent dinner to be served on the flight, but the flight was far from smooth and diversions had to be made to avoid storms. Entebbe was safely reached, but 20 minutes later a violent storm broke over the airport and delayed the departure of the Argonaut.

At Entebbe the queen asked Wing Commander Francombe to present the members of his crew. A few days earlier the wife of Mr Matthews, the steward, had given birth to twins and the queen, then princess, had visited the Nairobi hospital and seen her there. When Mr Matthews was presented to her at Entebbe the queen greeted him with the question, 'Tell me, Mr Matthews, how are the twins?' To Francombe this expression of human interest at such a time seemed the most memorable incident on that traumatic day.[4]

The next day the queen arrived in London. In Nairobi Mitchell wrote: 'All the world is paying tribute to George VI: if only all the world could emulate his conduct and character for a few weeks what might not be achieved!'[5]

Alas, on the local political stage 'the old rigidness and hates and bitterness' still prevailed among the die-hards, who fortunately were a dwindling element, and Mitchell reviewed the situation at length with Michael Blundell who was soon to become the leader of the European elected members. 'I propounded my thesis to MB,' he wrote, 'that by liberal measures now based on the Governor as Chief Executive we can in fact create conditions of justice and fairplay which will be satisfactory to the other races provided we also break the social ice as well.'[6] And a month later he saw that Blundell was 'plainly on the verge of breaking with Keyser'.[7] He had no doubt that constructive progress required a split in the European ranks, allowing the liberal element to escape from the fetters of the die-hards. The realization that such a split would occur before long gave him hope. Looking at the European community, he noted with satisfaction that Vincent 'now sees the total lack of realism "about this self-government", "cut Whitehall control" and all the rest of it, all of which ignore the simple fact that there is no alternative basis of authority which would be accepted by Indians, Africans or any conceivable Parliament or Government in the UK';[8] and he appreciated Derek Erskine's election address 'which, with naturally a lot of flamboyant Erskine, is very sound and sensible . . . and he at least comes out whole heartedly for friendship, tolerance and good will between the races'.[9]

Then on 19 June AB Patel and Eliud Mathu were sworn in to Executive Council. At last at the end of his governorship Mitchell had achieved the appointment of an African to the Executive Council. By bringing about this important step he cleared away the last barrier to constitutional advance on the basis of merit rather than race.

In June he opened the Royal Agricultural Show in Nairobi and made his farewell speech as governor to the people of Kenya. He told his audience that he and his wife would be returning to Kenya to become 'persons of no account at the north end of the Subukia Valley.' 'Indeed,' he said, 'I have been practising for some time going through doors last.' He finished his speech by saying:

> Will you excuse me if my last words are to utter a fervent prayer that we may all determine not to let ill-natured people sow the seeds of ill-will in this lovely country and to cut down at once any seedlings that may contrive to appear, for good will and friendliness are much better trees to plant and they will be grateful shade for us all in the years to come.[10]

As he showed by his mixture of the practical details of constitutional and agricultural policies and the pursuit of inter-racial aims by cultural means Mitchell was an idealist. He was an idealist with a strong practical sense, a realist with an ideal of inter-racial harmony on which to base his policy. Many years before he became Governor of Kenya he came to the conclusion that 'native affairs' was an 'unhappy phrase', which sounds so well and means so little, since native and non-native affairs are inextricably intermingled.[11] His life was based on a religious faith, which, as his diaries show, grew stronger with the years, and it was entirely in keeping that on his last day in Kenya as governor, before going to the final ceremony at the City Hall and then to the airport, he attended a service in the cathedral and laid up his full dress sword, the symbol of his duty as governor, in the keeping of the Church.

It might be suggested that consigning his sword to the keeping of the Church was a theatrical gesture. It was not that. It was an emotional gesture characteristic of a man who wept when hearing the broadcast of King George V's funeral service and stood in silent grief beside the body of his well loved friend and servant, Nasero. It was an emotional trait in his character which led him to pass hasty and violent judgements on people, but it was balanced by a willingness to admit that he was wrong and award praise in place of previous condemnation. To him the responsibilities of office were a trust and, if it was appropriate that the Church should be the repository of regimental banners, it would have seemed to him equally appropriate that the Church should be the guardian of the symbol of the trust which he had sought to keep for the 40 years of his colonial service.

Soon after his arrival in England Mitchell spoke at the East African dinner at the Connaught Rooms in London on 1 July. In his speech he said that it was 'unspeakable nonsense' to think, as some people thought, that East Africa was 'seething with African unrest'.[12] It was true that all East Africa was not seething with unrest, but the Rift Valley and the Kikuyu Districts certainly were. Three and a half months later the Mau Mau Emergency was declared and this speech was taken by many people in Kenya and Britain to show that Mitchell had been living in a fool's paradise and had done nothing to prevent the outbreak of a revolt which could not have occurred if he had heeded warnings sent to him from many quarters.

He had had first hand reports of Kikuyu disaffection many years before he became Governor of Kenya, but revolt had not broken out then. Later on he seems to have failed to realize that the nationalist aims of 1950 were of a different character from the African yearnings of 1935, in which year he stayed with Sir Joseph Byrne, the governor, on his way from Tanganyika to be Governor of Uganda. He saw then that Byrne was a worried man on account of the militant section of the European settlers. 'He does not know what his wild men are up to,' wrote Mitchell, 'but he thinks they mean serious mischief', and others told him that 'the wild men are bent on a row'.[13]

While he was serving in Tanganyika Mitchell had kept himself well informed about events in Kenya and in 1929 he thought that 'things seem to be drifting from bad to worse in Kenya and there is no doubt that important sections of the natives are becoming definitely hostile, which is a new spirit in Africa'.[14] A year later a visitor from Nairobi spoke about African hostility in the Kikuyu Districts. 'It may be exaggerated,' he conceded, 'but it is very disquieting, and I fear that an outbreak is unavoidable.'[15]

When he visited Kenya in 1930, Mitchell discussed the situation with the district commissioner at Nakuru who thought that there was not so much 'serious unrest' among the Kikuyu as 'a feeling of frightening uncertainty'. Mitchell felt that the position, as described by the district commissioner, 'is much the same as that which preceded the Zulu rebellion. The people are uneasy and scared: the personal rule of the DO and PC has gone and they do not know where to turn for guidance.'[16]

These two threads – the distrust of settlers caused by the 'wild men' and the breakdown of an administration which the Kikuyu could understand and appreciate – persisted throughout the 1930s. The chief native commissioner told him when he was in Nairobi in 1930 that there was serious unrest among the Kikuyu. Mitchell in Tanganyika reflected: 'How greatly simplified African problems would be if in addition to saying "the interests of the natives must be paramount" we actually made them so',[17] but in Kenya it was accepted that government policy must be based on agreement with the Europeans. When Mitchell arrived as governor, the Europeans assumed that this would continue. He soon made it clear that impartiality was embodied in his oath of office and they gradually came to realize that their agreement was no longer regarded as a necessary base for government policy to rest on.

Mitchell was handicapped by the very small number of educated Africans in Kenya at the time when he became governor. He would have liked to see more Africans in Legislative Council, but there were a mere handful with the necessary qualifications. In 1946 he and Creech Jones wanted to have five African Members of Legislative Council, but he was doubtful whether he could find so many. At that time Eliud Mathu was the only African Member of Legislative Council. In 1948 African representation was increased to four, and in 1952 to six.

Mitchell has been criticized for not nominating Kenyatta to

Legislative Council on his return to Kenya in 1946. It is a criticism which is easy to make years later but which ignores the conditions of the time and the image of Kenyatta which the African politicians had built up during the 14 years when he was away from Kenya. Mitchell met him first in 1931 at the Geneva conference referred to earlier and, as was his wont, he recorded the meeting in his diary: 'He seems to me to be a quite moderate and reasonable person, who might just as well be secretary or treasurer of a native administration. I really do not know what all the fuss is about.'[18] To a great extent that judgement was correct. If there had been better race relations before the war with some willingness on the European side to build a multiracial Kenya in which all races could share according to their capacity, it might have been possible for African aspirations to be satisfied by constitutional means, and Kenyatta might have become the leader of a nationalist movement willing to achieve its aims by cooperation. Instead, European attitudes were uncooperative and the effects of the war created a party of African militants who, although they later cast Kenyatta aside as being too moderate, hailed him on his return in 1946 as the leader of nationalist Africanism. The administrators in the districts therefore saw him as the leader of 'the bad men'. To have nominated him to Legislative Council would probably have been a wise, though dangerous, act of statesmanship. But could the governor and the secretary of state have dared to face the adverse reaction of the non-militant Africans and the violence of the European protest which would undoubtedly have resulted?

Kenyatta was in fact not just invited to sit on the Local Native Council at Kiambu. The government wanted to use his knowledge and prestige. Cavendish-Bentinck offered him a place on the African Settlement Board, which to Mitchell's great satisfaction he was willing to accept. That cooperative move was abandoned, however, because of the opposition of the administration in the districts, who feared that such recognition of Kenyatta would encourage the militant Kikuyus to intensify their clandestine activities, undermining the authority of the chiefs and the pro-government element around them and making the administration of the reserves well-nigh impossible.

Mitchell knew, when he was governor, that subversive elements existed and he contemplated the possibility of having to use force to quell a rising. He reassured himself by remembering that it would be easy to get aircraft from the Royal Air Force base at Aden to fly in troops, and for them to attack particular targets.[19] In 1949 Mitchell had been fully aware of Kikuyu cooperation with the Bataka, the anti-government organization in Uganda. On 17 June he presided over a meeting of the Executive Council when the security situation was discussed and he reported that the Kikuyu Central Association were in touch with the Bataka and that he had asked for a squadron of Tempests from Aden 'to show the flag' and had alerted all police, police reserves and army.[20] Missionaries, who spoke Kikuyu, repeatedly warned the district authorities of subversive unrest in the Central Province. Eliud Mathu told the Legislative Council about clandestine meetings of disaffection and district commissioners reported signs of political intrigue to Provincial Headquarters and to Nairobi.

The militancy did not originate in the Central Province but among the squatters in the Rift Valley and at the office of the Kenya African Union and the slums of Nairobi. Political militants were wont to go from the Rift Valley to Nairobi and from there agitators would go at the weekends to stir up trouble in the districts. The district commissioners and members of the district teams were then usually in their homes, not appreciating that it was then that they would have been most usefully employed moving around the *reserves*.

It was thought at Provincial Headquarters that the Kikuyu were disorganized and would never put up any sustained opposition to the government of Kenya. At this very key time the district commissioners were told not to send copies of their secret intelligence reports to the governor direct but to route them instead through the provincial commissioner and the Director of Intelligence and Security. It is possible that this information which finally reached Government House did not seem quite as critical as the district commissioners had considered it to be when they wrote their reports. Nor did there seem to be the sense of urgency at the higher levels of the administration which the gravity of the situation required. The official enquiry into the origins of Mau Mau, for instance, recorded that in April 1952 the Director of Intelligence and Security submitted a detailed report on Mau Mau. Instead of being given immediately to the governor this report did not reach Government House till August, a month after he arrived in London.[21] It would not have been possible to keep such information from the governor if Mitchell himself had moved about the country and talked with junior officers as he had done in former years. Unfortunately he depended too much on his senior officers.

The main ingredient of the growing anti-government feeling among the Kikuyu was the matter of squatters on European farms. The framework within which it has to be seen was set up many years before Mitchell arrived as governor. The Resident Native Labour Ordinance of 1937, which became operative in 1940, was sanctioned by the Colonial Office. It gave to the district councils in the scheduled areas control over the regulations affecting squatters. The war brought prosperity to many farms and the settlers used it to diversify their agriculture and build up dairy and beef herds, for which they needed land and whatever protection was possible against disease. Having been given control, the district councils were able to issue regulations reducing the size of squatter holdings and the number of squatter goats and sheep, and finally forbidding the keeping of squatter cattle altogether in much of the 'European Reserve'. The Jerseys, Ayrshires, Friesians and other imported breeds were highly susceptible to east coast fever and other diseases and even regular dipping could not fully protect them against infection by native cattle brought in from the reserves by resident labourers.

In 1946 a conference of District Councils with no African members adopted a resolution to eliminate native-owned stock on European farms within five years. As the reduction of squatter cultivation had drastically reduced the income of the squatters, this resolution could only mean the elimination of the labourer and his 'enforced return to already overstocked native areas', as Meredith Hyde-Clarke, the Labour Commissioner, pointed out to the chief secretary. In effect this would be contrary to the expressed policy in paragraph 54 of Sessional Paper No. 8 which reads as follows: 'It should be said at once that there is no question of the compulsory removal of these labourers back to the native areas.'[22]

Hyde-Clarke was correct in maintaining that, if they were deprived of their means of livelihood on the European farms, squatters would have no alternative to leaving and nowhere to go to but the reserves or the slums of Nairobi. But the Resident Native Labour Ordinance had the sanction of the Colonial Office and no secretary of state would have risked attacking what had become such a vital point in the economy of the European settlers. It was part and parcel of Kikuyu society that any of their numbers, whether landless or *ahoi*, were received back into the reserves whenever they wanted to come back. However, the influx of squatters from the European farms into the crowded Kikuyu Reserves increased problems there and so contributed to the causes of Mau Mau.

Mitchell saw that the question of squatters was basic to the problem and he wanted to lessen European privilege, but ordinances like the Highlands Board, stood in the way and the Colonial Office would not rescind them. Mitchell was thus powerless to deal with the matter and the Colonial Office kept in its own hands what was really the power of governorship. Even so, to the Europeans, who had limited detailed knowledge, it seemed that Mitchell, the governor, did nothing to heed warnings sent by missionaries and other Kikuyu-speaking people in close touch with the Africans. The Colonial Office in London kept in its own hands the power of governing instead of giving to the governor the authority without which he was powerless to govern. Mitchell himself told the author that what was needed was cancellation of orders-in-council and ordinances which put power into the hands of the Europeans and, like the

Highlands Board, took from the governor the power of governing as he felt was necessary.

In fact the Colonial Office held on to the power of governing
during the critical years when the squatter system was giving the
militant Kikuyus a clear way of building up revolt. The Colonial
Office unwisely tied Mitchell's hands at the time when his
knowledge of Africa ought to have been given full effect. He
saw clearly that cancellation of Colonial Office powers and
substitution of new ordinances could have enabled him to
govern instead of depriving him of the power to use the
knowledge for which he had been pressed to accept the
governorship.

The District Councils were right in concluding that the
squatter system, though useful in the past, could no longer
continue and that all labour in the future would have to be wage
labour, but they were insensitive and unrealistic in supposing
that this change could be accomplished quickly. The Labour
Department tried to persuade them that gradual change was
necessary and that wages would have to be sufficient to keep the
labourers and their families at a reasonable standard of living.
The District Councils, however, were unresponsive and the
resulting hardship suffered by the squatters drove almost all of
them into the arms of Mau Mau. Unfortunately the governor
could not quash the decisions of the councils, whose authority
over the squatters was sanctioned by the Colonial Office.
Mitchell's agricultural policy and his vision of solving the
problem of land on an East African basis required time for its
fulfilment, but the militancy of the nationalist politicians and
the hardships suffered by the Kikuyus were demanding more
urgent success.

It has sometimes been suggested that only the handing-over
to the Kikuyus of a substantial part of the European settlers area
could have prevented the outbreak of Mau Mau. Such a course,
which could have meant only a temporary postponement, was
unthinkable at that time. The Colonial Office and the Parliament
at Westminster would not have considered it, as the secretary of
state had said in the House of Commons in July 1952. The

249

African politicians, who roused Kikuyu opposition to cooperation with the government in measures such as terracing, on
which agricultural advance depended, wanted a purely African
– indeed a Kikuyu dominated – Kenya, but not a multiracial
nation. To disrupt measures for agricultural improvement and
so maintain African ill-will arising from poverty was a valuable
weapon in their armoury.

Mitchell wanted suitable Africans to be allowed to farm under
careful supervision as tenants on unused crown land in the
'White Highlands', but the Highlands Board refused to allow
this. As the matter of the Ithanga Hills showed, the board was
deaf to all pleading and the governor was unable to overrule its
decisions. His plan for the full use of land required 'sound
farming practice' and development throughout the colony.
There was unused crown land in the 'White Highlands' and on
European farms where the acreage was too large for the settler
to develop. As Mitchell was unable to change the 'Whites only'
policy of the Highlands Board, he could only ensure full use of
the land by increasing the number of European farmers there.

In the African Reserves the essential base for improved
agriculture was the consolidation of holdings, coupled with a
balanced agricultural/veterinary approach to land usage and the
development of cash crops. But consolidation was not easy to
achieve. Realities and legal impediments are sometimes overlooked. One critic for instance, writes that the proposition of
European soldier settler schemes after 'Hitler's War' was not
thought contradictory to a growing emphasis on the consolidation of African land holdings and the promotion of modern
agricultural techniques by Africans.[23] In fact, however, more
intensive farming in the Scheduled Areas was entirely unconnected with better agriculture, made possible by the consolidation of holdings, in the African Reserves.

Mitchell hoped that the efforts being made to improve race
relations would so much change the outlook of the majority of
Europeans that the Highlands Board would modify the rigidity
of its policy. In 1947 he even thought that before many years
had 'passed it would be possible to obtain agreement to the sale

of land to natives of the country irrespective of race, or at any rate to the sale of land on the borders of the European Reserve to adjacent Africans'.

In the meantime Mitchell was happy to act against the wishes of the board when the law allowed him to do so, as when in 1949 a South African white woman bought two farms at Kitale. Her husband was an Indian, and to save the district from having an Indian living in its midst the Highlands Board asked the governor to disallow the sale. He pointed out, however, that she, not her husband, was the purchaser and a white South African was entitled to buy land in the European area.[24]

Two years later Mitchell was plagued by the matter of Farm 12 at Nyeri. This land was adjacent to the farm of a European member of Legislative Council. It was farmed by an African although it was on the edge of but actually within the White Highlands. He had farmed it well for many years and Mitchell found it strange that his European neighbour was then asking that he should be turned off it on the grounds that his occupation of it contravened the Elgin Pledge. It would have made a pleasant addition to the European farm and Mitchell thought he noticed 'a bad smell' arising from the dispute. As governor he was put in a difficult position. The African had been occupying the farm for 35 years. 'How can I evict him now?' Mitchell asked. But the land *was* inside the scheduled area. Mitchell solved the problem by leaving the African in possession and excising the farm from the 'White Highlands'.[25]

In 1945 the Executive Council discussed the sale of a plot on the Ngong Road in Nairobi by a certain Mr Fox who wanted to sell it to an Indian. The area was inhabited only by Europeans and they wanted to prevent infiltration into it by Indians. The governor had the power of veto, but he explained that it was 'settled policy that there should be no racial segregation in towns' and so he approved the sale.[26] Two years later the Executive Council had what he described as 'some plain speaking' when they discussed the question of raising the Ruiru Dam to improve Nairobi's water supply. The plan entailed flooding 38 acres of African land and he told the Council that they must realize in such cases European land would have to be taken in compensation. Such 'plain speaking' had not been heard in Executive Council before, and Mitchell thought 'it did good'.[27] Instances such as these showed his racial impartiality, but the regulations sanctioned by London strictly limited his freedom of action.

Although he knew that there was unrest and discontent among the Kikuyus, it seems never to have been clear to his advisers in Nairobi that there was a coordinated movement of revolt. The security services were inadequate. Mitchell made a regrettable mistake by not calling provincial and district commissioners to regular meetings at Government House, a course which to some extent would have compensated for his lack of visits to the districts. If the state of his health caused a formerly active man to become a sedentary one, it would have been wise to keep in close contact with the officers in the districts by getting them to come to him. It was unfortunate that the Special Branch was confined to Nairobi until after the start of the Emergency when it was expanded to provincial and district levels.

In Nairobi the Special Branch, which had been in existence since the early days of the war, had a small office led by the Director of Intelligence and Security. That officer was in a specially advantageous position of influence, because he did not have to go to Government House by way of the secretariat but had direct access to the governor. In June 1952 Trevor W. Jenkins was appointed to the post. He had a clear perception of the growing state of subversion and wrote the report, already mentioned, which unfortunately went through the secretariat and did not reach Mitchell. In March his predecessor had written a short report of only three and a half pages which played down Mau Mau and said it was an isolated movement of little importance. The internal security plan for Kenya rested on the basic assumption that the Kikuyu presented no military threat to the peace of the colony.

Every year each district commissioner had to update his contribution to this intelligence and send his comments to the provincial commissioner in Nairobi. In January 1952 the District Commissioner at Nyeri had written a report saying that he considered it unsafe for Princess Elizabeth and Prince Philip to visit Nyeri, but the Office of Intelligence and Security caused Mitchell to write in his diary on 31 January (the day before the visit of Princess Elizabeth, so soon to become queen): 'Security reports that never have the people of all races been better disposed, more loyal or better pleased and that certainly is my own impression'.[28] It seems clear that Mitchell failed to see that trouble of a kind and magnitude never known before was growing in intensity.

Such additional security as was provided for the princess's journey through Nyeri District to Royal Lodge was given at the district commissioner's personal instigation by the local police. In the event the boys of the Kenyatta High School, past which the royal couple had to drive on their way to the lodge, lined the road and welcomed them with enthusiastic cheers. Mitchell may perhaps have sensed the distinction in African minds between the *Serekali* (the Government of Kenya) and the king and his family. During the Emergency, when D. H. Pratt, QC went to Kapenguria to defend Kenyatta at his trial, many of the peasants thought that the queen had sent her own lawyer, a Queen's Counsel, to defend the African leader. Everywhere during their visit to Kenya the princess and Prince Philip were greeted with affection.

Mitchell himself was much impressed by the friendliness of all the people he met during the last year of his governorship wherever he went in the country – often when fishing in the Tuso River in the Fort Hall Reserve on his own and, at his request, without police protection. Was he perhaps so trusting in the peasants that he allowed his idealism to warp his judgement, and so sure of himself, perhaps in part to compensate for his childhood insecurity, that he would not give sufficient weight to warnings of what he did not want to believe? He was generally very astute and always gave great thought to problems under discussion but, because he was more able than anyone around him, he always had things too much his own way and

253

was seldom prepared to modify his views. Nevertheless, behind the euphoria surrounding the royal visit the clandestine meetings in banana groves and caves, of which Eliud Mathu had given warning, continued unabated.

In April 1952 Mitchell urged on the chief secretary and other senior officers 'the importance of promoting some Asians and Africans to better posts – we cannot just go on saying we are going to and never doing it'.[29] Ten days later he attended the Annual General Meeting of the African Civil servants' Association, at which he recorded, 'Muchura, their President, made an absolutely first-class speech'. Muchura told the governor that the Africans were not willing to wait much longer for acceptance for what was 'called in the Army "commissioned rank".' They would doubtless make mistakes, but they 'were like a motorist with L plates on his vehicle. If he is not allowed to drive until he is efficient, he will never learn at all.'[30] If Mitchell had had the drive and energy of former years, he would probably have insisted on African promotion some years earlier with good effects, but the goodwill between the governor and the African Civil Servants' Association faded after his retirement and Muchura then felt that he was 'stifled'. Among Africans such as he the departure of Mitchell was greatly regretted. They recognized the sincerity of his work for African progress.[31]

When the Kikuyu reserves were aflame and a state of emergency had to be declared, the speech of 1 July was what was most remembered about Mitchell. It was felt that he could not have made it unless he knew nothing of the militant disaffection about which the administration had received warnings from many quarters. He might have postponed the revolt, but the danger would not have been removed unless he had been able to overcome the two racial extremes of political opposition and the secretary of state had annulled the existing authority of the Highlands Board and the district councils in the 'White Highlands'.

Years later the British Government allowed the winds of change to blow through its basic thinking and to abandon its assurance that European settlement was to be regarded as a permanent part of Kenya's development.

Notes

1. MD, 19 December 1951.
2. Ibid., 20 December 1951.
3. Ibid., 31 December 1951.
4. Information supplied by Wing Commander Francombe.
5. MD, 8 February 1952.
6. Ibid., 11 February 1952
7. Ibid., 5 March 1952.
8. MD, 12 May 1952.
9. Ibid., 14 May 1952.
10. EAS, June 1952.
11. MD, 1 January 1931.
12. There is a full report in EA&R, 3 July 1952, and in *The Times* and other papers.
13. MD, 1 October 1935.
14. Ibid., 30 October 1929.
15. Ibid., 16 February 1930.
16. Ibid., 10 March 1930.
17. Ibid., 14 August 1931.
18. Ibid., 21 June 1931.
19. Ibid., 4 May 1951.
20. Ibid., 17 June 1949.
21. Cmd. 1030, HMSO, 1960.
22. CO533/549/38232/15, Hyde-Clarke to chief secretary, 14 September 1940.
23. Gary Wasserman, *Politics and Decolonization: Kenya Europeans and the Land Issue, 1960–65*, (Cambridge, 1976) p. 101.
24. Ibid., 25 February 1949.
25. Ibid., 11 January 1951.
26. Ibid., 2 October 1945.
27. Ibid., 11 April 1947.
28. Ibid., 31 January 1952.
29. Ibid., 2 April 1952.
30. Ibid., 13 April 1952.
31. Muchura to the author, 16 April 1970.

XVIII
Retirement

M any people have thought that Mitchell was wrong to retire in Kenya, because it must have been difficult for his successor to have the former governor living in the colony. Before he bought Ndiloi at the northern end of the Subukia valley he told the Executive Council that he would like to buy a farm and retire in Kenya and no one saw any objection. When he met Sir Evelyn Baring, his successor, in London on his retirement leave, he assured him that he would 'keep right out of affairs' but would go to Government House to discuss any problems with him if he were asked to do so.[1] He kept strictly to his undertaking. It happened that Michael Blundell, the European politician whose inter-racial views were closest to his own, also lived at Subukia. He frequently discussed political matters with Mitchell and asked his advice. In February 1953 Humphrey Slade, the European elected member, who later became the elected speaker of the National Assembly of independent Kenya, asked Mitchell to advise him and those members with whom he was most closely allied, and Mitchell told him that they ought to give 'unqualified and unquestioning support to the Government and to Michael Blundell'.[2]

The new governor was told about these discussions which Mitchell had with Blundell and others and fully approved, and he himself often asked Mitchell to go to Government House to discuss problems and give his advice. In fact it seems clear that, because Mitchell kept in the background unless he was invited to enter the political arena, Baring was glad to have him in Kenya and appreciated his advice and the active help which at times he was able to give.

256

The Lyttelton Constitution, which was announced in March 1954, contained an important innovation: there were to be Asian and African ministers in the government. The first reaction of the African politicians was one of anger that the Asians were to have two ministers and the Africans only one, but they soon saw that this was not important. The breakthrough had been made and, as the number of educated Africans increased, an African majority in the Legislative Council and the appointment of more African ministers was inevitable. The die-hard element in the European community were bitterly opposed to sharing ministerial power with Asians and Africans, and they claimed that the Lyttelton Plan was imposed on the European elected members as a *fait accompli*. At every step, however, Blundell, their leader, had told them about his discussions with the governor and he had told Lyttelton that he thought an African ought to be included as a minister in the government, and Lyttelton welcomed the suggestion.[3]

Blundell's acceptance of the Lyttelton Constitution finalized the split which had been growing between the progressives and reactionaries among the Europeans. A split in the European political ranks was very pleasing to Mitchell, who thought at the beginning of 1953 that 'the Europeans must split or be for ever sacrificed to the die-hards'. Baring, the governor, put to Lyttelton the various ideas which became the ingredients of this plan, but Blundell had already suggested these ideas to Lyttelton and the governor. Blundell's liberal, inter-racial and realistic approach to the political and social problems of Kenya was in line with the aspirations of Mitchell, who saw in him a champion of the aims which he had followed for so many years, and he put his experience and intellectual powers at Blundell's disposal.

In October 1953 Mitchell wrote:

Michael Blundell came down to see me very cock-a-hoop. He has got the whole of his people less Grogan to accept documents based on those I prepared for him . . . a forthright declaration for equal rights, for racial toleration and cooperation and all the major things I have been campaigning for for so long. It will do great good.[4]

On 12 November on the BBC news service the European elected members issued a statement of policy. There were some members who disagreed with Blundell and his liberal majority – the die-hards who had to be left behind – but the progressive group was large enough to approve of a liberal, multiracial development in the future.

Blundell himself was convinced that it would be impossible to defeat Mau Mau unless the elected members had more say in the government, which, he stressed, must be a multiracial government. Lyttelton made it clear that no plans could be accepted unless all races were included. Much thought and much argument were expended in 1953 while constitutional changes were being discussed. The European elected members with few exceptions accepted the inevitability of the participation of other races in government, but Mitchell's papers gave a clear base for their final decision. At the same time as Mitchell was composing memoranda for Blundell he was writing notes for Baring himself and it was he who suggested that the 'Cabinet' should be composed of three European Ministers, two Indians and one African. Then again Baring asked him to go to Nairobi and Mitchell found him 'very appreciative and found most of what I had sent him fitted his ideas and Blundell's.[5]

Mitchell was always urging Blundell to form an inter-racial party, but in the year when the Lyttelton Constitution was introduced Blundell did not have sufficient support and was not strong enough for this. The die-hard Federal Independence Party was determined 'to oppose multi-racialism at all costs'.[6] Blundell felt then that the United Country party composed of Europeans who asked for cooperation with African and Asian political parties was all that was possible at that time. But the idea of multiracialism steadily gained ground and in October 1956 Mitchell wrote that 'The settlement of the political talks is now official and represents the whole of Michael's proposals ... A great triumph for M., Alfred and the Governor.'[7]

Cooperation between the past and present governors continued and in the following year Mitchell suggested that an
attempt ought to be made 'to get all parties into a temporary
Council for the purpose of working out some compromise'. At
Baring's request he agreed to see Blundell about this 'and
impress it upon him, while Baring would get Hill [the editor of
the *Kenya Weekly News*] on the job.[8] In such ways the *Karani
wa Shamba*, the farm clerk, as Mitchell called himself, was able
to help the politicians and officials who were trying to overcome
the racial approach to the problems of Kenya.

Mitchell had never had any private capital and had not been
able to save much out of his salary, so that in retirement he had
little money to spare. Indeed there was so little that he was
unable to go to London to attend the coronation of the queen.
He wrote sadly in his diary:

> Our mail contained a summons from the Queen to go to the
> Coronation in the Abbey! It must have been a personal thing,
> for when even peers have to ballot for seats retired Colonial
> Governors and their wives can't possibly rate them. It is
> miserable that we cannot possibly afford to accept; but I
> simply have not got £5 or £600 for such purposes, so it is no
> use repining. But it has deeply touched us both and is indeed
> a very moving thing.[9]

And on the day of the coronation, he wrote, 'We looked rather
wistfully at our invitation to the Abbey and were sad we could
not be there.'[10]

In 1954 a delightful visit to America was spoiled by his inability to take Lady Mitchell with him. He received a cable
from the British Ambassador in Washington via the governor
asking him to speak at a seminar on contemporary Africa held
by the Advanced School for International Studies of The Johns
Hopkins University in Washington. The fee offered would cover
all expenses and leave a little over but not enough to enable him
to take Lady Mitchell with him. He accepted the invitation,
which he received two months before the date of the seminar,

259

and in the interval worked hard in preparation for his talks at the university.[11]

The indebtedness of the farm without adequate capital to weather the storm caused him great anxiety. Things improved somewhat, because he was making money by other work, but with his wife's future in mind he looked gloomily at the farm's prospects and felt more strongly that he ought to sell Ndiloi and invest enough to secure her future if he died. In 1955 he accepted a directorship of Power Securities Corporation and became this corporation's director in the Kenya Power Corporation, a post in which he 'was expected to advise and help in negotiations over new concessions'.[12] A few days later he went to Nairobi to attend the first board meeting of the Kenya Power Corporation. When there, he was asked by the governor to go to breakfast to discuss with him and Sir Andrew Cohen (the Governor of Uganda, who was staying at Government House), a replacement for Colin Thornley, the Chief Secretary of Uganda, who had been appointed Governor of British Honduras. Three days later he talked all day till 11.00 p.m. 'with intervals for meals' about technical education with Sir David Lindsay Keir and Professor Vincent Harlow who were on an official visit from England'.[13]

Mitchell's diary shows that he was frequently feeling unwell. His health at that time was not good and he was doing too much work. 'I have too much to do with 20th Century Ford, Power Company and Nakuru Press, MIOME [Mombasa Institute of Moslem Education] and Kenya High School, [of which he was chairman of the Board of Governors] and the farm.'[14] He decided he must sell Ndiloi, though not in a hurry. 'If I can sell, I must, after 11 years struggle', and he worked out plans for his wife's financial security if he died.[15]

In October 1956 he was invited to the opening of the new harbour at Dar es Salaam by Princess Margaret and appreciated the 'pleasant gesture by Scup'[16] 'when he was the only guest in addition to the Princess's staff'. The racial relations in Dar es Salaam much impressed him: 'There is certainly a friendly camaraderie among all races and the natural good manners of

Africans were much in evidence. They have got to a point Kenya has not yet achieved.'[17]

He returned to Nairobi feeling 'certainly very much better if still easily tired', and had the great satisfaction of seeing Princess Margaret open the Royal Technical College of which he was the founder. But soon he was again suffering from 'a general lethargy'. On several occasions the governor continued to ask him to go to Government House to discuss political problems. His various appointments gave him outside interests and in 1960, when the Minister of Education formed a new Board of Governors, containing representatives of the public as well as the government, to frame the future policy of the Kenya [Girls'] High School, Mitchell was appointed chairman. A rowdy meeting was held, with the representatives of the Parents' Association strongly opposing a resolution to admit non-European girls to the school. Mitchell almost had to close the meeting, but with skill and persistence he managed to get the resolution passed by one vote. The racial barrier at the leading government girls' school having been breached, the two hitherto exclusively European boys' secondary schools in Nairobi had to follow suit. In 1950, by supporting the inter-racial primary school founded by John Karmali, Mitchell had shown that he was in favour of inter-racial education when and where social and economic conditions made it reasonable. The astonishing advances of the next ten years made inter-racial education reasonable at certain senior levels also and it was fitting that Mitchell, the governor who had supported the infants' school, should have been chairman of the board which swept away the racial barriers at the senior level in Nairobi.

During the later 1950s he was able to continue with a certain amount of public work, but his diaries show him becoming less and less active. Weeks passed with no entries at all except 'As usual' or 'As before'. By 1958 he was referring to his 'ageing' or 'decaying' memory and in the previous years he felt 'rather poorly and very depressed'; so depressed indeed that he told his doctor about his 'fits of depression and even thoughts of suicide'.[18]

261

The Mombasa Institute of Moslem Education continued to be of particular interest to him. He had always admired aspects of Islam and wanted to do what he could to raise the standard of education of the Arabs and other Moslems on the coast. From time to time he went to Mombasa for meetings of the council of the institute; but activities outside Subukia grew less frequent. In March 1958 he attended the opening of the East African High Commission Headquarters in Nairobi and was pleased by the recognition of his part in the formation of the commission: 'It is a magnificent building and I admit to being very gratified that in the centre of the ceiling of the main hall leading to the Council Chamber there is a plaster medallion enclosing my initials.'[19]

A year later when the Queen Mother was in East Africa and visited the Legislative Council in Nairobi, the governor with charming courtesy gave Mitchell the place of honour at the lunch party at Government House, seating him between the Queen Mother and Lady Mary Baring. A few days later he received another recognition of his work. In the 1930s Mitchell had reorganized Makerere in order to provide a university able to produce African graduates – an élite to lead the African people. The Queen Mother went from Nairobi to Uganda and conferred London University external degrees at Makerere on 20 Africans, including one young woman, while Mitchell was given an honorary fellowship.[20]

But the highlights grew fewer and fewer and on 2 May 1959 his diary contains the sad entry: 'Laid up with a stiff neck and unable to do much. I just sit and watch the days go by.' Then on 17 July he was staying in Nairobi and wrote: 'I loafed until tea time and then got Ali to drive me to the racecourse where I got a 1959/60 car badge and returned agreeably through Langata Forest.' That is the last entry in his diary, which he had kept since 1927. Even in his busiest years he had written daily about his official and personal activities, his conversations, his correspondence with the Colonial Office and his thoughts. This record of his life in the administration in Tanganyika, as Governor of Uganda, in Middle East Command and the western

Pacific and then as Governor of Kenya in the most difficult days of the colony's history ended abruptly with an agreeable drive through Langata Forest.

Mitchell retired in Kenya because he felt more at home there than anywhere else. At the beginning of his retirement he had to face the criticism of Europeans who laid the responsibility for Mau Mau at his door, and in Nairobi and Nakuru he had many painful encounters, when people turned away from him and ignored him. He kept silent and avoided discussion and argument, and two years after his return to Kenya the editor of *East Africa and Rhodesia* wrote to him that he 'has borne himself so composedly under great provocation at different times, and at none with greater dignity than in the past two years'.[21]

Although, as time passed, the hostility which he faced at the time of his retirement faded away, his hopes were not fulfilled. The violence and bestialities of Mau Mau profoundly shocked him, and on the personal side capital, insufficient to meet the hazards and uncertainties of farming in Kenya, brought him great financial anxiety. Before long, when he was fully rested, he found the society of Subukia small-minded and unable to meet the needs of his highly imaginative and intellectual mind. He used his powers to good effect as adviser to those who were actively engaged in the hurly burly of those difficult years, but he felt increasingly lonely and ate and drank too much. Lady Mitchell had to ration his consumption of Burgundy which, as she well knew, had a very bad effect on his gout and his heart. She was only partially successful. He became far too heavy, entirely lost his former desire to exercise and grew increasingly unfit and depressed. Finally in 1963 he decided that it would be wise to leave Kenya. He leased Ndiloi to his manager, Anthony Cartland, who bought it after Mitchell's death and after Lady Mitchell had gone to live in South Africa.

When they left Kenya Sir Philip and Lady Mitchell's intention was to make their home in Gibraltar or on the adjacent Spanish coast. He wrote to the Governor of Gibraltar but had no reply and early on Christmas morning the Governor's ADC telephoned to Mr Robert Broadbent, the security officer, to tell him that they had arrived in Gibraltar and were staying at the Bristol Hotel.[22] Mr and Mrs Broadbent immediately went to see them and were shocked to find them looking old and ill. The Broadbents took them to their home for Christmas Day and then moved them to a hotel at Rincón de la Victoria on the mainland. After a few months there they moved to a small, new villa called Catalina, belonging to the owner of the hotel. A maid came in daily to do the cleaning and Lady Mitchell did the cooking. Philip was a very sick man. The heart disease from which he had suffered for some years had become extremely serious and he could walk only for very short distances.

During 1964 Mitchell became steadily worse. At the beginning of October his condition was obviously critical and Mr Broadbent and other friends arranged for him to be admitted to the Royal Naval Hospital in Gibraltar, where he died on Sunday, 11 October 1964. It was both law and custom in those times that in hot countries anybody who died during the night should be buried that coming day. A funeral was therefore arranged for Sir Philip on the day he died. Unfortunately, although his family caught the first possible aeroplane from London to Gibraltar they were too late to attend the service. However, he was buried with full military honours in the civil cemetary. The only mourners were the Broadbents and the Governor's ADC. It was a sad end to such a distinguished career. Lady Mitchell stayed with Mr and Mrs Broadbent until she went to South Africa to live among her friends and relatives there.

Notes

1. MD, 27 June 1952.
2. Ibid., 4 February 1953.
3. Rhodes House, Oxford, Blundell 17/3: Lyttelton to Blundell, 26 November 1953.
4. MD, 31 October 1953.
5. Ibid., 27 November 1953.
6. EAS, 29 September 1954, Report of speech at Limuru by Major BR Roberts.

7. MD, 19 October 1956.
8. Ibid., 29 September 1957.
9. Ibid., 29 March 1953.
10. Ibid., 2 June 1953.
11. Ibid., 8 June 1954.
12. Ibid., 12 July 1955.
13. Ibid., 7 August 1955.
14. Ibid., 4 June 1956.
15. Ibid., 8 June 1956.
16. Ibid., 9 October 1956. 'Scup' was Sir WEH Scupham, Speaker of Legislative Council.
17. Ibid., 9 October 1956.
18. Ibid., 2 December 1957.
19. Ibid., 24 March 1958.
20. Ibid., 20 February 1959.
21. EA&R, 12 June 1954, p. 1324.
22. The information in this paragraph was given to the author by Mr Broadbent.

XIX
Epilogue

Historical assessment, like many other matters of opinion, swings from one bias to another. It became accepted in the 1960s and 1970s to view the colonial effort as a deliberate exploitation of less sophisticated societies by the industrially advanced nations. This view reflects a real truth, but not the whole truth. For many colonial servants, like Sir Philip Mitchell, the driving force was the idealistic concept of trusteeship.

For him, as for many, the ending of the British Empire was not seen as a regrettable decline, but as the goal. The emerging Commonwealth was the great ideal to be realised – a mutually supportive association of free nations.

Mitchell's own assessment of the responsibilities of the colonial powers was formed early in his career and remained to the end the guideline to which his policies and plans were attached. His military service with Africans during the First World War gave him affection for them and appreciation of many qualities and traditions in the African character and outlook. He soon became convinced of Africans' ability to rise to high levels of Western civilization and of the duty of the white people who had intruded into their lives to help them to do so. In 1930 Margery Perham, who became one of the leading authorities on African administration and had been given by the Rhodes Trust a travelling fellowship in 1929 to study 'Native Problems', met Mitchell at dinner at Government House in Dar es Salaam. She recorded this meeting with the Secretary for Native Affairs in an astute passage in her diary:

He is quite amazing. He is the youngest head of a department I have ever met, being only thirty-nine, very good-looking, Oxford, and a brilliant exploratory thinker. His view takes in the whole of Africa and he looks far ahead into the distant future. He talked better than any book I have read on Africa and I became almost uneasy lest his ideas should dominate me too much. He is emphatically pro-native – to use a bad term – he sees no hope in South Africa, nor in settler domination, and has every confidence in the development of the native from a tribal basis to some sort of self-supporting political organisation. He stands at the extreme opposite end from Smuts and Grigg and I marvel at the courage of Sir Donald Cameron in picking him for this post. I imagine he wanted a young and able man whom he could train and on whom he could cast his mantle, since he is soon to be translated to a higher and larger sphere – Nigeria – his former colony.[1]

In 1936 when Ralph Furse, who had interviewed Mitchell hen he applied for entry to the Colonial Service, was visiting ganda, he had asked Mitchell what he thought the adminis- ation was 'doing in these countries'. Mitchell replied:

I said I believed every man and woman had a common value for his (or her) own sake and a right to liberty of thought and soul and conscience, to justice and to decent Government. We were here to propogate these beliefs and to fit these people to secure these things for themselves so that they might become willing and loyal partners of the free system we were establish- ing – that was why our economic policy must accord with our philosophy and our benevolence.[2]

That ideal and aim, to lead the indigenous people to be able ﹥ share and enjoy the civilization which he himself prized so ighly, was basic to all Mitchell's political and economic plan- ing. The main objects of his policy in Kenya have been well

267

presented by George Bennett and Alison Smith in the Oxford *History of East Africa*. They write:

His aims were closely in tune with the current metropolitan ethics, in some ways even more closely when in 1945 a Labour government came into office. He believed firmly in the primacy of the economic base, in tackling the agrarian problem and in consolidating Kenya's wartime prosperity by internal administrative action and external co-ordination – in particular by continuing the inter-territorial economic co-operation of the war years. From his Fiji experience he brought – for the first time as a theory to East Africa – the concept of multi-racism as a positive principle of government. Further he was anxious to combat the caprice and frustrations of colonial government through the Legislative Council by introducing something like ministerial responsibility, with unofficials in charge of groups of department,[3]

Variations in the assessment of a historical figure can be on many levels, even the most personal. David Throup, writing in *Kenya: Economic and Social Origins of Mau Mau*, describes the Philip Mitchell who went in 1944 to be Governor of Kenya as a 'fat little man, without any social graces'.[4] A photograph of him as Governor of Fiji, the position he occupied in the previous few years, shows a man of very different appearance, a man who was described by a member of his family in earlier years as extremely handsome, who became the centre of attention wherever he went, 'larger than life' and 'socially very polished'.[5] People who knew him when he became Governor of Kenya found him attractive and understanding.

More important issues can also be seen from different perspectives. Mitchell's reputation has suffered from writers who have ignored the conditions existing in Kenya at the time of his governorship and who had not placed his plans within the context of the policies held by the Colonial Office and by both Labour and Conservative secretaries of state. For example, as Governor of Kenya Mitchell's hope was that race relations could be so much improved that a nation could eventually be created in which merit, not race, was the principle on which society was based. Marxist writers and African nationalists, for whom such an aim has no appeal, have regarded his hopes as acceptance of European privileges. The same criticism has been made by writers who have seemed oblivious both of the conditions of life in Kenya at the time and of the limitation of the governor's freedom of action imposed by orders-in-council and other edicts issued by London. The power of the Highlands board, for instance, prevented him from handing over the Ithanga Hills for settlement by the Kamba or allowing Africans to be tenants under supervision on crown land in the scheduled areas. Such moves would have paved the way for eroding the privileged 'whiteness' of the 'White Highlands' on a willing selling and willing buyer basis.[6] Mitchell himself bought land within the scheduled areas, but this was logical in a country which the imperial government hoped would develop as a multi-racial nation. Mitchell saw in the best of the settlers true allies in the task of bringing African advancement.

An American, Jack R. Roelker, in his book *Mathu of Kenya* condescendingly admits that Mitchell 'cannot be viewed completely as the settlers' ally.' This is very misleading. 'If,' this critic continues, 'his primary sympathies were in their camp, he was also intent on sheltering the "lesser breeds" from exploitation.'[7] Mitchell's whole career shows what he made clear from the very start of his governorship of Kenya, that his primary sympathies were *not* with the settlers or the European business community, but that '*ex hypothesi*', as he said. 'I am entirely impartial.'[8] His opposition to European attempts to continue indefinitely as the dominant community and to entrench their power is seen again and again in his diaries. To hint that he looked on the Africans as 'lesser breeds', to use Kipling's words, shows a sad lack of knowledge of his views. It implies a feeling of racial arrogance, which was far from Mitchell's outlook. He was a realist and understood the underdevelopment of the Africans of his time. To look on them as 'lesser breeds', however, would have contradicted his whole philosophy of life. Mitchell's diaries give an invaluable insight into his aims and the development of his policies which, adapted though they might be to meet changing circumstances, were always based on certain basic principles. Mitchell had a belief in the value of each man or woman, irrespective of race, and in the intrinsic capacity of Africans to reach the highest levels of civilization, as he saw it. He refused to be pushed into what he felt to be unwise or the acceptance of unwarranted privilege.

It has sometimes been thought that Mitchell's connections with South Africa must have influenced him in favour of South African racial attitudes and policies. In fact, however, his knowledge of South Africa reinforced his liberal approach to racial problems. His sympathies were with Reinhallt-Jones and the Durban Institute of Race Relations and with the opponents of the perpetual white domination.

In his book *Mathu of Kenya* Roelker seems to imply that Mitchell must have had a racial bias caused by his South African links. He correctly states that Mitchell saw his task as one of attempting to develop Africa as part of Western European civilization, but he goes on to write, 'Another dimension of his attitude is indicated by the fact that at this time [1947] he owned an extensive estate in South Africa and was to purchase additional land in Kenya's highlands before his administration had ended.'[9] To own an estate in South Africa does not convict a man of being an anti-African racialist and in fact Mitchell detested the general racial attitude of South Africa. But nor did Mitchell own an estate in South Africa in 1947.

Mitchell felt that Africa was his home and he had for many years had at the back of his mind the idea of settling in retirement not in South Africa but in East Africa. For a short time he did own a farm in South Africa – and for a very good reason. Lady Mitchell was a South African and, when wartime duties took Mitchell to Middle East Command, she and Philip agreed that the most sensible course for her to take would be to live among her relations in South Africa. After a while Lady Mitchell found a farm called Kingsley, near Grahamstown, which Mitchell bought for her to live on. On his way to Fiji

Mitchell went to South Africa to see his wife and to make arrangements for the running of the farm. A manager, a visiting agent and an accountant were appointed and Mitchell had no further anxiety on his wife's behalf. 'And so ends another phase,' he wrote. 'I am very happy about Kingsley, which I can see paying for itself, and that is all I ask.'[10]

As early as 1931, while he was serving in Tanganyika, Mitchell decided that to live in East Africa and serve the Africans there was his duty and his desire. Soon after he went to Uganda as Governor he wanted to buy some land at Nyeri in Kenya, but he was forestalled by another applicant and he suffered a similar disappointment in the same area in the following year. He did not make any further attempts to buy land in Kenya at that time, but six months after he became Governor of Kenya he decided to sell Kingsley and 'move up here'. Kingsley had served its purpose by providing a secure home for Mitchell's wife while he was away on wartime duty, but he did not need it any longer and wrote to his agent in South Africa to instruct him to sell it.

A month later Mitchell told the Executive Council in Nairobi about his wish to buy some undeveloped land in Kenya 'and no one could see any objections'.[11] He bought land at Subukia. He built a house which he called Ndiloi and which became his home on retirement.

Politics is, in the famous phrase, the art of the possible. Mitchell's critics have too often based their criticism on the time of writing and failed to appreciate the conditions existing at the time they were writing about. For instance, criticism of Mitchell for not at once ending the colour bar in hotels ignores the fact that the Race Relations Act, which would have been required, would most certainly not have been passed by Legislative Council. The desired result was achieved, however, by diplomatic and cultural means – a fact which such critics 'conveniently ignore'.

When Mitchell went to Kenya as Governor in 1944 he was only too aware that his years of colonial service and the arduous work during the war which had achieved great success had affected his health. The retirement which he was denied made it worse. Mitchell feared that this bad health would deprive him of the drive and stamina needed for the governorship of Kenya at that most difficult time, but his sense of duty persuaded him to agree to the appointment.

However, in addition to reduced physical powers, he suffered from a lack of cooperation from the Colonial Office, when he needed all the help possible from that Office. A minute in a Colonial Office file recommended that instructions given to him by the secretary of state should limit his initiative as firmly as possible – a minute which evoked no objection from the senior officer to whom it was addressed. The tragedy of Mitchell's years as governor was that the Colonial office would not hand over to him the power to govern. Instead it retained in its own distant hands the powers which Mitchell needed to act as he thought appropriate. He was perfectly clear about what he wanted to do, but the Colonial Office prevented him from acting as he thought necessary. The Governor was in Nairobi, but power continued to be wielded in London. After his retirement Mitchell regretfully told the author that this had been his failure, not to achieve the cancellation of orders-in-council and other edicts which limited his power of governing.

When he was governor of Kenya Mitchell told the Colonial Office that if he was to be able to attack the cause of Kikuyu militancy the orders-in-council and edicts issued in London must be revoked. Nothing, however, was done about this and Kikuyu discontent increased. He must have remembered that when he was Governor of Fiji he suffered a sad lack of help from the Colonial Office when he asked for action which he said was essential for ending the disastrous strike in the sugar industry. His request then was attended to only after he had written personally to the secretary of state, who told the Colonial Office that they must attend to the Governor's request. Before his request for help in Kenya was granted he went to England on retirement leave and made the famous speech at the East African Dinner.

One may wonder why Mitchell framed the speech exactly as he did. This speech cost him a peerage because it was interpreted

272

at the time as demonstrating a serious incompetence. The secretary of state felt he could not honour a governor who seemed to be unable to see that serious unrest existed in Kenya and would engulf the colony in the violence of Mau Mau. He had been offered a peerage some years earlier and Lennox-Boyd only withdrew the offer with great reluctance. He would have wished Mitchell's long and distinguished career to be crowned with honour.

It could be that the speech was a final act of service by Mitchell to the Kenya he loved. One may perhaps suggest that as his freedom of action was so greatly curtailed by the Colonial Office, all he could do effectively was to deprive the militant leaders of the publicity on which they tried to base their plans. These militant leaders were glad when the time came from Mitchell's retirement because, as already noted, they felt that he was 'too smart' for them. What he actually said in the speech was a true statement about East Africa in general. It was perfectly true that all East Africa was not 'seething with unrest', although Kikuyu areas certainly were. Later on, for example, the Governor of Tanganyika, Sir Edward Twining, admitting the failure of the ill-planned and poorly conducted scheme to grow ground nuts there, said that there were two things they did not have in Tanganyika – ground nuts and Mau Mau. It was the same elsewhere. It could be that he did not mention the serious situation in Kikuyu areas in the speech in order to deprive the militant leaders of the publicity they so greatly desired.

Worldly honours are not everything and honour is always founded on a purity of intent. After his retirement Mitchell looked back to the actions of the Great Powers and 'the relations of the African people with the great unknown world which suddenly fell upon them'. That they were caught up in that world was a fact, a process which could not be reversed. It laid a great duty on the Colonial Powers of the twentieth century. As he saw it and wrote in his autobiography:

What we have had to do since, and have to do still, is to help them to believe in that world, to feel at home in it and to look

273

with hope and happiness to their future in it: that, at least, is my conception of 'Colonialism', and explains what I have been trying to do, this thirty-odd years, with a growing consciousness that most of the answers were contained in the Book which the first missionaries carried with them into the darkness of the bush and forest.[12]

Mitchell wrote this near the beginning of his autobiography. A significant change was subsequently made. The lines about the early missionaries beginning 'The Book (that is the Bible) which the first missionaries carried with them into the darkness of the bush and forest' were changed into:

I do not delude myself that there will not be set-backs and failures, nor that envy, hatred and malice will be miraculously uprooted in a few years from the minds and hearts of men. But I do say that the task is tremendously worthwhile, that it is possible and practicable, and that I believe the young people now growing up will gladly and resolutely carry it forward: and I say, lastly, that when doubts and difficulties perplex and the way seems hard to perceive, there is always at hand a textbook for the business – the New Testament.[13]

Good intentions alone do not achieve desirable results. It is arguable nowadays whether Western man should have interfered at all with the sort of societies among which Mitchell worked. But even today it is also appropriate to defend an attempt to help such societies adjust to the consequences of being brought into juxtaposition with the industrial nations. For colonial servants like Mitchell it was apparent that these societies must adapt or be destroyed. He was also proud of the best that Western civilization had to offer.

Mitchell's gifts of idealism and a clear-sighted, long-term overview enabled him to design sound structures for the huge social changes envisaged. Throughout his career Mitchell was moved from one post to another before there had been time to see the result of some of his plans. The measure of his success can only be assessed if one looks at the flowering during another man's governorship of plans devised and set in train in his. It was so in Kenya. His economic policy set Kenya on the road to post-war prosperity and his creation of the East African High Commission and Central Assembly were of great value to East Africa as a whole. At the very end of his governorship an African was made a member of the Executive Council and his policies led logically to the inclusion of an African and Asians in the Lyttleton Constitution.

Perhaps his greatest achievements lay in the field of race relations. On his fortieth birthday Mitchell wrote, 'if there is a subject about which I know anything and might be of some use in the world, it is the race problem: if there is a job I have to do it is to try in some small degree to help the Africans in their encounter with civilization rampant and greedy'.[14] In spite of the violence which broke out so soon after his retirement, the history of post-war Kenya shows that his idealism and his striving for racial justice and harmony were rewarded by the goodwill which accompanied the transfer of power to African hands in 1963. The Trustee had discharged its Trust to a new nation with a large corps of educated nationals, a real experience of racial cooperation and a viable economic base.

In spite of the Colonial Office and the doubts about Mitchell's capacity to govern which it caused among the European population, his unswerving attention to his principles enabled the enigmatic Proconsul to ensure that in Africa the twilight of empire was followed by the dawn of an important part of the Commonwealth.

Notes

1. Margery Perham, *East African Journey*, (London, 1976) p. 42.
2. MD, 9 February 1936.
3. George Bennett and Alison Smith in DA Low and Alison Smith (eds), *History of East Africa*, (Oxford, 1976) pp. 112–13.
4 David Throup, *Kenya: Economic and Social Origins of Mau Mau*, (London, 1987) p. 33.

 5. See plates section.
 6. MD, 29 June 1954.
 7. Jack R Roelker, *Mathu of Kenya*, (Stanford, 1976) p. 87.
 8. MD, 19 January 1945.
 9. Roelker, *Mathu of Kenya*, pp. 86–7.
10. MD, 14 June 1942.
11. Ibid., 9 June 1945.
12. Mitchell, *African Afterthoughts*, p. 50.
13. Ibid.
14. MD, 1 May 1930.

Index

Index

279

maize, 83
Makerere, University of East
    Africa, 23, 63, 72, 86, 87–9,
    91, 179, 227, 262
Makerere Commission, 90
Makerere Conference, 92
Making of Modern Uganda, The,
    69
Makueni, 228
Makwaia, Chief, 24, 31
Malaya, 115, 139
Mander, Geoffrey, 130
Mange Alanga, 29
Mangu High School, 23
Mantolia, 153
Maori, 159
Maragoli, 233
Marchant, W. S., 146, 150
Margesson, David, 130–1
Marshall, Gen., 143
Masai Land Unit, 229
Masailand, 229
Masaka, 57
Mathu, Eliud, 191–2, 202, 217,
    232, 241, 244, 246, 254
Mathu of Kenya, 269, 270
Mau Mau,
  and Africans in Legislative
    Council, 201
  and voluntary funding, 211
  and repatriation of Kikuyu
    settlers, 229
  land question, 235, 249–52, 254
  and agricultural development,
    236
  Emergency, 243, 252, 254
  reports on, 247, 252–3
  and squatters on European
    farms, 247–9
  and Sir Philip Mitchell, 252, 263,
    273
Maxwell, C. V., 174
Mbeya, 37
Mboya, Tom, 233
Mechanical School, 88
Mehta, N. K., 81

Mengo Hill, 40, 57, 58, 63, 65
Merrick, 73
Middle East, 1217–8
Minaki, 23
Ministry of Food, 163, 167
Mitchell, Captain Hugh, 1, 2, 4
Mitchell, Katherine, 134–5
Mitchell, Kenneth, 4
Mitchell, Lady, 115, 116, 142
Mitchell, Mary Catherine, 1
Mitchell, Sir Philip Euen,
  see below *Buganda, Ethiopia,
    Fiji, Kenya*
  born, 1
  school, 2–3, 4
  'larger than life', 3
  Oxford, 3–4
  joins Colonial Service, 5
  Nyasaland, 5–6
  King's African Rifles, 6, 7–8
  and race relations, 21, 38, 42–3,
    112, 209–18, 268–70, 275
  diaries, 21, 107
  and education, 22–87, *and see*
    Makerere, University of East
    Africa
  'wards in trust', 44–5, 266–8,
    269–70, 273–4
  administration of justice, 96–105
    and the commission &
      Enquiry into the
      Administration of Justice in
      Kenya, Uganda, and
      Tanganyika Territory in
      Criminal Matters, 98–101
    and Chief's judicial role, 97–8
    and African marriage laws,
      102–5
  intellectual powers, 107–8
  death of Nasero, 108–9
  sailing, 109
  Star (his horse), 109–10
  religious faith, 110–11, 242–3,
    274
  Deputy Chairman of the
    Governors' Conference, 114

Index

coordination of East African
war-effort, 114–15
and Admiral Nimitz, 116,
143–4, 151, 155, 169
retirement, 256–64, 271
cannot go to coronation of
Queen Elizabeth II, 259
lectures to Advanced School of
International Studies at
Johns Hopkins University,
259–60
depression, 261
death, 264
and Margery Perham, 266–7
assessments of, 268–9
Buganda, 42, 45, 46–50
reform of the administration,
52–68, 61–2
and the Kabaka, 58–9, 61–6,
102
and see Buganda, and see
Kabaka
Ethiopia, 114–39
and Field Marshall (Lord)
Wavell, 115–6, 118–9,
120–1, 122, 123, 126–7
Chief Political Officer, 118
as Major General, 119, 138
and the Italian collapse, 122
and Haile Selassie, 124,
128–9, 131, 132–3, 135–6
and slavery, 125
High Commissioner for the
Italian Colonies and
Somaliland and Agent
General for Ethiopia, 127
and administration of Italian-
occupied territories, 126–7
and Ethiopia as a protectorate,
132
resigns, 134–5
withdraws resignation, 135–6
agreement with Emperor,
126–36, 142
Fiji, 24, 75, 154–72
Governor of Fiji and High

Commissioner of Western
Pacific, 142, 147, 158, 159
organizes war effort, 148
and Indians, 149
and New Zealanders, 149–50
Jonfrum cult, 151
and reconstruction, 152
and Tonga, 152
and American High
Command, 153
relations with Indians, 159
and constitutional reform,
159–60, 161–3
and education, 160–1
and sugar, 161–7
desire to leave, 168–9
Kenya, 8, 10, 29, 32, 35
refuses post of Chief Native
Commissioner, 174–5
reluctance to serve as
Governor, 175–7
accepts governorship, 176–7
the problem in Kenya, 178
Elgin Pledge, 179, 235
European settlement, 179–80,
197
and African agricultural
development, 180–1
trusteeship, 181, 196
opposes 'one man one vote',
181–2
and European settlers, 184–5
and constitutional reform,
185–8
appoints (Sir) Ferdinand
Cavendish-Bentinck as
Member for Agriculture,
186–8
financial reform, 188–9
development, 189–91
and the East African Central
Assembly, 197–201
and national registration,
201–2, 203–6
and race relations, 209–18

283

Index